THE
CHINESE
EXPERIENCE
IN
AMERICA

Minorities in Modern America

Editors
Warren F. Kimball
David Edwin Harrell, Jr.

THE CHINESE EXPERIENCE IN AMERICA

SHIH-SHAN HENRY TSAI

INDIANA UNIVERSITY PRESS
Bloomington and Indianapolis

To Sonia, Shirley, and Rocky

Manufactured in the United States of America

Library of Congress Cataloging-in-Publication Data
Tsai, Shih-shan Henry.
The Chinese experience in America.
(Minorities in modern America)
Bibliography: p.
Includes index.
1. Chinese Americans—History. I. Title. II. Series.
E184.C5T833   1986   973'.04951   85-45464
ISBN 0-253-31359-7
ISBN 0-253-20387-2 (pbk.)
1   2   3   4   5   90   89   88   87   86

CONTENTS

MAPS

TABLES AND CHARTS

ILLUSTRATIONS

following page 81

ACKNOWLEDGMENTS

In assembling the materials for this book, I had the advantage of relying upon the works of many who have done detailed research in various aspects of Chinese history, American history, and Chinese immigration to the United States. I wish to acknowledge my debt to them and hope that my efforts may serve to blaze a wider trail of richer Chinese American scholarship. I am particularly grateful to Professor David Edwin Harrell, Jr., for his painstaking and careful editing and unfailing cooperation. Sections of the manuscript profited from extraordinarily perceptive criticisms by Sucheng Chan, Him Mark Lai, and Timothy P. Donovan. Friendly but constructive advice from Professors Delber L. McKee, Noriko Kamachi, and Ronald Takaki also served me profitably on numerous points.

I am also indebted to Professors Willard B. Gatewood, Jr., Paul S. Holbo, Roger Daniels, and Ervin Lewis for their aid and encouragement. Many other colleagues, friends, and scholars also helped me at various stages in its preparation: Professors Lucie Cheng, Peter K. New, Thomas C. Kennedy, Elaine H. Kim, Lai To Lee, and Annie Soo of the Chinese Historical Society of America. For their friendship and professional assistance, this mere mention is inadequate payment. Thanks are also due Miss Lori K. Sletten and Mrs. Terry Garrity for typing the manuscript. Finally, my parents deserve a special note of appreciation. Without their constant encouragement and endless care, this work would not have been possible.

Drafts of this book were discussed at colloquia and seminars at the University of California at Berkeley, UCLA, and the University of Arkansas. The final version was written with the aid of a Fulbright College of Arts and Sciences Research Assignment from the University of Arkansas, and by a Post-doctoral Fellowship from the Institute of American Cultures, the University of California at Los Angeles.

PROLOGUE

During the 1984 Los Angeles Olympic Games, Chinese athletes surprised the world with their achievements. China laid to rest all doubts about its athletic prowess by winning 32 medals, 15 of them gold, and its 100-plus delegates charmed the American television audience with a mixture of competitiveness, grace, and modesty. Even before this event, Chinese baseball teams from Taiwan had won several Little League World Championships at Williamsport, Pennsylvania, and the excellent academic achievements of young Chinese Americans have frequently drawn the attention of the media. American youngsters at every level of education generally hold their Chinese peers in high esteem. In every Chinese community across the country, the Chinese minority has managed to pull itself up from hardship and discrimination to become a model of self-respect and achievement in today's troubled American society. And in spite of the fact that substantial numbers of Chinese are still economically disadvantaged, the 1980 census notes that the $22,075 median family income of Asian Americans—which also includes the Japanese, Koreans, and Filipinos—has surpassed that of white families, which averaged only $20,840. It is estimated that one out of every hundred Chinese in America is a holder of the Ph.D. The Chinese Americans are often characterized by a friendly media as fun-loving, industrious, honest, steady, loyal, and bright. Very few young Americans realize that their fathers and grandfathers did not think of the Chinese in the same way.

In 1927, social scientist Emory S. Bogardus surveyed 1,725 Americans and found only 27.0 percent who said they would accept Chinese as fellow workers, 15.9 percent as neighbors, and 11.8 percent as friends. The clearly unfavorable American perception of the Chinese was for the most part the product of the experience of the latter half of the nineteenth century when China was weak and poor, and the Chinese who came to America were largely uneducated and worked as cheap laborers. Pressed by poverty at home and attracted by job opportunities in America, hundreds of thousands of Chinese from the southern province of Guangdong flocked to the United States. They tunneled through mountains, cleared forests, reclaimed swamps, and helped to open up the great American West for settlement. In the course of their work, the Chinese were exposed not only to the inclemencies of the weather, but also to all the dangers of a region overrun by wild beasts and diseases. As a result, thousands of them perished.

The depression of the 1870s and mass unemployment caused growing tension between laborers and capitalists and accelerated the growth of organized labor in the United Sates. The Chinese, then appearing as a new ethnic group on the American scene, quickly became the target of racial hatred and victims of labor-management disputes. Anti-Chinese propaganda initiated by organized labor and the soapbox orations of wily politicians began to create a mythology of servile Chinese coolies and slave girls. The Chinese accordingly suffered from powerful prejudice, and for the next several decades, carried a stigma of villainy which became ingrained in popular American folklore. Sinophobic writers portrayed the Chinese as cowardly, dishonest, uncivilized, cruel, sinful, sick, degraded, and without any sense of decency or conscience. Occasionally, Chinese laundrymen, servants, or railway workers were described as hardworking, resourceful, thrifty, and docile; but even these humble virtues were viewed as only defensive mechanisms against the tyranny and lust of their employers. These distorted Chinese images lingered and were eventually exploited by the Hollywood movie industry. Movie such as *Mr. Wu* portrayed the Chinese as evil, wicked, and murderous while the slant-eyed *Dr. Fu Manchu* became the symbol of Chinese menace and terror.

Social Darwinists used those stereotyped Chinese images to argue that the debased Oriental blood might affect Anglo-American stock and that the Chinese should be excluded from the white man's land. Beginning in 1882, the United States government adopted a series of exclusionary laws to bar the entry of Chinese laborers. The American public, having been thoroughly conditioned to view the Chinese as "heathen," "yellow," and "inferior", went along with these anti-Chinese policies. Late nineteenth-century immigration legislation injured the Chinese more than any other immigrant group. In the meantime, those Chinese who remained in the United States were driven into Chinatown ghettoes, uncomplaining, withdrawing, apolitical, and passive. It should be pointed out, however, that this passiveness was not a cultural trait of the Chinese; it was the product of their experience as aliens. Until World War II, they were mostly limited to non-competitive jobs and were treated with benighted neglect.

When the Japanese attacked Pearl Harbor and the United States and China became wartime allies, American perception of China and the Chinese became more favorable. Three years after Japan's unconditional surrender, E. Elmo Roper reported that 85.8 percent of the whites then surveyed said they would accept Chinese as fellow workers, 72 percent as neighbors, and 77 percent as friends or guests. This more tolerant social environment along with better political conditions opened new educational and career opportunities to Chinese Americans, greatly improving their economic position. The 1950s saw a significant portion of Chinese easing into previously restricted areas of employment. In the 1960s and 1970s, the pace of of acculturation increased markedly. But in spite of these improvements, subtle racial barriers continued to exist and the Chinese are still employed mainly in jobs that require no public contact, such as bookkeeping, accounting, and engineering, and employment that requires patience and hard work. In the civil service and the professional groups, the Chinese still work mostly in engineering and as accountants.

However, with the rise of a Chinese middle class and the opening of housing opportunities in the post-World War II era, more and more Chinese moved out of the ghettoes. This has led many people, including the late sociologist Rose Hum Lee, to predict that all American Chinatowns would disappear. Yet, at the present time, Chinatowns remain alive and vibrant. This is partly due to the influx of new immigrants from Hong Kong and Taiwan since 1965. The newly arrived Chinese, especially those who do not speak English, often find themselves locked into low-paying menial work in and around Chinatowns. The persistence of Chinatowns is also due to the increasing demand for Chinese goods and services by those better educated newcomers who have found employment in their professions and have settled in suburbs, but desire to retain their Chinese culture and identity by establishing close ethnic ties. As a result of these new elements, a revitalization of commerce and a revival of interest in Chinese culture are taking place in America's Chinatowns. The influx of the immigrants has also dramatically increased the Chinese population in the United States from 237,292 in 1960 to 806,027 in 1980.

The newcomers have demonstrated during the past two decades that they, like the eighteenth-century French Huguenots, nineteenth-century German forty-eighters, and the twentieth-century Russian Jews, have adapted to American culture and therefore have succeeded in their diaspora experience. Statistics show that new immigrants were largely educated professionals, many of whom had achieved a certain degree of Americanization even before they disembarked. Others were capitalists, or *petit bourgeois,* nurtured in an urbanized setting, who had abandoned traditional Chinese religious beliefs in favor of Christianity and exhibited a high degree of individualism and economic motivation, traits frequently ascribed to American culture. Moreover, unlike the early wave of immigration, which was relatively homogeneous, most immigrants being Cantonese-speaking laborers from the rural villages of Guangdong, this new influx has been heterogeneous, made up of Chinese from many regions, speaking various dialects, and exhibiting a variety of political beliefs. At a time when China is still at a stage of "civil war," Chinese Americans confront the issue of their identity in relation to political events which take place in their homeland.

During the past century, the Chinese in America had the unique burden of responding to several major political changes in China, namely, the fall of a dynasty, the birth of a troubled republic, the turmoil of warlordism, the invasion of the Japanese, and the rivalry between the Communists and the Nationalists. These changes often divided America's Chinese community into various factions and intensified the identity crisis of Chinese Americans. In the late nineteenth and early twentieth centuries, the Chinese in America were wooed by three major political groups: the Manchu ruling class, the Reform Party of Kang Youwei, and the revolutionaries led by Dr. Sun Yat-sen. The early Republican era saw their political allegiance shifting from Yuan Shikai to Wang Jingwei to Chiang Kai-shek. Following the Communist triumph in 1949, cold-war politics complicated the political allegiance of Chinese Americans. The changing policy of the United States toward the "Two Chinas" divided the Chinese community into a pro-Peking group and a pro-Taiwan group, with the latter further split into a pro-Kuomintang faction and the Taiwan Independence Movement. At present, the Chinese in America are as politically fragmented as they were at the turn of the century when the reformists and the revolutionaries were fiercely competing for money and support. This situation, plus a prevailing civil rights awareness, has stimulated political activism among Chinese Americans.

With this brief introduction, the reader must be aware that American images of the Chinese as shaped by changing circumstances, the United States immigration laws specifically aimed at the Chinese, and other facets of Sino-American relations have, to a great extent, influenced the Chinese experience in America. The Chinese occupational adjustment throughout the years, the evolving Chinatowns, the process by which the Chinese entered the mainstream of American life, their subordination, assimilation, and integration with the host country—all these themes and many more have made up the Chinese experience in America.

The Chinese experience in America has been quite different from that of other subordinated ethnic minorities (with perhaps the exception of the Japanese Americans) and voluntary European immigrants to this country. This study discusses the differing experiences of three groups: sojourners, ABC (American-born Chinese), and student-immigrants. The sojourners, who were China-oriented and non-English-speaking, suffered from persistent inequality, racial conflict, alienation, and subordination. Their experience in America was one of tragedy and travail. In the end, they remained "truly Chinese." The ABC, who constantly faced conflicting values and had to deal with various assimilation problems, generally led a dual life and bore feelings of ambivalence. Even though most of them were completely acculturated, they were not fully integrated. Their experience was, therefore, a mixture of expectation, struggle, and inevitable confusion and anger. The highly educated student-immigrants, who indeed are modern China's "cream of the crop," tend to emphasize cultural pluralism and national diversity; accordingly, they emphasize the persistence of ethnic cultural traits, family practices, subcultural activities, and distinctive identities. They belong to America's middle class, and in spite of their color and physical appearance, are occupationally integrated, though some of them are not yet completely acculturated. Their successful and pleasant experience in America has earned them the "model minority" title.

While assessing the successes and failures of each of the three groups in historical context and exploring theories of assimilation, this study also strives to acquaint the reader with the evolutionary patterns of Chinese-American interaction. While it describes Chinese life in the United States, it also examines an American national character that is filled with paradoxes: narrowness and magnanimity, benevolence and exasperation, sympathy and hostility, Christian love and racial hatred. It hopes, therefore, to serve as a reflection of the evolving American mentality as our nation gradually overcomes bigotry and racial prejudice, and grows into maturity.

A distressing aspect of writing about the Chinese minority in America is the agonizing problem of romanization. Many important names and institutions were traditionally romanized according to the pronunciation in their particular Cantonese dialects. Added to that difficulty is the unsettled debate over use of the established Wade-Giles system versus that of the Hanyu Pinyin more recently developed by the People's Republic. The solution adopted here is to retain some of the romanization of Cantonese as the names and terms appeared in historical records, official documents, and newspapers. Otherwise, names and terms are romanized according to Hanyu Pinyin, except for a few universally recognized post-Atlas spellings, such as Peking instead of Beijing.

I

THE NINETEENTH-CENTURY CHINESE IMMIGRATION

It is easy to stay home for one thousand days; it is hard to stay outside for a short period.

—Chinese proverb

East or West, home is best.

—Western saying

1. Problems in the Old Country

Recent archaeological finds off the Palos Verdes Peninsula, just south of the California coast, briefly caused a delirious speculation that America was discovered by Chinese Buddhist missionaries in the fifth century. Thirty coral-encrusted rocks were found, each weighing from 500 to 700 pounds, with man-made holes and inscribed with identifiable Chinese characters. These artifacts correspond to a passage in the *History of the Liang Dynasty* that records how Huishen, a leader of the group, discovered the Kingdom of Fusang, possibly the West Coast of North America, in A.D. 459. However, descriptions of what he saw are too vague to be accepted as positive proof.[1] Nearly a thousand years later, during the first quarter of the fifteenth century, the Chinese launched a series of phenomenal maritime explorations, but no record told of encounters with American Indians.

According to legend, the first Chinese to land in the New World were three seamen, Ashing, Achun, and Accun, crewmen on the ship *Pallas.* In 1785 they were stranded in Baltimore by their captain, John O'Donnell.[2] In the following decade, a trickle of Chinese merchants, carpenters, coopers, and servants were said to have arrived in Phila-

1

delphia, as well as at Nootka Sound in Canada, and the Hawaiian Islands. Other notable visitors before 1847 included a Chinese merchant who visited his friend John Jacob Astor while collecting debts in New York, five Chinese students who came to Cornwall, Connecticut, for education, and three young Cantonese who attended the Monson Academy in Massachusetts.

In 1820, the United States began to keep immigration records, but for almost three decades, up to 1849, the records show a total of only 43 Chinese. This, however, did not include Chinese immigrants to the West Coast as it was not a part of the Union at that time. According to historian Hubert Howe Bancroft, two men and one woman from China, probably servants of Charles Gillespies, stood on the deck of the ship *Eagle* on February 2, 1848, as it came into San Francisco Harbor; they were the first Chinese settlers in California. By January 1850, the Chinese population of San Francisco had increased to 787 men and two women, and the first mayor of San Francisco, John White Geary, invited them to participate in a memorial funeral procession for the late President Zachary Taylor.[3] In the next few decades, tens of thousands of Chinese, most of them young men between the ages of 15 and 40, poured into America. Suddenly, the influx of the Chinese became an international issue that concerned both Peking and Washington.

Chinese immigration to the United States was but one aspect of a greater Chinese exodus during the nineteenth century. Since 1644 China had been under the autocratic rule of the Manchu, or Qing, dynasty. For several decades after its conquest of China proper, the Qing government feared a possible alliance between anti-Qing forces at home and Chinese rebels abroad; consequently, it refused to sanction the emigration of Chinese people. One statute stipulated: "Those who find excuse to sojourn abroad and then clandestinely return home, if captured, shall be executed immediately. Those who smuggle abroad cattle, horses, ammunition, metal . . . , shall be whipped one hundred times. Those who smuggle human beings or weapons out of the country shall be hanged."[4] By the nineteenth century, however, the dynasty had passed its pinnacle and was on the decline. Heavy taxation, corruption, and oppression caused discontent among the people. The rapid increase in population, which was estimated at about 143 million in 1741, 286 million in 1784, and 430 million in 1850, further aggravated the situation.[5] Population pressure, bureaucratic incompetence, and natural disasters created food shortages that led to social unrest and rebellion. Many chose to risk the perils of travel and punishment to go to Southeast Asia and America in search of greater economic opportunities.

A majority of those who chose to emigrate came from the two

coastal provinces of Guangdong and Fujian, which are hilly and not well endowed with natural resources. More than sixty percent of the Chinese in the United States trace their roots to a small region in Guangdong Province. This area contains eight districts, each about the size of an average American county. Between 1833 and 1882, the region was hard hit by an unusually large number of natural disasters—droughts, storms, typhoons, blights, earthquakes, and plagues. Whenever the region's river system could not cope with a sudden rise in the volume of water, floods and famines occurred.[6] Moreover, since the late seventeenth century, the population of Guangdong had swelled every year, reaching the 16 million mark in 1787 and 28 million in 1850.[7]

The increase in population was not accompanied by a comparable increase in arable land; to make matters worse, most of the land was concentrated in the hands of a few landlords. A majority of the Cantonese peasants were tenants who, in order to make ends meet, often had to work as part-time laborers, servants, watchmen, and the like. Much of the cultivated land, which as late as 1955 constituted only 16 percent of the total area, was used to grow such commercial crops as tobacco, sugar cane, and fruit instead of rice, the staple food of the southern Chinese.[8] Consequently, the common folk suffered from the rapidly rising price of rice while the rich landlords and merchants accumulated wealth. The corollaries of these circumstances were a string of domestic revolts, rampant piracy, and the establishment of secret societies. In 1849, for instance, a rebellious group ambushed a detachment of government troops, and in November, 1850, the Taipings, first in Guangxi, then in Guangdong, launched an open revolt. In the ensuing years, the revolts in Guangdong increased in number and scale and severe fighting continued throughout the 1850s. Such turbulent events resulted in political disorder, social chaos, and economic dislocations. A local gazetteer graphically described the situation: "The fields in the four directions were choked with weeds. Small families found it difficult to make a living and often drowned their girl babies because of the impossibility of looking after them."[9]

2. The Myth of Chinese Coolies

Compounding the desolate circumstances in these regions was a series of foreign invasions and encroachments upon China's sovereignty. The Opium War (1839–42) resulted in a humiliating treaty, in which China granted all English nationals the privilege of extraterritoriality. By virtue of the most-favored-nation clause, other European nations and the United States eventually were also awarded the same privilege. The degradation of extraterritoriality allowed "merchant vessels of the treaty powers, lying in the waters of the five treaty ports of China" to engage in commerce and trade "under the jurisdiction of the officers of their own governments without control on the part of China."[10]

At this juncture, the Spanish Republics had begun to enforce measures against the slave trade with new stringency and, suddenly, the planters in Latin America, especially those in the West Indies, were in great need of labor. After learning of the availability of cheap, hard-working Chinese labor and of the loopholes made possible by extra-territoriality, many resorted to fraud and coercion to induce the Chinese to emigrate to work in the region. In the 1840s, an illicit trade in Chinese contract laborers, known as the "coolie trade," sprang up in various Chinese ports, the center being Macao, a Portuguese colony not far from Canton and Hong Kong.

The first recorded shipment of coolies to the American continent was from Amoy, one of the treaty ports in Fujian province, in 1847. About 8,000 coolies were carried to Cuba that year. In 1849, two Peruvian capitalists, Domingo Elias and Juan Rodriguez, brought 75 Chinese coolies to work in Peru's guano pits.[11] During the following year, an American businessman, Henry Chauncey, recruited several thousand Chinese to build a railroad from Panama to Colón. News of the possibilities in the coolie traffic soon spread throughout the New World; from 1847 to 1859 the number of Chinese coolies transported by American shippers to Cuba alone averaged over 6,000 per year.[12]

The coolie purveyors erected barracoons or "pig-pens" and made arrangements with pirates, Chinese brokers, and others to secure workers. A great number of poor Chinese peasants were induced to leave their homes by misleading promises and were detained in the barracoons. Some were kidnapped while asleep in their junks or taken out of their fields or gardens with hands and feet tied. They were then hurried off to the barracoons where they were imprisoned until a ship was ready to sail. Some were victims of clan fights and were sold by their captors to coolie brokers. Still others were gamblers who, on losing, surrendered themselves in payment according to the Chinese custom of the time.[13]

Treatment of the Chinese coolies on board ship was inhumane. Usually the transport ships were badly equipped and overcrowded. Food was poor. Sanitary facilities were nonexistent. Brutality against the coolies was common. The American ship *Waverly*, bound from Swatow to Callao, Peru, with 450 coolies aboard, was typical. On October 27, 1855, while preparations were being made to bury the body of the captain at Carito, Philippines, the coolies believed that they had arrived at their destination. They wished to go ashore and attempted to take possession of the boats, but the new captain fired at them. After a short struggle with the armed crew, the Chinese were driven below deck and the hatches closed. Some twelve or fourteen hours later, when the hatches were opened, it was found that nearly 300 of the Chinese had perished by suffocation.[14]

Coolies who could not endure the treatment committed suicide or instigated mutinies. Many stabbed themselves with pieces of wood or hanged themselves from the masts. Others jumped overboard and drowned. Mutinies frequently erupted when the coolies discovered they had been tricked into bondage. Angry and desperate coolies sometimes butchered crew and officers or set fires aboard their ships in midpassage. One case that attracted the attention of the United States government occurred aboard the American ship *Robert Browne,* sailing from Amoy in 1852. When the 400 Chinese emigrants due for shipment discovered they had been deceived and were to be carried into contract bondage, they killed all the officers. Afterwards, they testified in a Chinese court that they had been promised four dollars a month for working in the United States as hired laborers, not as contract coolies.[15]

Upon arrival at their destination, the fate of many coolies was unpredictable and extremely precarious. They frequently were bound to colonization companies by contracts they had never examined. Sometimes the coolies would be sold at auction in open market to the highest bidder, who held them virtually as slaves for as long as seven years. In many cases the coolies were sent to labor, contrary to their agreements, in the sugar plantations of Cuba or in the foul guano pits of the Chincha Islands and other guano islands off the coast of Peru. They were forced to toil in gangs under the charge of an overseer armed with a cowhide lash. Of the 4,000 coolies who had been fraudulently consigned in 1860 to the guano pits of Peru, not one survived.[16] Of the 150,000 coolies taken to the Spanish and South American colonies before 1865, fewer than 500 lived to return to China.[17]

It is impossible to secure accurate figures on the number of Chinese coolies who were carried to Latin America, but statistics on the coolie trade for 1855 at Swatow (Table 1) may indicate the extent.[18]

TABLE 1

Ships		Tonnage	Coolies
American	5	6,592	3,050
British	3	3,821	1,938
Chilean	1	500	250
Peruvian	3	1,860	1,150
	12	12,773	6,388

From 1847 to 1862, American shippers monopolized the coolie traffic between Macao and Havana, as United States Congressional documents reveal. Table 2 represents the total number carried by American ships.[19]

TABLE 2

Year	No. of Vessels	Tonnage	Shipped	Landed	Died
1847	2	879	612	571	41
1853	15	8,349	5,150	4,307	843
1854	4	2,349	1,750	1,711	39
1855	6	6,544	3,130	2,985	145
1856	15	10,567	6,152	4,968	1,184
1857	28	18,310	10,116	8,547	1,509
1858	33	32,800	16,413	13,385	3,029
1859	13	10,283	6,799	6,027	772
	116	90,081	50,122	42,501	7,562

The Qing government did little to ameliorate the situation because it looked askance at emigrants for leaving their ancestral land. But as reports of atrocities against the coolies continued to pour in, Peking finally drew up, in December of 1866, a set of twenty-two rules regulating the recruitment and working conditions of coolies. Furthermore, in 1874, the government sent investigation teams to Peru and Cuba to look into the Chinese problems there. These two missions resulted in two bilateral treaties with Peru and Spain, both of which guaranteed better treatment of the Chinese coolies. Nevertheless, due to the lack of resources and insufficient personnel, the Qing government did not accredit any representatives to protect Chinese interests in the Americas until 1878.

Since American vessels frequently took Chinese coolies from the treaty ports of China, United States authorities were aware of the abusive operation. As a mater of fact, in their messages to the Congress, Presidents Pierce, Buchanan, Lincoln, and Grant deplored the illegalities, immoralities, and revolting atrocities of the coolie trade. The United States, to all intents and purposes, prohibited coolie immigration; it allowed only free and voluntary immigrants from China. Because of American involvement in the coolie traffic between China and Latin America, the term "coolie," which carried with it connotations of servitude, slavery, or peonage, came to be used loosely in the United States to designate all Chinese immigrants. But however restricted the rights of early Chinese immigrants in the United States may have been, the term coolie is an inaccurate name for them.

Two U.S. laws and one Sino-American treaty worked to virtually prohibit bond coolies from coming to this country. A law enacted in February, 1847, provided that the master of a vessel taking on board any greater number of passengers than the ship can accommodate and causing the detriment of the lives and health of the passengers, with intent to transport the same from the United States to any foreign port or place, or from any foreign port or place to the United States, was guilty of a misdemeanor.[20] This law, however, did not prohibit the transportation of contract laborers from one foreign port to another foreign port, say from Macao to Havana. American shippers took advantage of the loopholes in the law and entered the lucrative coolie traffic. As abuses grew, the United States Congress, in February, 1862, passed the Prohibition of Coolie Trade Act which prohibited American shippers from engaging in any form of the coolie trade.[21]

Six years later, the 1868 Supplementary Articles to the Sino-American Treaty of Tianjin, commonly known in this country as the Burlingame Treaty, not only repealed the century-old Chinese prohibitory emigration laws but also repeated the American principle of free immigration. Article V of the treaty stipulated:

> The United States of America and the Emperor of China cordially recognize the inherent and inalienable right of man to change his home and allegiance, and also the mutual advantage of the free migration and emigration of their citizens and subjects respectively from one country to the other for the purpose of curiosity, of trade, or as permanent residents.[22]

The anti-coolie acts and free migration agreement between China and the United States set the legal framework for nineteenth-century Chinese immigration. The Chinese emigration to California was free and voluntary, confined to independent emigrants who paid their own passage money and were in a condition to look to their arrangements.[23] The Chinese ministers who were in charge of the 1880 Sino-American migration negotiation characterized the Chinese in America as "wild geese" who had flown to the United States not as a result of deceit or by being kidnapped but because they regarded America as a land of abundance and as furnishing great opportunities.[24] Moreover, Congressional documents reveal that the early Chinese in the United States were free immigrants, at the very worst coming on the so-called "ticket system" or on money borrowed at a high rate of interest. In spite of such evidence, the myth of "Chinese coolies" has persisted in America; it has had a mischievous effect on American perceptions of the Chinese.

3. Coming to the Gold Mountain

Chinese immigrants to Gum Sann, or the "Gold Mountain" of California, usually traveled in junks, lorchas, or rafts over the waterways of the Pearl River Delta from their native villages to Hong Kong or Macao, then took a steamship for the trans-Pacific voyage. American and British ship masters afforded a variety of facilities to accommodate the immigrants, then charged them high passenger rates, ranging from $40 to $50 one way and $60 to $70 for a round trip. During 1852, about 30,000 Chinese embarked at Hong Kong for San Francisco and paid a total of approximately $1,300,000 for the voyages. At the beginning of 1856, the Reverend William Speer calculated that Chinese immigrants to California had paid a total $2,329,580 for trans-Pacific trips. Understandably, transportation companies became powerful supporters of Chinese immigration. In 1866 the Pacific Mail Steamship Company entered the China trade, and a little later the Occidental and Oriental Steamship Company was organized as a competitor. During the peak years of the Chinese immigration, from 1876 to 1890, steamships carried an estimated 200,000 Chinese to West Coast ports and over half that number back to China where they visited or remained. American and British companies probably realized more than $11 million in steerage ticket fees.[25]

Some emigrants were able to put up enough cash for the passage fees; others who were poor and could not raise the necessary money usually entered a "credit ticket agreement." The Wells-Fargo Bank History Room in San Francisco displays a contract, signed in 1849 between an English company in Shanghai and a group of Chinese laborers, that illustrates how the credit system worked. From the time the workers left Shanghai, the expenses for their provisions and transportation were defrayed by the company. On arriving in San Francisco, the company was obligated to seek employment for the Chinese mechanics and laborers; the money the company had advanced would be returned when employment was secured. A moiety of each immigrant's wages would be deducted monthly until the debt, which amounted to $120 each, was absorbed. After that, the Chinese would receive their wages in full every month.

While an overwhelming majority of the Chinese immigrants settled on the West Coast, a trickle journeyed to the South to seek employment. During the Reconstruction era, some white Southerners decided to bring Chinese into the Mississippi Delta region. Several white planters in the South hoped to use Chinese to replace black labor and undermine the growing political power of the freed blacks. They often resorted to the credit ticket system, revising the agreements to allow for a longer period of service. An 1872 agreement was typical:

Article I:　The undersigned has borrowed $100 from an American businessman for voyaging purpose to Louisiana.

Article II:　On arrival, employment for the said laborer should begin for the next five years. The said laborer agrees to work 20 days a month, from dawn to dusk except breaks for meals. The plantation owner agrees to pay the said laborer $7 a month as wages.

Article III:　In case of night work, the owner should pay 50 cents for every six hours' work.

Article IV:　The said laborer pledges to follow the plantation rules and be honest and industrious; and he'll get Sunday off.

Article V:　The plantation owner may volunteer to give the said laborer a private lot for gardening. Every month the owner should give the said laborer 45 pounds of rice, 15 pounds of smoked pork, and ⅓ pound of tea.

Article VI:　If the said laborer falls ill, the owner will pay for his medical expenses but will not pay his regular wages. If the said laborer declines to work without good reasons his wages will be deducted accordingly.

Article VII:　Should Article V fail to satisfy the needs of the said laborer, he may exchange the listed items for $5.50 cash, but he would have to take care of his own food bills.

Article VIII:　It is expected that after a period of five years, if the owner is satisfied with the work of the said laborer, the $100 passage loan would be absorbed by the owner. And an additional $150 will be given to the said laborer as reward.[26]

Some Southern planters even offered opium as an inducement. As an example, Arkansas planters in the 1870s promised to pay every Chinese worker half a pound of opium per month in addition to wages fixed in the contract. When the price of opium later went up to $15 and $18 per pound, the planters decided that they could no longer afford Chinese labor.[27]

Most Chinese, after working for only a brief period of time, left the Delta region. Had they been "coolies," like those kidnapped or tricked into going to Cuba and Peru by unscrupulous brokers, they would not have been able to leave at their option. The Chinese laborers, whether working on a Louisiana plantation or mining in California or building a section of railway in the High Sierras, were clearly not drones, criminals, or bond slaves. They were mostly poor and uneducated, but they were responsible free men. Many were married and had families to support in China. While generally accommodating and easily governed, they cherished high hopes of getting a good price for their labor.[28] As the trans-Mississippi West captured the imagination of the world during the mining rushes, the Chinese flocked to the region in response to the same hopes for riches and adventure that attracted other migrants.

A typical Chinese immigrant wore coarse gray, wide-legged trousers, a broad-brimmed straw hat, and a pair of sandals or wooden shoes. The few merchants who joined the gold rush usually wore silk caps, mandarin-style gowns, and cloth shoes. During the trans-Pacific voyage, which took between two and three months, he used his rationed water to brew hot tea, and ate lemon peal or salted, dried plums to prevent scurvy and seasickness. Together with his fellow passengers, he was crowded into the steerage of the ship and spent most of his time dozing in his narrow cot. When his ship arrived in San Francisco or Eureka, he wadded his body with personal belongings and brought his small bundle of clothing and blankets with him. After clearing the dreaded customs house, he was met by a Chinese representative who registered his name and sent him to join his provincials in some sort of caravansary boardinghouse. There the weary immigrant could rest and arrange for a portion of his wages to be remitted home periodically to his relatives in China. He also immediately arranged for his body to be shipped to China for burial in case he should meet with an accident in America; he believed that if his body was buried in a strange land, untended by his family, his soul would never stop wandering in the darkness of the other world. After taking care of such details, he left for the gold mine, railway construction site, or marshy field, in express wagons or on foot.

4. In the Mines

During the early days of the gold rushes a cosmopolitan assortment of humanity gathered on the mining frontiers of the American West, including white Americans, British subjects, Germans, French, Indians, Mexicans, Spaniards, Negroes, and Chinese. By the 1860s, when the gold bonanza yielded only modest pay dirt, most of the white miners had forsaken the gulches and canyons, but the Chinese stayed on and made up almost two-thirds of the mining labor force in the states west of the Rocky Mountains. The United States census of 1870 counted 17,069 Chinese miners, more than 11 percent of the total 152,107 in the country. But in the western states, the number of the Chinese miners was very significant. For example, of Oregon's 3,965 miners, 2,428 or 61.2 percent were Chinese; in Montana, of 6,720 miners, 1,415, about 21 percent, were Chinese; in Idaho, among the 6,579 miners, 3,853 or 58.6 percent were Chinese; and out of the 36,339 California mining laborers, 9,087 or 25 percent came from China.[29] According to mining expert Henry Degroot, during the period 1849–1870, the value of the precious metals produced upon the Pacific coast approximated $1.2 billion, and in 1871 alone Chinese miners extracted and put into circulation something over $27 million.[30]

The first three Chinese in the California gold field apparently arrived only one month after James Marshall had found gold in Sutter's Mill in January, 1848. As the bonanza grew, more and more Chinese caught gold fever and joined the fortune hunt. During the next two decades, thousands of Chinese were digging in the mines of Mariposa, Placer, and Pine Tree of California. It was difficult to ascertain how many worked their own stakes and how many were hired by Chinese contractors or American companies. It is clear that, once the shallow deposits were exhausted and larger mining companies began to move to deeper deposits and use hydraulic mining, the Chinese drifted back into the foothills to continue their more elementary operations.

The general impression that the shallow placers had abandoned California by 1865 is unfounded. River and bar mining was still extensively carried on by the more patient and more poorly equipped Chinese in many parts of California. As late as 1871, the Chinese were still prospecting on the banks and bars of the American River with satisfactory results. Several Chinese camps in the great canyon of the North Fork of the American River between Jehoval and Cape Horn still existed in the 1870s.[31] In the often all-male mining communities, Chinese were much sought after as laundrymen, cooks, and servants. As a result, mining counties in California also found a larger Chinese population[32] (see Appendix 1).

From California, the Chinese ventured on to Oregon, Washington, Nevada, and Idaho. Along the Rogue and the Umpqua Rivers in southwest Oregon, Chinese miners built houses with cedar boards and roofed them with logs and brush; by 1858 nearly 1,000 Chinese resided in the mining center of Josephine. The principal mining area in Oregon later moved to the eastern part of the state, on both sides of the Blue Range. By the late 1860s, the mining industry in Oregon had fallen mainly into the hands of Chinese who, in most cases, purchased placer mines formerly operated by whites. Using superior patience and economy, the Chinese continued the production of gold in many Oregon localities after other prospectors had left.[33] One writer described the situation at Auburn, a typical eastern Oregon gold town: "The Chinese patiently panned the gulches until there was scarcely an ounce of gold in the tailings of other days. . . . When the Chinese miners had gleaned the last meager clean-up of dust from the gulches, the story of Auburn was ended."[34]

In the early 1860s, Chinese miners moved to eastern Washington. Up and down the Columbia River and its numerous tributaries, Chinese worked and panned. They established a village where the Chelan River joins the Columbia. By 1864, hundreds of Chinese were operating along the river east of Rock Island. As they did in California and Oregon, the Chinese bought large gravel bars from white miners and worked them for the last traces of gold. They searched every creek and channelled every small brook; they ditched and flumed for long distances to get the last meager returns.[35]

In Nevada, some fifty Chinese dug a canal to bring water from the Carson River, and founded a town called Dayton in 1855. Placer mining by Chinese was concentrated, however, on the north side of the Owyhee River and at Silver Peak. The entire force in the Red Mountain mines was said to have been at one time all Chinese. One mining company manager in the Morey district of Nevada declared in 1869 that the Chinese gave him perfect satisfaction, doing as well as an equal number of white men.[36] Although gold and silver mining were the main attractions for Chinese in Nevada, they found other work as well. Some were engaged in the hotel, grocery, laundering, restaurant, and even gambling businesses. In the 1870s, there was a "Chinatown" in practically every major Nevada city; in Carson City, the Chinese population numbered more than 2,000. When the first Chinese minister to the United States, Chen Lanpin, visited Nevada in 1878, he reported large Chinese communities in Reno, Battle Mountain, and Carlin.[37]

From Oregon, some of the Chinese moved into Idaho, and in the mid–1860s they arrived in the Boise Basin. In spite of the exhaustion of the creek and gulch claims of the older placer mining, the Chinese purchased abandoned fields and for several years maintained a moderately productive industry. The Chinese in Idaho in 1870 totalled 4,274, but mainly because of the decline of the mining boom, the population had decreased to 2,007 by 1890.[38] Other Chinese miners continued to follow the rivers and streams to their sources in the Rocky Mountains and inevitably reached the diggings in Montana, Colorado and the Dakota Territories. A. K. McClure, a famed newsman, reported in 1869 that there were at least 100 Chinese in and around Virginia City, and twice as many in Helena, Montana.[39] The 1870 federal census showed a total of 1,949 Chinese residing in Montana, including 1,415 engaged in mining. In 1870, the Colorado legislature passed a joint resolution welcoming Chinese laborers to "hasten the development and early prosperity of the Territory." Chinese worked in the Gilpin's mining area, in the Hope Valley, and also in Denver, all as employees in American-owned mines. In spite of a horrible anti-Chinese riot in Denver in 1880, the Chinese population in Colorado increased from 612 in 1880 to 1,398 in 1890. In South Dakota, Chinese miners lived mostly around Deadwood, a small town north of the Black Hills range. The tiny Chinese community organized a team of 12 firemen who, on July 4, 1888, won first prize in a fire-drill contest.[40]

Like other prospectors, Chinese miners used the pick-axe, the pan, the sluice box, and the water wheel, known in America as the China pump, to work the gravel heaps and tailings of the mines. Living conditions in the mining camps were primitive and often unsanitary. At the camp site, workers slept in small tents, on the ground, or huddled together in cabins or tents abandoned by the whites. Some of them even burrowed caves, using a blanket to cover them. They retained their blue cotton tunics and broad trousers, their wooden shoes and broad-brimmed hats with a queue, or pigtail, hanging down their backs. Since most Chinese spoke little or no English, those who worked for American companies were usually hired through a broker who would recruit miners from among his relatives or fellow villagers. The employer would pay a lump sum to the broker who provided the daily necessities and dispensed wages to his crew. This system was also practiced for hiring in railroad construction, wheat harvesting, and in the canneries.

Chinese miners were particularly subject to danger from the lawless outcasts attracted to the camps. They were also confronted with discrimination in the form of confiscatory taxes and other legal obstructions. For example, the Oregon Constitutional Convention in August, 1857, ruled that Chinese should not be allowed to own mining claims or land. Two years later, when Oregon achieved statehood, its legislature levied a $5 poll tax on every Chinese.[41] In 1864, Washington Territory passed an act designed to disfranchise the Chinese in the mining field. A special quarterly capitation tax of $6, called the "Chinese Police Tax", was levied on every "Mongolian" in the territory. The sheriff in each county was responsible for collecting the tax and was entitled to keep 25 percent of the money he collected.[42] Moreover, if there were disputes between whites and Chinese, the latter were prohibited from giving testimony in the courts. In Montana, Nevada, and Idaho, similar discriminations were imposed on the Chinese, while the California legislature, beginning in 1852, passed a series of laws against the Chinese miners. The Act of 1855 required the owner of a vessel to pay $450 for each passenger who was ineligible for citizenship and the Act of 1862 required a monthly payment of $2.50 by each "Mongolian" over eighteen who had not paid the miner's license fee.[43]

The intent of these various tax measures seemingly was to protect

white miners against competition from the Chinese and to discourage
the immigration of the Chinese. Such official restrictions probably encouraged white men's contempt for and violence against their Chinese counterparts. The yellow skins, strange features, small figures,
and incomprehensible language of the Chinese led whites to believe
that the Chinese were an inferior race. White jailbirds, gamblers, de-
serters, desperadoes, thieves, and frequently even respected citizens
used such epithets as "John Chinaman," "Chink Chinamen," or "heathen," when they talked to the Chinese, refusing to address them by
name. During the anti-Chinese movement of the late 1870s and 1880s,
labor unions further propagated the myth of the inferiority of the
Orientals. But in spite of adversity, the Chinese doggedly pursued
their right to stand beside other miners as equal partners. They resisted the collection of these confiscatory and clearly discriminatory
taxes. Most of these acts were later declared unconstitutional by state
or federal courts.

Chinese mining activities, working conditions, wages, contributions, and problems were described in a congressional report prepared in March, 1871, by Rossiter W. Raymond, the United States
commissioner for the collection of mining statistics. After making a
long and thorough investigation of the western mines, the commissioner praised the qualities of the Chinese miners and concluded that
their presence in this country was highly desirable. He found that the
Chinese were willing to work for modest wages, but were very firm in
the matter of payment. Because they had little faith in the promises of
their employers, they would stop work if not paid promptly. Raymond
believed that Chinese skilled miners were equal to those of any other
race, and in some instances, they even surpassed white men employed
in the same mines. The greatest asset of good Chinese miners, as opposed to the Europeans, was their fidelity. The commissioner said
that the latter, if working for hourly wages, had a habit of idling and
malingering, and, if working by contract, were constantly angling to
get the better of the bargain. The Chinese, on the other hand, were
far more earnest and faithful. In every area he investigated, the commissioner found that the Chinese enjoyed the "universal reputation of
conscientious fidelity." In his conclusion, the commissioner emphasized that the Chinese were not "coolies" and predicted that Chinese
labor would come to be valued in this country not because of its
cheapness, but because of its excellence.[44]

Many employers shared Commissioner Raymond's views and actively sought the services of the Chinese. In the 1860s, Chinese were
hired to work in salt basins around San Francisco Bay and to gather
borate from deposits in Oregon, Nevada, and California. From 1870
until the turn of the century, Chinese miners also found jobs in many

coal mines of Washington, Wyoming, and Utah, and were employed in the quicksilver mines of California's Napa and Lake counties.

5. Building the Railroads

The one employer of Chinese who most enhanced their reputation as good and reliable workers was the Central Pacific Railway Company. Incorporated on June 28, 1861, it was controlled by four Sacramento merchants—Leland Stanford, Collis P. Huntington, Mark Hopkins, and Charles Crocker. These fortune-builders realized that the best means to conquer and exploit the great American West was by railroad construction. They knew that public enthusiasm for railroad-building was at its height and that even the enemies of the railroad could not deny its importance.

As the government at all levels thrust credit and resources upon the railroad-promoters, the Central Pacific and the Union Pacific, by a Congressional act in 1862, were chartered to build the first American transcontinental railroad. The former was to start work in Sacramento and push its way eastward through the Sierra Nevada Range while the latter was to start from Omaha and work westward until it joined with the Central Pacific. By 1866, the two companies had begun a race to secure the largest possible federal subsidy. The Central Pacific had a more formidable task because its track had to cross the Sierra Nevada—a solid wall of granite—and the arid plains and deserts of Nevada and Utah. Shortly after Congress approved the project, the Central Pacific formed a subsidiary company called Crocker and Company, to take over construction contracts; but after two years, less than fifty miles of track had been laid. Crocker and his associates realized that each week lost meant the loss of hundreds of thousands of dollars in land and cash subsidies and that whichever road reached Salt Lake Basin first would probably come to dominate the entire system.[45] They also were aware that while their construction was bogged down because of climatic and engineering difficulties, the rival Union Pacific could build two-thirds of its road before encountering any appreciable engineering problems. Under these circumstances Crocker and Company decided, in early 1865, to draw on the Chinese for its labor supply.

When the decision to hire Chinese was made known, Crocker's European employees, including his superintendent, James Harvey Strobridge, protested that the Chinese were too small and frail to take on heavy construction jobs and that they were not fit to become masons or to handle explosives. Crocker was said to have reminded his skeptics that the Chinese had built the biggest masonry structure in the world—the Great Wall of China—and had invented gunpowder, introducing Westerners to its uses.[46] Strobridge first agreed to try fifty Chinese, using them to cut down trees, root out stumps, break and cart rocks, and lay down rails and ties. The results were so gratifying that Strobridge agreed to accept fifty more and, by the spring of 1865, more and more Chinese were employed by the Central Pacific. E. B. Crocker, former Chief Justice of the Supreme Court of California and brother of Charles Crocker, described the situation:

> A large part of our forces are Chinese, and they prove nearly equal to white men, in the amount of labor they perform, and are far more reliable. No danger of strikes among them. We are training them to all kinds of labor, blasting, driving horses, handling rock, as well as the pick and shovel. . . . We want to get a body of 2,500 trained laborers, and keep them steadily at work until the road is built clear across the continent.[47]

Through a contract with a Dutch trader named Cornelius Koopmanschap and the firm of Sisson and Wallace in San Francisco, the Central Pacific brought large groups of Chinese to the rail camps. After receiving training in basic skills, the Chinese were immediately put to work, leveling the roadbeds, digging the tunnels, and blasting the mountains. Before the completion of the project, between 12,000 and 14,000 Chinese were on the payroll of the Central Pacific.[48]

The Chinese were hired in groups of fifty to a hundred, and as practiced in the mining industry, their broker received the wages for the group in monthly lump sums. On average, a white laborer was paid $35 a month plus board and lodging; a Chinese laborer, however, received between $26 and $35 per month and had to provide his own food and housing. The broker furnished his workers with supplies of food and supplied a cook to prepare meals, make tea, and keep a large boiler of hot water for the group's bathing. The Chinese menu included pork, poultry, rice, bean sprouts, bamboo shoots, various kinds of vegetables, dried fruit and fish, Chinese sausage, and peanut oil, some of which were imported directly from Hong Kong and Canton. The workday began at sunrise and ended at sunset, six days a week. They spent Sundays doing laundry, mending, talking, smoking, and gambling. By the end of the month, the broker deducted all the expenses that had been defrayed, then distributed earnings to each individual. Most Chinese laborers probably saved around $20 a month.[49]

The quality of Chinese rail workers was severely tested when the railhead had to cross the Sierra Nevada Range. Often ridges jutted up from the valley floors below; in the winter heavy snows made sure deathtraps for anyone in an exposed area. In the spring of 1866, when assaulting Cape Horn Mountain, the Chinese devised a solution to a difficult tunnelling problem. They wove reeds into large wicker baskets which were hauled to the top of the cliffs where one or two Chinese got inside. By a pulley system, they were then lowered over cliffs two thousand feet above the base of the American River Canyon. They chiseled holes through the granite escarpments, scrambled up the lines and placed the dynamite and lit it before they were pulled up to the top of the cliff, usually just in time to escape the explosion. A white foreman with a gang of 30 to 40 Chinese generally constituted the work force at each end of a tunnel.[50]

Central Pacific records indicate that Chinese workers advanced the railroad an average of 1.18 feet daily and that sometimes it took 300 Chinese ten days just to clear and grub a mile of roadbed. Climbing through the High Sierra was difficult enough, but working in the freezing cold of the winter season made it even more dangerous. Accidents and severe weather took a heavy toll among the Chinese laborers. A good many died when baskets were not pulled up fast enough or a rope broke. Uncounted numbers froze to death when unexpected blizzards caused shelters, often old barns or wooden sheds, to collapse. Many who were covered by snow slides were not found until the next spring when the snow melted. It was estimated that more than 1,200 Chinese perished before the golden spike was driven at Promontory junction in Utah.[51]

Chinese workmanship elicited praises from their bosses and newspaper reporters who visited the construction sites. Strobridge, who at first strongly objected to hiring the Chinese, ended believing that the Chinese were the best workers in the world. The *Alta California* characterized the Chinese as "competent and wonderfully effective" because they were "tireless and unremitting in their industry."[52] Leland Stanford, president of the Central Pacific, praised his Chinese employees:

> As a class they are quiet, peaceable, patient, industrious and economical. Ready and apt to learn all the different kinds of work required in railroad building, they soon become as efficient as white laborers. More prudent and economical, they are contented with less wages. . . . No system similar to slavery, serfdom or peonage prevails among these laborers. Their wages, which are always paid in coin each month, are divided among them by their agents who attend to their business according to the labor done by each person.[53]

Despite the fact that Chinese surplus labor had contributed to Stanford's enormous wealth, he later turned his back on the Chinese and acquiesced to the exclusion laws against his once-favorite employees.

On May 10, 1869, the race between the Central Pacific and the

Union Pacific came to an end, with both sides claiming victory, when formal junction of the two rails took place. The entire country joined in a paean of praise; parades, speeches, celebrations were held throughout the United States. Ironically, the Chinese were not allowed to take part in the festivities either at Promontory Point, Utah, or at Sacramento when the Crocker brothers celebrated the landmark achievement.[54] Nevertheless, news of the usefulness and reliability of the Chinese laborers quickly spread. In June, 1870, for example, the Union Pacific started to employ Chinese as section hands. In 1875, during a strike of white workers, the same railroad introduced 150 Chinese to work in the coal mines of Rock Springs, Wyoming. Subsequently, Chinese miners and rail workers also settled at Evanston, Wyoming, and at Brigham City, Park City, and Scofield in Utah.

The joining of the transcontinental lines completed the antebellum dream of spanning the continent by rail, and soon after Promontory, Chinese appeared as construction workers on a variety of other major rail projects, including that of the Canadian Pacific. In 1868, the Northern Pacific Railway Company began recruiting workers in Hong Kong, bringing over 430 Chinese to begin working south of Portland. Before the end of 1872, more than 1,500 Chinese workers were laying rail tracks and telegraph lines in Oregon. Henry Villard, owner of the Northern Pacific, reportedly employed about 15,000 Chinese to lay rails in northern Washington and, in 1882 and 1883, used about 6,000 of them for similar work in Idaho and Montana. Although these figures may be exaggerated, there is good evidence that Chinese graded all the railroad mileage in Washington's Whitman, Spokane, and Stevens counties.[55] In the course of these operations, the Chinese encountered no animosity from their white counterparts. As a matter of fact, the Oregon Railway and Navigation Company employed 5,000 Chinese and 1,500 whites for the joint construction of the line that linked with the Northern Pacific at Wallula. The *New Northwest* reported that near Lake Pend d'Oreille in northeast Washington, 1,800 Chinese and 900 white laborers worked together without tension or incidents.[56]

Railroad construction in the Northwest stimulated the area's lumber industry, which also employed a substantial number of Chinese for cleaning up sawmills, storekeeping, cooking, and other logging-related labor. As more and more Chinese came to the Pacific Northwest, a number of general stores were set up to serve them. Among these was the well-known Wa Chong Company of Seattle, founded in 1868 by Chin Chun Hook. Chinese stores usually opened up in a cluster of adjacent streets, and Chinatowns, like those in Portland and Seattle, began to take shape. Some Chinese who acquired initial capital and a basic knowledge of railway construction later made significant contributions to their native land. A Seattle labor contractor by the name of Chin Gee Hee decided, in 1905, to raise money among his fellow Cantonese in America for the construction of a railway in southern Guangdong. Called the Xinning Railroad, the line was 127 kilometers long and ran from Taishan district to Xinhui district southwest of Canton. Completed in 1908, it was the first railway in China entirely designed, financed, and built by Chinese.

The remarkable performances of the Chinese on the Pacific Coast also sparked an interest in them in the deep South. On November 10, 1869, General John G. Walker of the Houston-Texas Central Railway Company signed a contract with Chew Ah Heang, a Chinese labor contractor in San Francisco, for the services of 300 Chinese workers. A few weeks later, some 250 Chinese left San Francisco by train. After reaching Council Bluffs in Iowa, they traveled on planks laid over the ice to reach the train which carried them to St. Louis, then to Houston via New Orleans. According to the contract, each Chinese was to be paid $20 in silver monthly, but due to financial difficulties in the company, many of the Chinese were later laid off.

A somewhat similar situation faced the Chinese in the construction of the Alabama-Chattanooga railroad. During the winter of 1870, between 600 and 700 Chinese did work on the Alabama-Chattanooga line; apparently none of them stayed in the area after completing their work.[57] But in the Southwest, a few pockets of Chinese settlement grew out of the ambitious project of Collis P. Huntington, who was determined to build the Southern Pacific southward from San Francisco through California and eastward across Arizona, New Mexico, and Texas. Huntington, who promoted unrestrained capitalism and preached the Gospel of Wealth, acquired a crew of 1,200 Chinese to help fulfill his dream. The Southern Pacific finally reached El Paso, Texas, on May 19, 1881. Once again, Chinese footprints followed the Southern Pacific railwork and, with its completion, small enclaves of Chinese were found in Phoenix, Tucson, Tempe, Albuquerque, El Paso, and San Antonio. Most of the discharged railroad crews remained to work as laundrymen, cooks, barbers, servants, grocers, and truck gardeners.[58]

6. In Agriculture, Fishing, and Other Industries

At a time when labor was scarce and expensive in the West, the Chinese proved indispensable for all kinds of jobs. Even the most prejudiced employers were glad to avail themselves of Chinese labor. Among the white employers were California's wheat growers, many of whom testified to a special Congressional committee in 1876 that without Chinese labor they could not raise wheat and sell it in the market, and that their crops would have been failures entirely had there been no Chinese to gather them.[59] In the mid-nineteenth century, gold mining and railroad building were the most talked-about bonanzas in California, but wheat growing was also an important source of wealth. According to an 1868 article in the *Overland Monthly*, California produced about 20 million bushels of wheat. That amounted to about one-tenth of the yield of the whole United States and was valued at $20 million dollars, nearly as much as California's total production of precious metals during the same year.[60] Harvesting the wheat required an extensive labor supply and it was natural that farm owners turned to the Chinese. They were used as binders, as threshers, and often as cooks for the other laborers. The binding and threshing usually began long before daylight and sometimes continued into the night. The Chinese set up a dirty tent in some corner of the field near the water supply, slept on the ground, worked by starlight, and lived on a diet of rice.

After completion of the transcontinental railroad, California farmers, now having easier access to the markets of the East Coast, gradually switched from wheat to more perishable but more profitable crops, such as grapes, fruit, and vegetables. Once again, the Chinese furnished the most available, reliable, and satisfactory labor in the planting, grafting, pruning, and harvesting of these labor-intensive crops. They dispersed throughout the state of California, with larger concentrations in such areas as Alameda, Sacramento, Fresno, and Santa Clara counties. By 1882, the Chinese made up between 50 and 75 percent of the harvest labor in some counties in California.[61]

But California was not the only state that benefited from Chinese agricultural labor. In the farms of the Pacific Northwest and the deep South, Chinese were used for tending orchards, picking cotton, harvesting rice, and building canals. Among the more outstanding individual Chinese was a horticultural expert named Ah Bing. For several years he worked in Milwaukie, Oregon, and in 1875, introduced a hybrid cherry tree which has carried his name ever since. Another Chinese, Lue Gim Gong of De Land, Florida, developed in 1888 the famous frost-resistant orange of Florida that made possible the great citrus industry of that state. Lue was later awarded a Wilder Medal, the highest honor of the United States Department of Agriculture. Other less-known Chinese were instrumental in pioneering new brands of rice and in turning celery into a commercial crop in America.

Chinese laborers also reclaimed thousands of acres of tule swamps. Californians called the overflowed lands of the Sacramento-San Joaquin Delta tule-lands. Beginning in the late 1860s, some 200 Chinese were hired by the Tide-Land Reclamation Company to build levees along the river banks. Using only shovels and wheelbarrows and working in waist-deep water, they dammed sloughs, cut drainage ditches, constructed floodgates, and built levees. By 1876, the Tide-Land Reclamation Company hired between 3,000 and 4,000 workers, most of them Chinese, to cut blocks of peat to form levee walls and fill the interior with sand. The Chinese made about one dollar a day or $27 a month and were required to provide their own food and board. After the levees were completed, many Chinese stayed on to work in the fruit orchards along the Sacramento River banks from Freeport to Isleton. Several of them leased ranches and became truck gardeners, growing and selling sweet potatoes and vegetables. In 1889, about 2,000 Chinese were living in the Delta, thinning, hoeing, and harvesting sugar beets, growing hops, and doing the greater part of the agricultural labor in the area.[62]

Before the mass migration of Japanese into the Delta in the 1890s, the Chinese composed the predominant race of tenants and laborers, with Portuguese and Italian immigrants being the next most numerous. The Chinese and the Southern Europeans settled in the newly reclaimed areas while their Northern European counterparts stayed on the high ground, away from the unhealthy lowlands. The Southern Europeans soon tired of living behind a levee and subleased their lands to the Chinese. In the 1890s, partly because of the exclusion laws, Chinese population in the Sacramento Delta gradually decreased. At the present time, only Locke still exists, representing the last concentration of Chinese in rural California.[63]

While some Chinese turned to agricultural labor to replace mining and railroad work, many found employment in the factories of San Francisco and other California cities. Chinese competition in manufacturing industries, however, increased apprehension among white laborers and often created hostility against Chinese laborers, particularly when they were used as strike breakers. For example, early in 1869, workers in the shoe industry formed a national craft union called the Knights of St. Crispin, and about 500 of its members went on strike in April of that year. Employers refused their demand for higher wages and, in retaliation, hired Chinese laborers. By 1873 Chinese labor was producing over 50 percent of California's boots and shoes. Chinese also competed with white labor in the woolen industry. Heyneman, Pick and Company pioneered woolen production in San Francisco, and the Chinese were among the company's first workers. In 1867, as a recession set in, white labor accused the Chinese of causing unemployment, and it was true that Chinese labor was much cheaper. In 1876, Chinese woolen workers were paid from 90 cents to

$1.20 per day while the white workers demanded much higher wages for the same job. The mill owners continued to resist the pressure but bitterness and hostility grew thicker as depression lingered on. Similar problems also arose in the sewing and clothing industries of the West Coast.[64] When the labor movement turned surly and violent in the late nineteenth century, the Chinese were obvious targets of the pent-up anger.

In the cigar and tobacco industries, the Chinese fared better because many of the cigar factories, which required little capital investment, were Chinese-owned. In the 1860s and 1870s, between 60 and 70 Chinese merchants in San Francisco were engaged in this business. In 1876 alone, about 7,500 Chinese were employed in this industry, and the output of cigars manufactured in San Francisco increased from 35 million in 1868 to 107 million in 1879. Accordingly, the Chinese tobacco manufacturers purchased two-thirds of the San Francisco cigar revenue stamps sold by the Bureau of Internal Revenue.[65] As the influence of organized labor grew, Chinese cigar workers formed a labor union called the Tang Dak Tong, or Hall of Common Virtue. Union members were not permitted to work alongside non-union members and fair wages were demanded. Unfortunately, the Chinese cigar union was not recognized by the white Cigar Makers Union of California. Their actions indicated that whatever their common class interests, white workers' racial prejudices were too strong to cooperate with the Chinese.

The nineteenth-century Chinese sojourners never did venture into the cattle industry, but they did make significant contributions to America's merchant marine service and fishing industry. The crews of the Occidental and Oriental Steamship Company and the Pacific Mail Steamship Company often included Chinese boatswains, seamen, firemen, coal passers, stewards, cooks, cabin boys, storekeepers, bakers, porters, pantrymen, and waiters. It was estimated that in the year 1888, American vessels, both commercial and government, employed a total of 1,280 Chinese workers.[66] Those steamships regularly engaged in trade between San Francisco and Asian ports used Chinese exclusively as deckhands and as helpers in engineer's and steward's departments. The crews were usually engaged in Hong Kong for a round trip voyage to San Francisco; they were then discharged at the end of the completed voyage. Sometimes a few additional crewmen were hired in San Francisco. But there was a major wage differential; Chinese hired in Hong Kong were paid $7 to $15 dollars per month, while seamen hired out of stateside ports received from $25 to $55 per month. One scholar estimated that the number of Chinese crew members carried on the steamships ranged from 29 to 227 and that the total number of Chinese so engaged over the thirty-year period 1876–1906 amounted to 78,433.[67]

Apparently, the courage and skill in navigating and seamanship of the Chinese sailors, long experienced in sailing junks in the South China Sea, made an impression on American naval authorities. During the Spanish-American War, eighty-eight Chinese seamen were reported aboard Admiral George Dewey's Pacific fleet and nine Chinese were among the crew of the battleship *Oregon* when it bombarded Santiago, Cuba.[68] Unfortunately, because of restrictive immigration laws, the Chinese, since 1884, were required to carry a white tag for identification and needed permission to move about when they visited American port cities. This was later to cause a real problem for Admiral Dewey when he invited his Chinese crew members to participate in a hero's welcome parade in San Francisco. In the late 1890s, new constraints were placed on Chinese seamen, and the 1915 Federal Seamen's Act further restricted the hiring of Chinese, drastically reducing the number of Chinese seamen employed on American vessels. As in the cases of mining and railroad construction, Chinese labor had contributed in a small but not insignificant way to the development of the nation.

If the Chinese were good sailors, they were even better fishermen, as they had proved for millennia before coming to America. In the 1850s, they were among the first to engage in commercial fishing on the West Coast. As they had in Guangdong, the Chinese made mesh nets, gear, and hooks for fisheries. For offshore fishing, they built small wood sampans, about 15 feet long, for gathering operations, and constructed large junks for transporting their catch. During the 1860s, Chinese fishing activities in California, notably at Humboldt Bay, increased steadily. In 1863, several Chinese companies of fishermen settled on what is now Marine Laboratory Point near Pacific Grove. By 1870, Chinese fishing activities had spread up and down the Pacific Coast of the United States with San Francisco, San Diego, and Monterey as the principal centers. In 1888 in California alone, over 2,000 Chinese in 30 camps were engaged in the fishing business.[69]

Chinese fishermen could be found in a wide variety of places in the 1870s and 1880s. Chinese fished both bay and river for salmon, crab, sturgeon, squid, and other marketable fish. In the waters off Santa Catalina in the 1860s and for the next 20 years, many Chinese caught sharks for a living. Shark's fins—a great delicacy in Chinese cuisine— and shark's liver, which yields a lubricating oil, were marketed for high prices. In the Monterey peninsula, the Chinese gathered huge amounts of seaweed off the rocky shores and sold it as food after it had been dried and processed. The Chinese also introduced abalone for the commercial market. They sold its shell to the East Coast and Europe as raw material for jewelry while they made its meat into an expensive food commodity. In the 1870s and 1880s, several hundred Chinese worked in the shrimp industry of California and Louisiana. The Chinese proved to be experts in drying shrimp in the sun and packing them in barrels. They were also good at salting trout and canning salmon. As early as 1871, Chinese workers were employed by R.D. Hume's salmon cannery plant on the Rouge River of Oregon, and in subsequent years, in the canneries of Washington, British Columbia, and Alaska. Gordon B. Dodds reported that in the late 1870s nearly 80 percent of the cannery workers on the Columbia River were Chinese.[70]

Chinese expertise and competition in the fishing industry once again aroused opposition. White fishermen charged that the Chinese were destroying young smelt, killing baby fish, and harvesting small abalones. The California legislature bowed to pressure from white fishermen and passed laws to discourage and curtail Chinese fishing activities. In 1860, a discriminatory tax of $4 a month was imposed on every Chinese fisherman. Though this law was repealed in 1864, the California legislature later restricted the use of mesh nets and limited the shrimp fishing season. As these measures proved ineffective in discouraging Chinese fishermen, a law was passed in 1905 to ban the exportation of dried shrimp from California. In addition to these legal limitations, Chinese fishermen often became the victims of intimidation and violence; their boats were frequently sunk and their nets slashed. After the 1882 Exclusion Act went into effect, fewer and fewer young Chinese fishermen were able to continue the business established by aging veterans.[71] By 1900, only a few decaying Chinese fishing camps remained along the Pacific shores.

7. Chinese Communities Outside of the West Coast

During the heyday of Chinese immigration, between 1868 and 1882, almost four-fifths of the Chinese resided in California, digging mines up and down the state, working in the manufacturing industries of San Francisco, raising hops and fruits in Santa Clara and elsewhere, reclaiming marshy lands in the Sacramento-San Joaquin Delta, and fishing along the California coast. In 1870, only 13,972 Chinese lived outside of California, but by 1880, the figure had increased to 30,333 (see maps 1 and 2). With recession bearing down hard on California in the late 1870s, more and more Chinese sought employment in other states and territories. Oregon, Nevada, Idaho, and Washington absorbed many Chinese while Montana, Arizona, Wyoming, and New

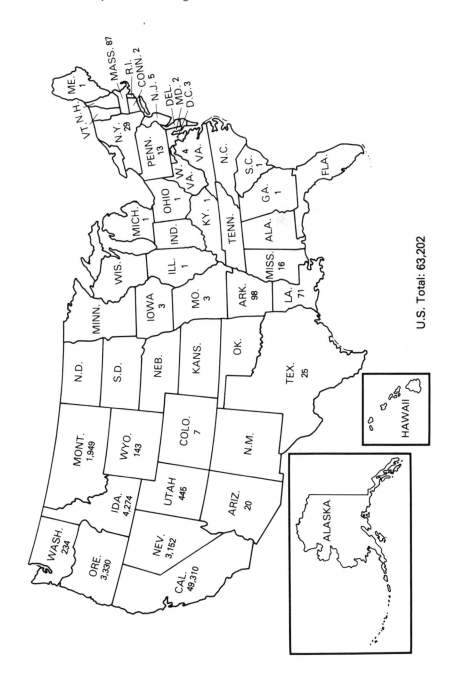

Map I. Distribution of the Chinese Population, 1870

U.S. Total: 63,202

MASS. 87
R.I. 1
CONN. 2
N.J. 5
DEL. 2
MD. 2
D.C. 3
ME. 1
VT. N.H. 1
N.Y. 29
PENN. 13
W. VA. 4
VA.
N.C.
S.C. 1
FLA.
OHIO 1
KY. 1
TENN.
GA. 1
ALA.
MICH. 1
IND.
ILL. 1
MISS. 16
WIS.
IOWA 3
MO. 3
ARK. 98
LA. 71
MINN.
N.D.
S.D.
NEB.
KANS.
OK.
TEX. 25
MONT. 1,949
WYO. 143
COLO. 7
N.M.
IDA. 4,274
UTAH 445
ARIZ. 20
WASH. 234
ORE. 3,330
NEV. 3,152
CAL. 49,310

HAWAII

ALASKA

Map II. Distribution of the Chinese Population, 1880

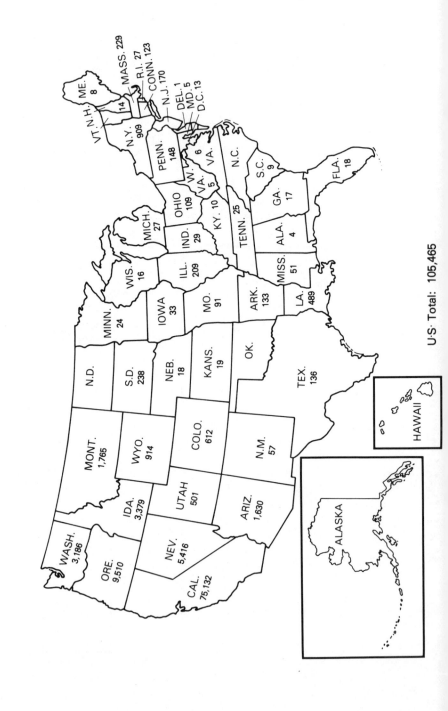

U.S. Total: 105,465

MASS. 229
R.I. 27
CONN. 123
ME. 8
N.H. 14
VT.
N.J. 170
N.Y. 909
DEL. 1
MD. 5
D.C. 13
PENN. 148
W. VA. 6
VA. 5
N.C.
OHIO 109
KY. 10
S.C. 9
MICH. 27
IND. 29
TENN. 25
GA. 17
FLA. 18
WIS. 16
ILL. 209
ALA. 4
MINN. 24
IOWA 33
MO. 91
MISS. 51
LA. 489
ARK. 133
N.D.
S.D. 238
NEB. 18
KANS. 19
OK.
TEX. 136
MONT. 1,765
WYO. 914
COLO. 612
N.M. 57
IDA. 3,379
UTAH 501
ARIZ. 1,630
WASH. 3,186
ORE. 9,510
NEV. 5,416
CAL. 75,132
HAWAII
ALASKA

York also received a sizable number of Chinese immigrants. A few Chinese even ventured into the South where their industriousness and "cheapness" made them attractive to Southern planters and railway magnates.

Even before Charles Crocker put the Chinese on his payroll, the *Montgomery Daily Mail* and a few other Southern newspapers had already discussed the possible use of Chinese labor in the South. In 1866, the Louisiana Commission of Immigration took the lead and brought some 200 Chinese from Cuba to work on Louisiana sugarcane plantations. In the next few years, several colonies of Catholic Chinese from the Philippines were established in the state. As it turned out, Louisiana planters could not compete with the wages offered the Chinese in California and by railroad builders. Others deserted the plantations to become fishermen, mainly along Louisiana's Barataria Bay, or engaged in truck gardening for the New Orleans market.[72]

The completion of the transcontinental railroad in 1869 sparked an increased interest in bringing more Chinese to the South. A convention of Southern planters and businessmen met in Memphis, Tennessee, in July, 1869, to discuss the feasibility of encouraging Chinese to come to the South. Attending the convention were Cornelius Koopmanschap and Kim Wing, the largest two Chinese labor contractors in San Francisco. In addition to making keynote speeches for the convention, they toured the Southern states to make arrangements and to take orders for Chinese workers. They offered to supply Chinese agricultural laborers for five-year terms at a wage of $8 to $10 per month.[73] In the wake of the Memphis convention, several local meetings were held in Southern towns and "the efforts of the planters were especially exerted for the substitution of Chinese immigrants . . . for Negro labor."[74] By the end of 1870 at least 200 Chinese had moved to work in the cotton fields of the Yazoo-Mississippi Delta region of Mississippi and Arkansas.

Small numbers of Chinese laborers continued to trickle into the South. In November, 1873, 25 Chinese arrived in Augusta, Georgia, to work on a canal that was to bring water from the Savannah River to the city. Several dozen Chinese laid off by the Houston-Texas Central Railway Company found employment on the rich cotton farms of the Brazos River Valley of Robertson County, Texas. Some Chinese farm laborers became southern sharecroppers. A Texas farmer named James Scott Hanna contracted with two Chinese workers to farm 30 acres of land, 20 in cotton and 10 in corn, with half of both crops going to Hanna and the other half to the Chinese. But most remained simply hired hands. Another nineteenth-century contract provided for a group of 17 Chinese to work as field hands at a monthly wage of $15 to $18, besides room and board.[75] Generally speaking, however, the efforts to utilize Chinese for cotton-field work in the South was a failure. The Chinese simply could not compete with cheap black labor, and the post-Reconstruction racial settlement in the South made them less suited to replace blacks. Many Chinese laborers deserted the fields to settle in St. Louis and other Midwestern and Southern cities. Others, after working out their contracts, went to the West Coast or returned to China. Nevertheless, small contingents of Chinese remained and established colorful enclaves in Mississippi, Arkansas, Louisiana, and Texas.

While the South never received a significant migration of Chinese in the nineteenth century, Hawaii, before its annexation by the United States in 1898, had experienced a major influx. Only six years after Captain James Cook discovered the Sandwich Islands in 1788, another famed English navigator, Captain George Vancouver, noted the presence of the Chinese in this archipelago. But instead of calling them the Sandwich or Hawaiian Islands, the Chinese named them the Sandalwood Mountains. Since the early years of the Canton trade, the Chinese had coveted the sandalwood produced in Hawaii. Known for its fine-grained quality and unique fragrance, sandalwood was used by Chinese for making small ornamental articles, jewelry, cosmetic boxes, cabinets, and incense.

The early Chinese immigrants to Hawaii were not seeking sandalwood; rather, they were brought to Hawaii to work on the sugarcane plantations. Beginning in 1820, after the arrival of missionaries from New England, Hawaii came increasingly under the influence of Americans, who owned most of the sugarcane plantations and dominated the sugar industry of the islands. By the 1850s the sugar industry began to assume a dominant position in Hawaii's economy; because of the scarcity of satisfactory labor the American planters looked to China for a possible solution. The Royal Hawaii Agricultural Society was founded in 1850 and, two years later, the society engaged a Captain Cass and the ship *Thetis* to bring 195 Chinese to Hawaii. Later in the same year, 100 more Chinese arrived in Hawaii; all of them were dispatched to work in the sugar fields. The planters were highly satisfied, finding the Chinese to be "quiet, able and willing men."[76]

Still, the number of Chinese in Hawaii remained low until the American Civil War, which stimulated a rapid expansion of the sugar industry. According to Katharine Coman, an authority on the history of Hawaii's sugar industry, the islands produced 4,286 pounds of sugar in 1837; by 1868 the figure was 18,312,926 pounds.[77] Moreover, in 1875, the United States and Hawaii signed a treaty allowing Hawaiian sugar to be admitted to the mainland free of duty in exchange for the establishment of a naval base at Pearl Harbor. This treaty greatly stimulated development of the sugar industry in the islands. Accordingly, in the ten-year span 1876–1886, large numbers of Chinese arrived in Hawaii as a direct result of initiatives taken by white sugarcane planters. By 1884, there were 18,254 Chinese in Hawaii; they composed 22.26 percent of the population.[78] Until the influx of Japanese workers in the 1890s, the Chinese were the main labor force in Hawaii's production of sugarcane.

In general, Chinese laborers in Hawaii worked under three- to five-year contracts at a starting wage of $3 a month. They were also provided with free passage, food, clothing, shelter, and medical attention. The cost of transportation from China to Hawaii was about $50 per person and maintenance costs were approximately $5 a month. The labor was difficult, beginning before daybreak and ending after sunset. Living conditions were primitive—groups as large as fifty workers were packed into one barracks room. An outbreak of disease could have a devastating effect. In December of 1899, two cases of bubonic plague were reported in Honolulu's Chinatown. The Hawaiian Board of Health removed 4,500 Chinese to a quarantine camp, and the Chinese quarter was incinerated.[79] Chinese suspected of carrying smallpox were housed in makeshift quarters with a guard to prevent escape. In 1881, the *Septima* arrived at Honolulu with 699 Chinese aboard and all the passengers were detained in quarantine.[80] The mortality rate among the Chinese laborers was high, and rumors of inhuman treatment at the hands of plantation overseers were often heard. With such harsh working conditions, it was no wonder that the majority of Chinese, at the expiration of their contracts, abandoned agricultural labor in favor of a trade.

The resulting dispersion of the Chinese brought them into contact with other races on the islands, particularly the Hawaiians who were friendly toward them, showing them the same hospitality they had accorded the whites. The Chinese mingled freely with the Hawaiians; some married Hawaiian women. The census enumeration of 1896 recorded a total of 1,387 part-Hawaiians with Chinese fathers, a number large enough to be significant.[81] The family life of intermarried couples required adjustment on both sides and took several forms of mutual accommodation. According to Doris M. Lorden, three main types of accommodation were reached by early Chinese-Hawaiian families: first, complete adoption of the Chinese pattern by Hawaiian wives; second, complete adoption of the Hawaiian pattern by Chinese husbands; and third, the adoption of a biracial cultural pattern with both Chinese and Polynesian elements. Lorden found that the majority of the Chinese-Hawaiian families followed the third pattern and that their racially mixed children often formed a distinct and segregated community. Such communities were found in rural villages such as Kau; others were formed in the larger towns such as Hilo and

Honolulu.[82] After the immigration of Chinese women made possible the establishment of a large number of Chinese families, the inter-marriage between Chinese and Hawaiians became relatively rare, as the Chinese men preferred brides of their own race.

After leaving the plantations, many Chinese took up residence in small rural villages. By using a part of the wages they had accumulated as capital, Chinese men, mainly bachelors, established small businesses or engaged in commercial agriculture. Sometimes groups of former laborers would pool their funds to begin rice growing, poultry farming, or gardening. They leased land that was not suitable for plantations, improved it, and produced diversified crops for the Hawaiian market. They introduced to the Hawaiian consumers a variety of Chinese fruits, vegetables, and flowers, including Chinese cabbage, water chestnut, jasmine, pomelo, lychee, and longan. Land leasing and truck gardening led others to establish country stores to supply goods needed by the laborers or city stores to dispose of the farm produce. As Chinese immigrants accumulated more and more capital, they began to compete with white businessmen in Honolulu. By the 1880s, most of the Chinese had joined a growing Hawaiian middle class. The Chinese owned over 30 percent of businesses in Honolulu and had become prosperous merchants in many Hawaiian towns.

Chinese business success and their increasing urbanization created much apprehension among the American whites in the 1880s. The anti-Chinese movement in California and the passage of the 1882 Exclusion Act inspired the Hawaiian government to adopt similar restrictive measures against Chinese immigration. At the prodding of American officials in the islands, the Hawaiian government began in 1885 to limit to 25 the number of Chinese who might be brought in on any vessel. In 1887, the Hawaiian legislature completely excluded the Chinese.[83] Consequently, between 1884 and 1890, the Chinese population in Hawaii dropped by about 2,600. However, in 1889, because of a labor shortage, several planters petitioned the government to amend the act so that Chinese might be admitted to the islands as agricultural laborers. The petition was first refused but eventually prevailed and, in 1895, a further modification of the Exclusion Act was allowed. As a result of these changes, the more prosperous Chinese were able to bring wives and children from their homeland. The United States Census of 1900, the first in which Hawaii was included, revealed that the Chinese population had increased to 25,767. Restraints remained strong, however, and the growth of the Chinese population was slow in Hawaii[84] (see Appendix 2).

Chinese assimilation in Hawaii was more rapid than on the mainland. Chinese families became rapidly dispersed throughout Honolulu and across the islands; the Chinatown in Honolulu, unlike its counterparts in San Francisco and New York, was never exclusively a Chinese residential area. Nevertheless, it was and continued to be a nucleus for Chinese business, cultural, and organizational activities. Numerous huiguan (clan/family organizations), blood-tie, trade, and secret-society organizations, were formed by the Chinese immigrants to provide mutual aid. Among cities in the Western Hemisphere (until after World War II, when New York's Chinese population grew very rapidly) Honolulu was second only to San Francisco in numbers of Chinese inhabitants.

By the beginning of the twentieth century the Hawaiian Chinese had far outstripped their brethren in the Atlantic states who were still running laundries, small grocery stores, and Chinatown restaurants. Under a relatively less open pattern of ethnic relations, the Chinese on the East Coast encountered much more cultural and racial prejudice. Generally, Chinatowns in the East were located close to transportation terminals, growing first around the railway stations, the immigrant's place of entry and his lifeline to his friends. This pattern was clear in Boston, St. Louis, and Pittsburgh. In New York, where a majority of the Chinese arrived by steamer, Chinatown was near the harbor. According to sociologist Louis J. Beck, the early Chinatown in New York covered the triangular area bounded by Mott, Pell, and Doyers Streets, as well as Chatham Square; later the Chinese moved into Bayard Street.[85] As anti-Chinese violence increased in the West in the late nineteenth century, New York became something of a haven for those who could not or would not tolerate the persecution. In the late 1880s and early 1890s, New York saw a steady increase of Chinese population, from 29 in 1870 to 2,935 in 1890 and 7,000 in 1900. Before the outrages of the 1870s and 1880s, very few Chinese went to the East. A few Chinese were imported in the 1870s as strike breakers in Belleville in New Jersey, Beaver Falls in Pennsylvania, and North Adams in Massachusetts. Most of these workers eventually drifted into the major cities of the East. By 1900, every major Eastern city—New Haven, Philadelphia, Pittsburgh, Boston, Baltimore, Detroit, and Washington, D.C.—had a Chinese population, ranging from 300 to 1,000 persons.[86] Most were doing strenuous jobs, working long hours for low pay. But they survived, sojourning in a strange land. And so, though the nineteenth-century Chinese immigration remained essentially a California issue, by 1900 the American Chinese population, increased greatly by the acquisition of Hawaii, was becoming both scattered and diverse.

It is generally believed that the Chinese population in the United States reached a peak in the early 1880s although the actual number will probably never be known. The 1880 census counted 105,465 Chinese plus some 10,000 living in Hawaii, and immigration records indicate that in the first two years of that decade, 57,271 arrived and 26,788 departed, leaving a net gain of 30,483. When the Chinese Exclusion Law passed the United States Congress in 1882, the probable Chinese population in America (including Hawaii) was about 152,000. By 1890, the number had fallen to 122,789, a figure that still exceeded that of 1880. However, a drastic decline took place in the 1890s and continued until World War II when the new immigrants and students and the birth of a second generation caused the number of Chinese in America to climb slowly upward again (see Appendixes 2 and 3).

The 1890 census provided no information on occupations of the Chinese population yet it is certain that the 1882 Exclusion Law and other legal restrictions had greatly affected the social-economic conditions of the Chinese. For instance, increasing numbers of Chinese moved to other sections of the country, and the ratio of urban to rural Chinese in Hawaii and California, as well as in the rest of the nation, increased substantially during the last two decades of the nineteenth century. This urbanized population found it more difficult to find manufacturing jobs and discovered the environment was different from their agrarian background in Guangdong. Lacking large amounts of capital and fearing racial violence, more and more Chinese congregated in Chinatowns and engaged either in small-scale commerce or worked as common laborers, cooks, and servants, occupations that did not carry high status in Amerian society.

Struggling in an age when white Americans applauded Rudyard Kipling's "White Man's Burden," subordinated Indians and Mexicans by conquest, and harnessed blacks by Jim Crow laws, the Chinese, whose motherland had already become a victim of white supremacy and imperialism, quickly learned that they were a despised and unwanted minority. Their hope of escaping the miseries of life in old China, a hope that had sent them flocking to a dream of a Golden Hill, turned into a harsh experience in reality. In America, they were denied egalitarian or democratic treatment; their labor and service were no longer appreciated. Chinatown hence became their safety valve and ethnic frontier. Unfortunately, it was also to become a barrier to acculturation and to doom the first wave of Chinese immigrants to "failure." This isolation also explains why the cultural connections of the American Chinese with their ancestral country persisted so powerfully for more than a century.

II

THE DEVELOPMENT OF THE EARLY CHINESE COMMUNITY

A guest from the Gold Mountain, if he has
not one thousand dollars, at least he has
eight hundred.

—*Gazetteer of Kaiping District*

To stay in a distant foreign country is a
tragedy long grieved since our forefathers.

—General Li Ling of the Han Dynasty

1. Chinese Culture Transplanted to America

The Chinese who came to America in the late nineteenth century were mainly poor peasants and workers who had to struggle to survive in the destitute circumstances of their times. The well-to-do Chinese gentry class—scholars, officials, and landowners—were the elite of Chinee society and had no need to leave their ancestral homes to pan for gold or to work in rail gangs in a distant land. But whether they were poor or rich, the Chinese rarely abandoned their homeland to search for another. When they went abroad, a wife and children frequently were left behind. Almost all emigrants hoped to return after having accumulated a fortune by trade or by labor in a foreign country. In America a Chinese laborer who could save up a few hundred dollars would consider it a small fortune and would usually retire to his native village in Guangdong. He could expect to spend his declining years surrounded by his filial sons and grandchildren, and when he died be laid to rest among the honored dead of a long ancestral line. Such a "situation-centered" Chinese culture, as cultural anthropologist Francis L. K. Hsu has called it, is quite different from the "individual-centered" American culture.[1] This cultural gulf was the source of much of the subsequent friction between Chinese immigrants and white Americans.

In spite of their strong ties to the homeland, Chinese immigrants did not establish a miniature replica of traditional Chinese society in America. They lived in an abnormal society full of young males, wandering sojourners, whose dream was to put in a few years of hard labor and to return home wealthy and respected "Gold Mountain Guests." This "sojourner's mentality" had deep roots in Chinese cultural tradition. Nineteenth-century China was an unsophisticated agrarian society. The great majority of the Chinese people still embraced both Confucianism and Taoism, religious systems which, to a great extent, reflected the inspirations and aspirations of peasants. A typical peasant, who lived in a small rural village, rarely traveled, and had insufficient knowledge of geography to go far unless he was directed or accompanied by someone else. He idolized Lao Tze's famed Utopia in which "the next place might be so near at hand that one could hear the cocks crowing in it, the dogs barking; but the people would grow old and die without ever having been there."[2] He observed Confucian filial duties as binding restrictions: "While father and mother are alive, a good son does not wander far afield."[3] Emigration was generally looked upon as banishment, a severe punishment next only to death. Out of these beliefs grew the concept of sojourning, an idea that stressed the temporary nature of one's absence from home.

The Chinese sojourner's society in America was markedly different from the home country in two ways. First, the population was almost totally transient and, second, there was a great scarcity of females. Mainly because of the seasonal or temporary nature of available work, there was scarcely a Chinese laborer in America who had not lived in several places along the coast. The fluidity of Chinese society was best demonstrated by the phenomenal increase in the Chinese population in the 1870s and by the fact that every year hundreds of Chinese returned to their native land because of seasonal unemployment. As a result, relatively few Chinese owned property, real or personal, in America, a situation that often led to the complaint of American local governments that the Chinese did not pay a fair share of taxes.[4]

This social instability also made possible the rise of Chinese quarters or Chinatowns in American cities. In the late 1870s, between one-fifth and one-fourth of all Chinese in the United States were in San Francisco; most of them resided in seven or eight blocks of that city. The situation was more or less the same in Sacramento and in other urban communities. In these small and often crowded quarters, the Chinese built temples and public halls, established stores and businesses, and opened restaurants and wash houses. They retained their native customs and formed a nation within a nation; a tendency characteristic of all immigrant groups in America. The men continued to wear their hair in queues—a peculiar hairstyle imposed on them since the seventeenth century by their Manchu conquerers—while most of their women practiced the tradition of foot-binding. They also retained their national habits in food, reading, and mode of life, a capsule of which was the popular reader titled *Mirror of Mind*.

This book was made up of selections from a great number of Confucian writers. It also contained anonymous sayings and proverbs that had been handed down by tradition. A work of twenty chapters, its subjects included: "The Practice of Virtue," "Heaven by Rules," "Filial Duties," "On Restraining the Passions," "Diligence in Study," "Peace and Righteousness," and "On Sincerity." The book was much studied by all classes of Chinese; a quotation from it was generally recognized and applauded in whatever company the quotation might be repeated.[5]

Confucian emphasis on reciprocity and righteousness undoubtedly had exerted great influence on the Chinese immigrants, some of whom frequently formed close and respectful personal relationships with Americans. During the Civil War, Leland Stanford employed a 15-year-old Chinese, Moy Jin Mun, as a garden boy. During his three years' service, Moy won the affection of Mrs. Stanford, who wanted to adopt him. But Moy's older brother, who had also cooked for the Stanfords, objected on the grounds that it would violate Chinese custom. The brother sent young Moy away, but before Moy departed the Stanfords gave him a gold ring as a token of remembrance. Moy Jin Mun carefully kept the ring until his death in 1936.[6]

A similar story is that of Dean Lung, who was a long-time servant of General Horace Walpole Carpentier, a Columbia University graduate and a successful California entrepreneur. Carpentier retired in New York, taking with him his Chinese house servant Dean Lung. One evening, in a drunken frenzy, Carpentier beat his servant into unconsciousness. The next morning, when he regained his senses he was surprised to find Dean Lung attending to his usual household chores. Carpentier asked how he could prove his gratitude for Dean Lung's impeccable loyalty? Dean Lung replied that he wished the general would do something to help the American people understand Chinese culture and history. Carpentier subsequently donated $10,000 to his alma mater in the name of Dean Lung. Dean Lung also contributed his lifetime savings of $14,000, and in 1901 Columbia University established a Chinese Department and a Dean Lung Professorship of Chinese Studies.[7] Typical products of Chinese culture, Moy Jin Mun and Dean Lung won the respect of their American employers and displayed their strong sense of righteousness and their fidelity, which were among several virtues the Chinese brought to America.

Chinese festivals and seasonal celebrations became important social events for the Chinese living in America. The Chinese Lunar New Year, which usually falls in late January or early February, was the occasion of a gala atmosphere in every Chinese-American community. A thorough cleaning of the household ushered in each new year. Workers, craftsmen, farmers, merchants, and professionals collected debts, paid their bills, and settled all accounts in order to begin the year with a clean slate. On New Year's Eve, a rich dinner which symbolized the hope for abundance for the forthcoming year was attended, in cases where that was possible, by every member of the family, and presents of money in red envelopes were exchanged. But the height of the celebration took place on New Year's Day when people put on their best clothes and offered greetings to relatives, friends, and acquaintances. A dragon or lion parade was staged in the midst of thundering firecrackers, designed to chase away evil spirits and bring good luck in the new year. For several days, Chinatown would bloom with colorful lanterns and bright banners; its inhabitants were aglow with smiles and optimism.

The Chinese also celebrated lesser festivals while sojourning in America, although some observances have been slightly modified. One favorite was Spring Festival, known also as Qingming or Pure and Bright. This festival took place in early April; in it the Chinese paid respect to the dead by visiting and sweeping the tombs. They also offered meat, vegetables, cakes, fruit, and the like to the spirits of the dead. Flowers and make-believe paper money were laid on the graves and, if the dead were cremated and ashes preserved in a temple, incense was burned in front of the urns containing the remains. Another popular festival was the May Fete, known also as the Dragon Boat Festival. It occurred on the fifth day of the fifth lunar month. The May Fete commemorated the patriotic deeds of an ancient poet named Ch'ü Yüan (343–290 B.C.) who, after losing favor with his prince, drowned himself in a river. Ever since, Chinese people have wrapped cooked rice in leaves, rowed their boats out, and thrown this food into the river so that hungry fish and spirits would not bother their dead hero. Finally, there was the Mid-Autumn Festival, which took place on the fifteenth day of the eighth lunar month. It was a time for making and eating moon-cakes and for family reunions. Women took this occasion to offer peanuts, melon seeds, water chestnuts, sugarcane and other gifts to the Moon Goddess while men prayed for prosperity and bright futures for their careers.

Between the more elaborate festivals, Chinese immigrants took time from their work to enjoy opera and other forms of Oriental music and to play chess. Chinese opera, a dramatic art form that possesses the elements of action, dialogue, and singing, was the most popular pastime among the Chinese working class. Most of the opera plots were based on familiar stories, hence the audience could actually learn a few lines from the actors and actresses; female roles were usually played by beardless males. As San Francisco's Chinatown grew, several theaters were built; one was called the Ascending Luminous Dragon, another claimed to be the Newest Phoenix. Later, when opera became increasingly in demand, traveling troupes were brought from China and regularly visited small Chinatowns across the country. Chinese chess, which has 16 pieces on each side and is quite similar to Western chess in rules and strategy, was widely played. Any game was likely to draw a crowd of spectators. For those who did not like chess, mah-jong was often an alternative amusement. Still a few others, who brought Chinese musical instruments across the Pacific, could play moon guitar, gong, harp, flute, and drum.

Life in Chinatown was bustling, noisy, and colorful. A typical street included signs advertising fortune tellers, barber shops, butcher shops, doctors' clinics, and a variety of stores. For a few cents, a fortune-teller would predict a customer's destiny, dissect the characters forming the customer's name, or read his palms. For a few more cents, the fortune-teller could even decipher the "eight diagrams" for his customer and could conjure up his dead relatives to talk with him. Not far from the fortune-teller was a barber shop, whose trade emblem was a washstand and basin placed just outside the doors. On the same block, Chinese doctors and druggists abounded. Some specialized in feeling the pulse and dispersing herbal prescriptions; others claimed to be experts in curing wounds and fixing broken bones. Inside a typical Chinatown store were scrolls hanging on the walls and Chinese characters written upon red papers which were pasted on doors or over money chests. On the scrolls were quotations from the classics and famous poets, while on the red papers were popular rhymed verse, such as "Wealth Arising Like Bubbling Spring," and "Customers Coming Like Clouds." Chinese merchants and customers frequently began their bargaining with polite conversations about the quality of the scrolls and the philosophical meaning of the verses.

2. The Dark Side of the Old Chinatowns

Most Chinatowns also included narrow streets or alleys given over to shabby apartments, dens for opium smoking, gambling joints, and brothels. From these unsanitary areas came the Chinese criminals; their existence had an important negative impact on the image of the broader Chinese community. According to San Francisco police records, which are probably typical, during the period from 1879 to 1910, Chinese arrested on criminal charges constituted 8.8 percent of all arrests. Of the Chinese arrested, only 11 out of 100 were convicted, the majority for violations of municipal health and fire ordinances. The San Francisco Board of Health was controlled by anti-Chinese physicians who credited "Chinatown with introducing and disseminating every epidemic outbreak to hit San Francisco." To them, Chinatown was more than a slum, it was "a laboratory of infection, peopled by lying and treacherous aliens who had minimal regard for the health of the American people."[8] But Dr. Joan B. Trauner has argued that the pronouncements by the Board of Health were often characterized by political and social expedience, rather than by social insight. The Chinese were made medical scapegoats in San Francisco.[9]

Chinese wage earners, while holding or looking for jobs, usually sought temporary accommodation in the most inexpensive place possible. It was not uncommon for 15 or 20 bachelors to share a small room. In San Francisco's Globe Hotel in the 1860s, some 300 to 400 transient Chinese laborers were housed in extremely congested conditions, highlighting for the authorities their housing problems. In 1870, the California legislature passed a "Cubic Air" law which required a lodging house to provide at least 500 cubic feet of clear atmosphere for each adult person in an apartment. When the Chinese landlords and lodgers resisted complying with the law they were put into prison *en masse*. Later, the Cubic Air Board adopted the notorious "Queue Ordinance" whereby every male prisoner was required to have his hair cut by a clipper to a uniform length of one inch from the scalp. In carrying out the ordinance, a San Francisco policeman named Matthew Noonan cut the queue of Ho Ah-kow, a Chinese prisoner, to the very inch prescribed in the ordinance. The Circuit Court in California in 1879 ruled that the ordinance was unconstitutional and that Ho be awarded a $10,000 compensation by Noonan and the San Francisco city government.[10]

In addition to housing-ordinance violations, Chinatowns were notorious gambling havens. The most common forms of Chinese gambling were fan-tan and lottery. Fan-tan players guessed the exact coins or cards left under a cup after the pile of cards had been counted off four at a time. Fan-tan later became very popular among the Japanese and Filipinos; some lost all their hard-earned money before they could return to their native lands. The same consequences befell many a Chinese worker; many were so impoverished they could not pay for their ashes to be sent to their native villages in China for permanent burial. The lottery game was also known as the white dover card sweepstakes. Any person who wished to enter the game bought a randomly assigned sweepstakes number. In the lottery saloons, about ten of which existed in 1868, drawings were held twice a day; and the odds of winning were probably about the same as in modern-day "keno" in a Las Vegas casino. Many white Americans were attracted to the lotteries; but the unquestioned winners were the saloon owners. There are indications that the gambling-house operators received protection from corrupt police officers. In his testimony before the California Senate Committee in 1876, a Chinese witness estimated that there were about 200 Chinese gambling houses in San Francisco and probably a dozen in Sacramento. He indicated that fan-tan gambling operators were required to pay police officers $5 in "hush money" each week and lottery owners $8 a month for the privilege of keeping their businesses open.[11]

Another factor that contributed to a negative Chinatown image was opium smoking. Originally introduced to China by English merchants from India in the late eighteenth century, this vice not only drained gold and silver out of China but enfeebled the Chinese population and demoralized their society. When pressed by the English to legalize the opium trade, the Chinese Emperor Daoguang (1821–1850) was reported to have vehemently exclaimed: "I know that wicked and designing men, for purpose of lust and profit, will clandestinely introduce the poisonous drug, but nothing under heaven shall ever induce me to legalize the certain ruin of my people."[12] Chinese refusal to legalize the opium trade ultimately led to the infamous Opium War, in which China suffered her first defeat at the hands of a European nation. But the war did not solve the opium issue and for several years opium was not contraband in the newly annexed British colony of Hong Kong, from where the Chinese carried opium into the United States.

The biggest supplier of opium was Hong Kong's Fook Hung Company, which annually paid an opium monopoly tax of between 200,000 and 300,000 dollars to the British authorities. Since the United States did not have specific laws against opium, the drug was sold openly in the streets. Opium dealers did not advertise their business, but smoking dens could easily be located by their red cards, which announced: "Pipes and Lamps Always Convenient!" An 1876 estimate noted more than 200 opium dens operating in San Francisco's Chinatown; the addicts, mostly Chinese, exceeded 3,000.[13] Although opium was not declared illegal until 1909, it was listed as "special merchandise" on which the United States Customs imposed a heavy import duty. In 1887 a Chinese minister reported that, of the tariff revenues levied on Chinese imports by the United States Customs, 840,000 Chinese silver dollars were for rice, 150,000 for silk and cloth, and more than 750,000 for opium.[14] The high duty rate on opium encouraged smuggling. In 1886, the San Francisco Customs authorities broke a smuggling ring and confiscated $750,000 worth of opium. When the United States Congress finally banned opium, the price per pound jumped from $12 to $70. The high price caused most of the opium dens to close their doors; nevertheless, illicit activities continued because desperate dealers knew how to operate around the law and squeeze profits from die-hard addicts.

Another Chinatown social evil, prostitution, was exacerbated by the shortage of Chinese women in America as Table 3 shows.

TABLE 3

Year	Number of Chinese males per 100 females
1860	1,858
1870	1,284
1880	2,106
1890	2,678
1900	1,887

This skewed sex ratio of the Chinese population existed even in Hawaii; there, in 1890, of the 16,752 Chinese, only 1,409 were females and, in 1900, among the 25,767 Chinese, only 3,471 were females.[15] "There were more monks than rice porridge," as the Chinese described the situation; prostitution was inevitable.

Prostitution, the world's oldest profession, was, of course, not a unique Chinese vice. All seriously deprived classes in American society have been plagued by this evil. But anti-Chinese agitators in the late nineteenth century nonetheless held the Chinese particularly culpable. They charged that Chinese prostitutes, who demanded less money for their services, spread the practice among young white males, exerting a bad influence on the entire community. Whether such charges were true or not, government investigations made clear that the Chinese were not solely responsible. Prostitutes received protection from corrupt policemen and other officials and could not have operated without such cooperation.[16]

Chinese prostitutes were mostly imported from Hong Kong and held under contract by underworld figures. The Reverend Otis Gibson, who provided shelter for runaway Chinese prostitutes, testified in 1876 before a special Congressional committee that he had seen some of the contracts and found them to be replete with false promises and outright fraud. Once in America, the girls were quartered in the small alleys of Chinatowns, notably on Jackson Street of San Francisco and I Street of Sacramento. They lived in small filthy rooms of 10 by 10 or 12 by 12 feet.[17] If the girls failed to attract customers, or refused to receive company because of illness or other reasons, they were beaten with sticks. When such punishment did not work, the house mistress tortured them in a variety of sadistic and cruel ways. A great many, terrified by such savage treatment, ran away before the expiration of their contracts. Some slipped back to China, others went to the country for temporary hiding; the most fortunate found shelter in the Gibson station-house. However, countless numbers of unfortunate girls were passed from owner to owner, never escaping their vicious captivity.

It was impossible to ascertain the exact number of the Chinese prostitutes in America. Conservative estimates put the figure between 1,500 and 2,000 in 1870, but a Chinese official who visited California in 1876 reported that there were approximately 6,000 Chinese women in the United States and that 80 to 90 percent were "daughters of joy."[18] Although some municipal laws were passed and sporadic enforcement measures were taken, the problems remained, mainly from police corruption and the ease with which brothels were moved from place to place. Since there was no local supply of Chinese women, some reformers hoped to end the evil by cutting off the supply from Hong Kong and other Chinese ports. Consequently, in 1875 the United States Congress passed the Page Law to stop women "of disreputable character" from coming to America. Nevertheless, pimps continued to find ways to elude the authorities, and prostitution, like opium, remained a problem in Chinatowns.

In order to protect the interests of brothel owners, an association of Chinese villains, known in San Francisco as "the highbinders," was formed. The highbinders, who lived off the prostitutes by levying upon each girl a weekly fee, left behind them a trail of mayhem, blackmail, and murder. It was this lawless element in Chinese society which led many Americans, such as Frank M. Pixley, spokesman for the municipality of San Francisco, to conclude: "I believe that the Chinese have no souls to save, and if they have, they are not worth saving." Pixley's ethnocentric view of the Chinese was typical of nineteenth-century America; it was echoed in a special Congressional committee report: "Upon the point of morals, there is no Aryan or European race which is not far superior to the Chinese as a class."[19] Of course, such racist expressions were not unlike those of the chauvinistic mandarins who, as late as the 1870s, continued to call the Europeans and Americans "Western barbarians."

The problem was that opportunistic American politicians could easily portray the Chinese opium smokers, hookers, gamblers, and highbinders in San Francisco as typical representatives of the Chinese race, just as the narrow-minded mandarins' perception of Westerners was limited to a handful of European drunken sailors, greedy American merchants, and unscrupulous vagabonds lurking in China's treaty ports. In actual fact, the Chinese community in America consistently denounced prostitution, gambling, and other vices which they knew gave Chinatown an unsavory reputation. When Mayor Andrew J. Bryant of San Francisco chided the Chinese leaders about prostitution problems, the president of one of the Six Companies replied: "Yes, yes, Chinese prostitution is bad. What do you think of German prostitutes, French prostitutes, Spanish prostitutes, and American prostitutes? Do you think them very good?"[20] Realizing the harm prostitution had done to their community, several Chinese civic groups, such as the Chinese Society of English Education, the Chinese Students' Alliance, Chinese Native Sons, and Chinese Cadet Corps, took steps in the late 1890s to drive the practice out of Chinatowns. Leaders of these organizations monitored the wharfs to prevent suspicious Chinese women from landing, while young students went directly to the brothels, destroying buildings and furnishings, to drive out the offenders. Such actions were dubiously legal and probably inefficient, but fair-minded Americans could not deny that most Chinese immigrants were as opposed to corruption and vice in their communities as was anyone else. Furthermore, Chinese lawless activities, which were part of the unsettled frontier society, were more of an American than a Chinese phenomenon.

3. Chinese Religious Life

As soon as the Chinese arrived in America, church workers sought to convert them to Christianity, but the majority of nineteenth–century Chinese retained their religious traditions, which were syncretic, tolerant, and nondogmatic. Chinese religious concepts pictured the universe as a trinity of heaven, earth, and man; heaven directs, earth produces, and man cooperates. When man cooperates, he prospers; on the other hand, if man does not cooperate, he destroys the harmonious arrangements of the universe and suffers the consequences in the form of natural disasters, such as floods, droughts, and famines. Heaven replaces the Judeo-Christian concept of God. In Confucianism, one of the most important duties of the Chinese emperor was to maintain the proper relationship beween himself and heaven. By moral conduct, he set an example and maintained harmony between the processes of heaven and of mankind. Hence, the emperor was called the Son of Heaven; his life had cosmic, universal significance, not merely national, and he ruled with the Mandate of Heaven. Within this general context, a Confucian could be an agnostic or even an atheist, or he might worship a variety of local deities.

Confucianism allowed the widest individual discretion in matters of personal belief, and paid little attention to matters of God and afterlife. This tolerance was difficult for Christians to understand because they generally demanded an unflinching faith in a fixed creed.[21]

The Chinese also practiced Taoism, a religious idea centering around a search for a long and serene life, to be attained through simplicity, tranquility, and harmony with nature. Some Taoists pursued not only health but immortality, or at least longevity, by means of physical exercise, breathing control, diet, alchemy, the use of medicine, and good deeds. Having no sense of orderly divine revelation, Chinese Taoists resorted to extreme means to ascertain the future. Various kinds of divination developed, such as the use of phrenologists, geomancy readers, physiognomists, mediums, and fortunetellers. Taoists also promoted the multiplication of gods and goddesses, and believed that famous people enter their pantheon after death. Accordingly, most Taoists did not have an overpowering attachment to any one deity.[22]

Many Chinese were also influenced by yet another religion, Buddhism. The fundamental truths on which Buddhism was founded are not metaphysical or theological, but rather psychological. Buddha taught that suffering results from desire; therefore, the goal of his religion is the extinction of desire, the end of pain, and entry into nirvana. After its Sinicization, Buddhism played down its foreign elements and made itself as Chinese as possible. The abstract concept of nirvana was replaced by a concrete idea of happiness, hence the Western Heaven of Amida Buddha was given prominence.[23] Chinese Buddhism increasingly accommodated itself to the already present Confucian and Taoist beliefs by the Later Han Dynasty (A.D. 25–220) and the three great religions survived and generally mingled peacefully into modern times. It was entirely possible for a Chinese to consider himself a loyal adherent to all three systems. The Chinese call this the harmony of the Three Teachings; they developed a classical, syncretic religious tradition. Many Chinese therefore had a Confucian cap, wore a Taoist robe, and put on a Buddhist sandal.

With such a seemingly rational religious tradition in China, it is understandable that American missionaries had difficulty in converting the Chinese to the more exclusive and dogmatic Christianity. But they quickly seized the opportunities afforded by racial discrimination and social injustice as issues to make their Christian God omnipresent to the Chinese immigrants, and to act as liaison between Chinatowns and white society. Among the more prominent early Christian workers were the Speers, the Loomises, and the Gibsons. In 1852 Dr. and Mrs. William Speer, who had been Presbyterian missionaries in Canton from 1846 to 1850, established a medical clinic in their

San Francisco mission to try to gain influence in the Chinese community. They also established a newspaper called *The Oriental,* a bilingual periodical with printed matter suited to American readers on one side of the paper and the other side printed in Chinese for Chinese readers. They worked hard to allay prejudice and to help the Chinese and the Americans better understand each other. Because of Speer's poor health, the paper operated for only two years; the clinic was closed after four years.[24]

In 1859, the Speers' mission was reestablished under leadership of the Reverend A. W. Loomis and his wife, also former missionaries to China. They set up a free school to teach the Chinese the English language and the gospel. Their activities set a precedent that was followed by most of the Chinese Christian churches. In 1868 the Reverend Otis Gibson organized a Methodist Episcopal Church in the San Francisco Chinatown with a social-welfare program to aid the poor; similar mission programs were also established by the Reverend W. C. Pond for the Congregational Church and by the Reverend John Francis of the Baptist Church. Social programs, however, did not result in mass conversions of Chinese to Christianity, but did slowly expand church influence in the Chinese community. By 1892 Chinese were listed as members of 11 denominations in North America and had established 10 independent congregations and 271 Sunday Schools in 31 states of the Union. The expansion of Chinese Christian faith was accompanied by the appearance of numerous denominational associations. By the turn of the century, the Association of the Presbyterian Mission, for instance, claimed to have a membership of more than 1,000 in 12 states.[25] Impressive as these gains seemed, many Chinese Christians continued to hold syncretic religious views; Christians frequently practiced ancestor worship, followed traditional Chinese wedding and funeral rituals, and paid occasional respect to Taoist gods in Chinese temples. Before World War II, except among the native-born, orthodox Chinese Christians in America were still scarce.

In addition to loyalty to their own religious traditions, Chinese resisted Christianity because of sojourner mentality, American racism, and community pressure. For a sojourner, his mind, heart, and soul remained in China, and he satisfied his social and psychological needs through clan/family organizations and community activities. This mentality was reinforced by flagrant anti-Chinese racism. If the Chinese were encouraged to go to the white man's heaven, why could they not freely immigrate to the white man's country? In his reasoning, the Chinese immigrant could discern a patent hypocrisy among white Christians whose Bible taught justice and love but whose deeds against the Chinese were a shameful and undeniable record of injustice and violence. Finally, community pressure was also an important reason for the church's failure to convert large numbers of Chinese immigrants. Leaders of the Six Companies, for example, viewed Christianity as a threat to Chinese culture and Chinese social institutions. On a few occasions they made desperate moves, using harassment and social ostracism to discourage the increase of Chinese Christians.[26]

4. The Six Companies

The Six Companies' attempt to dissuade early Chinese immigrants from becoming Christians was only one of the hundreds of incidents that placed this powerful organization at the center of controversy. Chinese immigrants were not only socially and economically divided, they also represented a variety of regions, cultures, and languages. The rich and more respectable merchants were generally the San-yi (from the three districts of Nanhai, Panyu, and Shunde), the petty merchants, craftsmen, and agriculturalists were mainly among the Si-yi (from the four districts of Enping, Kaiping, Taishan or Xinning, and Xinhui) while the laboring class came from a variety of regions. For example, the San-yi people at times controlled wholesale merchandising, the garment industry, and overall manufacturing. The Hakkas (Guest Settlers) dominated the barber business; the tenant farmers engaging in fruit growing in the Sacramento-San Joaquin Delta were mostly Zhongshan immigrants.[27]

Each region spoke its own local variation of Cantonese, so there was a basic correspondence between Chinese class structure and dialect groups. The people from Guangzhou (Canton) and the San-yi spoke Cantonese, and that dialect came to be considered standard. Most people from Zhongshan district, about 30 miles south of Guangzhou, spoke a dialect closely resembling the standard Cantonese, but the surrounding countryside spoke a dialect akin to Amoy. Except in the Sacramento Delta and Hawaii, the Zhongshan immigrants have always been a minority in America's Chinese communities. On the other hand, the Si-yi people, who made up the bulk of Chinese immigrants, spoke a dialect almost totally incomprehensible to the city dwellers. Finally, among these heterogeneous groups were the Hakkas. Originally migrating from North China, the Hakkas were quite scattered with strong concentrations in Jiaying and Chaozhou and other districts of Guangdong province and Fujian province. They spoke a dialect more akin to Mandarin than the other groups. Though the Hakkas never comprised more than 10 percent of the Chinese population in the continental United States, they made up about 25 percent of the Chinese in Hawaii.[28] Among these dialect groups there was a long history of rivalry, and sometimes conflict. The Cantonese called themselves Puntis, which meant "the natives," and considered the Hakkas invaders. The Hakkas and the Puntis had long felt hostile to each other in China, and a dreadful internecine strife between them had taken place in the southwestern districts of Guangdong from 1864 to 1868. Both parties procured arms and even armed steamers from Hong Kong, and inflicted heavy casualties on each other.

The instability of the bachelor society and the dialect/regional divisions in America were cornerstones of the social organizations that emerged. In China, social organizations were normally formed on the basis of a common regional origin. One of the most important types of organization was the huiguan. A huiguan was a traditional and lawful association of fellow-provincials away from home, either visiting or on business. In the nineteenth century, when mercantile pursuit was not encouraged by Confucian ethics, the status of merchants was much lower than that of scholars, officials, and landowners. Since there were no specific laws to protect their interests, merchants needed patronage from officials, who could benefit from certain financial arrangements the merchants might consider it wise to make. As a result, in major Chinese cities all kinds of huiguan were organized by merchants. In Shanghai, for example, one could find the Canton Huiguan, the Ningpo Huiguan, the Fijian Huiguan, and the like.

A second basis of social organization in China, and a much tighter one, rested on a coincidence between blood and region. In an agrarian society, the people of any one clan, those claiming a common ancestor, usually inhabited a village or cluster of adjacent villages. Agnatic descendants maintained these lineage alignments by keeping a common estate and by forming a clan association for the control, protection, and general welfare of their kinsmen. Another basis of organization, again agnatically defined, was the blood-ties association. Chinese who have the same surname, though they might come from different parts of China, could organize a huiguan on the grounds that they had a common ancestor in the distant past. In the modern city of Taibei, Chinese mainlanders have formed many such associations since 1949. The same situation existed when the Chinese emigrated to America.

When a Chinese laborer arrived in the United States, the first thing he did was to seek people who spoke his dialect, and a bond of solidarity soon arose. This tendency was naturally strengthened by his inability to communicate with Americans and those speaking other Chinese dialects. The linguistic bond accounted to a great degree for the rise of so many huiguans in Chinese communities. It is believed that in 1851 an influential Si-yi leader named Yu Laoji founded the first huiguan, the Kong Chow Company (or Gangzhou Huiguan), in San Francisco with membership open to all Chinese except San-yi and Hakkas. Within a year, the more affluent San-yi immigrants organized their Sam Yup Company (or Sanyi Huiguan) with branches in San Francisco and Stockton.[29]

In 1853, the Si-yi immigrants felt that the Kong Chow Company could no longer accommodate their needs, so more than 10,000 of them organized a new huiguan called the Sze Yup Company (or Siyi Huiguan). Shortly thereafter, the Zhongshan immigrants founded their own Yeong Wo Company (Yanghe Huiguan) and the Hakkas their Yan Wo Company (or Renhe Huiguan).[30] With the founding of these last two organizations a huiguan existed for all Chinese in America. Near the end of 1853 the presidents of these various organizations (Kong Chow Company excluded) met to form a federal association called the Four Houses. Then, in 1854, over 3,000 Taishan natives left the Sze Yup Company in order to form a more exclusive huiguan, the Ning Yeung Company (or Ningyang Huiguan). The Ning Yeung Company proved so successful that the rest of the Taishan people soon joined it, leaving the Sze Yup Company defunct; ultimately the Sze Yup Company lost its representation on the council of the Four Houses to the Kong Chow Company.[31] The spin-off process continued when, early in 1862, the remaining Kaiping and Enping Chinese left the Sze Yup Company to form yet another huiguan called the Hop Wo Company (or Hehe Huiguan). Soon after that, both the Ning Yeung Company and the Hop Wo Company joined the Four Houses, which changed its Chinese name to the Zhonghua Huiguan and its English name to the Chinese Consolidated Benevolent Association; it was widely known to Americans as the Chinese Six Companies. A similar evolution took place in the Hawaiian Islands among the Chinese plantation workers, who also established a Chinese Consolidated Benevolent Association. When the Chinese in America ventured farther to the East Coast, they carried their huiguan identifications with them and quickly founded clan/district associations in Boston, New York, and other cities.

In addition to the Six Companies, the Chinese established the Zhonghua Gongsuo, Congress of the Six Companies, consisting of elected officials of the huiguan organizations. Housed in a building at 709 Commercial Street in San Francisco, this congress had a permanent headquarters and full-time officials, as with each of the six companies. All matters affecting the general interests of the Chinese in America were referred to this body. It settled disputes between individuals and the companies, decided strategies for contesting or seeking relief from unconstitutional or burdensome laws, devised ways to curb the importation of prostitutes, and arranged for public dinners and other celebrations.[32]

Anti-Chinese partisans claimed that the Six Companies extended oriental despotism to the United States, placing Chinese laborers under tyrannical control. They accused the Six Companies of importing "coolies" and prostitutes under contract; of operating gambling and opium dens; of establishing secret tribunals and codes of laws; and of illegally extorting money from Chinese immigrants. A. W. Loomis, who worked in the Chinese community for years, branded such charges "popular fallacies" and "groundless assertions."[33] In fact, the huiguan was designed to protect newly arrived kinsmen and fellow-provincials from those who otherwise might take advantage of them. The company building, therefore, served the same functions as the caravansary of Eastern countries in the Middle Ages.

As soon as an immigrant ship arrived from China, the company sent an interpreter to the wharf to welcome the arrivals. In the company headquarters, the new immigrants were furnished water, fuel for cooking, and a room in which to spread their mats. Chinese laborers from inland towns and mining camps, embarking for return to China, often stayed in the company houses instead of in the more expensive boarding houses. The sick and indigent were also welcomed; the idle and irresponsible, however, were quickly weeded out. The company houses forbade the concealment of stolen goods. No strangers could be brought to lodge; no gunpowder or other combustible material stored. Gambling, accumulation of baggage, drunkenness, storage of victuals, and disposal of garbage were not allowed. Serious offenders were turned over to the police of the city; lesser offenses could result in expulsion from the company. For all except transients and invalids, the membership fee was $10, in the 1850s. Finally, members intending to return to China were required to make that fact known, so their accounts could be examined and measures taken to prevent their departure if debts remained unpaid.[34]

In most of the company buildings there were special sections devoted to religious purposes. These areas were furnished by voluntary contributions and were not usually provided for in the constitutions of the companies. However, as a means of gaining prestige among their fellow-provincials, wealthy merchants, whether or not they were believers in idols, gave money to religious causes. Some individuals obtained the privilege of taking care of the idols and earned money from the sale of incense sticks, candles, and charms, and from donations and fees from worshippers. In some company buildings an apartment was devoted to worship of the spirits of deceased members. In it was an altar before which a light was constantly kept burning. Friends and relatives of the deceased made offerings on the altar, behind which was the list of names of the company members who had died. Because of religious beliefs and strong ties to China, bones of the deceased were usually exhumed as soon as possible and sent home for permanent burial. But gathering bones of the dead and sending them back to China was not a part of the work undertaken by the company. Clan or blood-ties groups represented in America in some instances undertook separately the performance of this obligation; but very many remains were sent home by personal friends in America, the expenses being paid by relatives in Guangdong.[35]

The Six Companies kept a register of names and addresses of all the Chinese in the United States; in 1876, for instance, it listed a total of 150,130. Li Gui, a Chinese official on his return trip from the Philadelphia Exposition, interviewed leaders of the Six Companies, and noted in his travel journal: "The Chinese of both sexes in America amount to a total of about 160,000, of which roughly 40,000 reside in San Francisco, 100,000 in other cities, and the rest spread out in the hinterlands . . . Only about 2,000 non-Cantonese do not belong to the Six Companies."[36] Two years after Li Gui's visit, the first Chinese minister to arrive in San Francisco recorded these population statistics in his diary: "Sam Yup Company has 12,000 members, Yeong Wo 13,000, Kong Chow 16,000, Yan Hop a few thousands, Hop Wo Company has 40,000, and Ning Yeung 70,000."[37]

The leaders of the Six Companies were mostly successful businessmen who were wealthier and better educated than most of their fellow immigrants; many occupied positions of honor and power. However, realizing that in the old country they would not have a high social status, these merchant huiguan leaders promoted Confucian ideology, stressing the importance of clan/regional ties and choosing the company president from among those members who had obtained the best Chinese education. By the 1890s the huiguan made efforts to bring from China scholars who had successfully passed the Chinese civil-service examinations, to serve as company officials. In 1906, for example, there were four Juren (holder of the second examination degree) among the company presidents and they were paid handsomely for coming to America. Of the 14 presidents of the Sam Yup Company from 1881 to 1927, three had Jinshi degrees (holder of the first examination degree), nine had Juren degrees, and one had a Gongsheng degree (holder of the third examination degree).[38]

The Six Companies were often viewed as secretive, extralegal organizations because they arbitrated cases of misunderstanding or quarrels among the Chinese. The fact that thousands of Chinese acquiesced in the huiguan arbitration decisions led many white Americans to believe that the Chinese in America feared jurisdiction of the companies more than they did American laws or courts. Such Americans did not understand the strong Chinese tradition of respect for elders, superiors, and all those who occupied positions of authority and honor. Moreover, since Chinese laborers were frequently represented in economic matters by the Six Companies, those officials became the natural representatives to resist, in any possible way, legal impositions and social indignities imposed upon the Chinese immigrants. Accordingly, the huiguan officials often attended to cases in the civil courts, hiring American lawyers and assuming responsibilities for legal costs. Thus many poor and illiterate Chinese laborers who could not afford to retain an attorney were defended in the courts. One of the leading scholars on the Chinese Americans, Stanford M. Lyman, correctly characterized the Six Companies as "an official government inside Chinatown and . . . the most important voice of the Chinese immigrants speaking to American officials."[39]

Before the establishment of the Chinese legation at Washington, D.C., in 1878, the Six Companies functioned as representatives for the whole Chinese population in America. After the Qing emperor sent diplomatic agents to this country, the Six Companies and the Chinese legation worked together and continued to control the internal affairs of the Chinatowns. Whenever a high-ranking official visited or passed through California, the Six Companies leaders seized the opportunity to entertain and consult with him. As a matter of fact, the Qing imperial decrees and proclamations were, in most cases, conveyed to the Chinese through the Six Companies. Nevertheless, the leadership of the Six Companies began to shift its allegiance to the anti-Manchu forces in 1911.

San Francisco early became and long remained the cultural center of Chinese Americans. However, by the end of the nineteenth century, there were communities of Chinese in other American cities, and these communities, because of their small sizes and sectional characteristics, did not always follow the pattern of San Francisco. Clan competition was characteristic of the larger Chinese communities in such cities as San Francisco and Honolulu, but small Chinatowns were usually dominated by a single clan/regional association and, therefore, had fewer conflicts. Although such communities maintained close political, economic, and social ties to San Francisco's Chinatown, they enjoyed a local autonomy. For instance, theoretically, all Chinese clan/regional associations in America belonged to an umbrella organization called the Chinese Consolidated Benevolent Association (CCBA) with headquarters in San Francisco. The CCBA in Honolulu or in New York, however, probably paid only lip-service to San Francisco's CCBA. On certain controversial issues they functioned as autonomous and holistic entities.

5. Other Chinese Community Organizations

Although the Six Companies were the most important and most famous, Chinese immigrants designed a wide variety of other organizations to meet their needs in the new world. Typical were benevolent societies, clan/family groups, trade and craft guilds, and several secret societies. In 1903 the eminent Chinese scholar Liang Qichao visited San Francisco and reported the existence within Chinatown of 10 public Chinese organizations (including the Six Companies), 2 trade organizations, 9 benevolent organizations, 24 clan organizations, 9 combined clan (blood-ties) organizations, 25 secret societies, and 5 cultural societies.[40] Most of these organizations were called tongs, which means hall or parlor. Because of the proliferation of tongs, there was much confusion about the use of the word. The American public often identified a tong as a group of criminals who lived off the opium smugglers, gamblers, and prostitutes. But the clandestine organizations of the so-called highbinders or hatchet men actually constituted only a small percent of the Chinese tongs in America. Furthermore, even these martial tongs had religious aspects and political origins as distinctively Chinese as the Six Companies.

In traditional China the secret society was an underground seditious organization directed against unpopular government authority. The societies constantly changed their names to divert the attention of the authorities. In the nineteenth century the most prominent included the Pure Water Society, Small Dagger Society, Big Sword Society, and Copper Coins Society. The origins of these societies are shrouded in mystery, but it is generally believed that Chinese secret societies in America stem from the notorious Triad Society of South China. The Triad Society was originally a quasireligious fraternity established in the seventeenth century by a sect of militant Buddhist monks of the Shaolin Monastery in the Fuzhou area. The name Triad, or Three United Society, is apparently derived from the trinity of Heaven, Earth, and Man; hence, it was also known as the Society of the Three Dots and as the Heaven and Earth Society. Because of its connection with the Ming Dynasty (1368–1644) founded by the Emperor Hongwu, it also received the names Sect of Hong, Family of Hong, and Red League.[41]

The Triad Society, or the Hong League, was in some ways like Freemasonry, professing such virtuous aims as obeying heaven and acting righteously. Bound by oaths of blood-brotherhood, the members pledged to overthrow the Manchus and restore the Ming house to the throne. This goal was captured in such slogans as "By patriotism and loyalty we support the Han House, with unity and cooperation let us annihilate the Qing Dynasty." The Hong League led several rebellions against the Qing regime in the late seventeenth century, but was defeated by the superior forces of the government. Many members paid with their lives for their audacity; others went underground or escaped abroad. In spite of these setbacks, Hong League loyalists embraced the idea of nationalism and preached it, handing it down from generation to generation.[42]

When transplanted overseas, the Hong League generally lost its religious and political significance and became rather a fraternal order which offered aid to travelers and the indigent. In America secret societies were sometimes organized to unite members of minority family clans against economic exploitation, including the invasion of their business interests by a major family group. Since the American West lacked effective legal institutions, the secret societies grew into mafia-type organizations, using violence and intimidation to punishing enemies and to accumulate wealth. Emphasizing fraternity and mutual assistance, the secret society had a three-point code: secrecy, help in time of trouble, and respect for one another's womenfolk. This code had its legendary origin in the third century A.D., when China was divided into Three Kingdoms. Three strangers, named Liu Bei, Guan Gong, and Zhang Fei, met in a peach garden and bound themselves under an oath of brotherhood to be loyal to each other until death, to save the declining Han Dynasty and to serve the people. Guan Gong was later idolized as the God of War and as the symbol of loyalty and integrity. The Shaolin monks and Ming loyalists of the seventeenth century perpetuated the code when they founded the Triad Society.[43]

According to Liang Qichao, many members of the Hong League went overseas after the defeat of the Taipings in 1864.[44] Taiping historian Ling Shanqing wrote:

> Yang Fuqing, the younger brother of Eastern King Yang Xiuqing . . . in the seventh month of 1864, changed clothes and escaped out of the fallen city of Huzhou with a foreigner. He went to Shanghai, then Hong Kong, and from there he emigrated to San Francisco. After selling his jewels he got more than a hundred thousand dollars. Using this fortune, he started the Three United Society, a secret society aiming to rebuild the Taipings . . . Through this secret society, he supported many Chinese who came to America.[45]

The date of the founding of the first Hong League in America is still debated. It is generally believed that even before Yang Fuqing came to America, followers of another Taiping general, Chen Jingang of Guangdong, had founded the first Hong League lodge at Barkerville, Canada. But the celebrated San Francisco Chee Kung Tong, or I Hsing or Patriotic Rising Society, was probably not founded until 1863, by either Lin Yin or Luo Yi. Others maintain that the lodge of the Hong League began in the Rocky Mountain mining communities and subsequently moved to Chinese settlements in northern Montana and Canada. It is even possible that an authentic Hong League organization was in full operation in British Vancouver as early as 1858.[46]

It is not clear, then, whether the secret societies in America were simply different branches of the parent Triad of China or emanated from one branch of the Triad which first came to the New World. It is evident, however, that the American Hong League was never a united body; it developed as several separate societies, each claiming membership in the Triad family and acting independently of the others. American ethnologist Stewart Culin notes that by the 1880s Hong League organizations were active not only along the Pacific Coast but in most major American cities. There was the Yi Xing or Righteous Rise in Philadelphia, which adopted the name Hongshun Tong, or Hall of Obedience to Hong, for its lodge. The New York Triad group called its headquarters Lianyi Tong or Hall of United Righteousness, while the lodges in Boston and Baltimore, which were handsomely decorated with votive tablets, were said to have been founded by the same elderly man. In the mid-West the Triad societies, notably those in St. Louis and Chicago, chose Hongshun Tong as their names.[47]

One interesting aspect of the secret society was its unique Cantonese origins, a fact that has long intrigued Chinese officials and American writers. According to Ji Ying, the Chinese Imperial Commissioner who concluded a treaty in 1842 with the British to end the Opium War, the Cantonese were "violent and obstinate," and "all classes were fond of brawls and made light of their lives." He also characterized them as a people who "loved to display their spirit and bravery," making them "habitual disturbers of the peace."[48] Other Chinese officials, such as Minister Zhang Yinhuan, noted the same Cantonese qualities—clannishness, courage, and alertness—qualities which had in the past fitted them as leaders of rebellion and underworld activities. When these qualities were transplanted overseas, combined with racial solidarity and tightly guarded directorates, the secret societies became powerful organizations. They commanded allegiance, collected money, and controlled external relations of the overseas Chinese. Indeed, secret societies reflected the peculiar genius of the Cantonese for political organization and social control. The secret societies confined their interests exclusively to the Chinese population and rarely terrorized non-Chinese residents. Their intersociety feuds, however, were so frequent that the so-called tong wars were viewed with alarm by outsiders.

It is not clear when true tong wars began in America, but, by the late 1880s, the word "tong" had come to have negative connotations outside of Chinatowns. Actually, in the long list of Chinese tong organizations a large number remained altogether free from intersociety feuds and unlawful activities. These were often referred to as the non-fighting tongs.[49] Even so, it was difficult for outsiders to distinguish a militant tong from a pacific one. This difficulty was compounded by overlapping membership, since many people belonged to more than one tong. A respectable merchant, for instance, had automatic membership in one of the Six Companies; he probably held membership also in one or two benevolent tongs and at least one clan tong. He might also join a secret society tong for protection against fighting tongs. Economic motives and the preservation of clan prestige were the most important causes of tong violence. Accounts of battles arising from these causes were indeed numerous. In early May, 1869, for example, a battle occurred between two rival groups of Chinese railroad workers near Camp Victory in Utah. The dispute erupted over a $15 debt owed by a member of one tong to a member of a rival tong. After the usual braggadocio, both parties sailed in, at a given signal, armed with every conceivable weapon. Several shots were fired and all indications of the outbreak of a riot appeared until a superintendent of the Central Pacific restored order and averted a major disturbance.[50]

The tong wars began escalating in the 1880s. For several years the Six Companies attempted to make peace among the tongs, but to no avail. The problems eventually drew the attention of Chinese officials when a vicious San Francisco tong feud in 1886 resulted in heavy loss of lives and property. The Chinese legation in Washington issued a proclamation warning that if "gangsters" continued these senseless feuds, the guilty would be deported to China and their relatives in Guangdong would also be held responsible.[51] The proclamation did little to quell the increasing violence in Chinatowns; more and more Chinese were jailed because of their involvement in the intertong strife. One consul-general named Zuo Geng decided to spy on the troublemakers and tipped off American officials to aid in arrests and quick convictions. Another, named He You, resorted to the radical method, which authorized Chinese officials to jail the gangsters' relatives in Guangdong for crimes allegedly committed in America. Measures such as these helped to combat the tong wars and, by 1900, violence in America's Chinatowns had declined dramatically.[52] Furthermore, by the turn of the century, there were more native-born Chinese Americans and they were less easily intimidated by criminal elements. Since 1921, tong wars have been practically nonexistent in

American Chinese communities.[53] With the passing of the fighting tongs, a new era of healthier growth in Chinatowns had begun.

Looking at these community organizations, it is clear that the Chinese sojourners tried to maintain indigenous Chinese culture in a hostile new land. Chinese values, norms and historically derived beliefs were distinctly expressed in their political, social and religious behavior. Anthropologist Clifford Geertz, in relating culture to behavior, wrote: "Culture is best seen not as complexes of concrete behavior patterns . . . but as a set of control mechanisms—plans, recipes, rules, instructions (what computer engineers call 'programs')—for the governing of behavior."[54] Chinese informal political organization of the Six Companies, the subterranean social structure of the tongs, and the fact that the Chinese embraced traditional Chinese religions instead of Christianity set them off from the American mainstream.

These community organizations were designed to meet all the needs of Chinese residents and to promote their interests. But because they were based exclusively on Chinese ethnicity, the Chinese ended up exploiting themselves and pitting one group against another; for the most part, the organizations failed to bring about planned social change for group development. They failed to deal with the issues most vital to the improvement of Chinese life in America. Efforts to stop anti-Chinese exclusion laws, on which they expended so much energy and money, proved to be impractical and misdirected. Chinese Americans did not have the power to change the direction of United States policy to any significant degree. In the final analysis, their lofty effort to maintain Chinese heritage, language, and religion in America retarded the acculturation of the first and second generations of Chinese in the New World.

III

AMERICAN EXCLUSION AGAINST THE CHINESE

> Goods become dearer when they leave
> their native places; people become cheaper
> when they leave their native lands.
>
> —Chinese proverb

> The friendship of officials is as thin as
> paper.
>
> —Chinese proverb

1. Public Debate Over the Chinese Issue

California was both the first home of Chinese immigrants and the place where they made their greatest contribution; it also was where anti-Chinese sentiment first turned ugly. The anti-Chinese movement in America has been carefully studied in recent years. Some experts, like Stuart C. Miller, believe that hostilities toward the Chinese were a part of the general xenophobia of white Protestant Americans, who also resented Catholics and immigrants from southern and eastern Europe. The racist views that supported these fears included the belief that "Mongolian" blood was debased, that the Chinese mind was politically retarded, and that further Chinese immigration would threaten Aryan dominance in America. Other scholars, like Elmer C. Sandmeyer, have argued that economic considerations were most important in causing anti-immigrant feeling, particularly because Chinese laborers became unwitting pawns in American labor-management disputes during the vicious economic cycles of the late nineteenth century. Mary R. Coolidge, on the other hand, has blamed anti-Chinese agitation squarely on wily demagogic politicians who, in order to win the support of the working classes, hysterically fanned anti-Chinese sentiment. A few clergymen did all they could to give a

more rounded picture of the Chinese community in America and portray the Chinese residents as a variety of decent individuals rather
than an undistinguishable mass, but the public was generally swayed
by shriller voices. Finally, cultural anthropologist Francis L. K. Hsu
sees the problem as a classic cultural misunderstanding: the majority
of white Americans were ignorant of Chinese culture and their ignorance produced prejudice. On the other hand, because of the language barrier, different customs, syncretic religion, and other traditions, the Chinese held aloof from the whites. They tried to place
a comfortable distance beween them and the unfriendliness in the
looks and acts of their coworkers or neighbors. Unfortunately, the
voluntary Chinese separation stamped them with a badge of inferiority. [1]

Before the United States Congress took up the "Chinese issue" in
1879, anti-Chinese attacks and political agitation were confined to the
West Coast. Early oppression included violent attacks on Chinese
workers and their property, and the enactment of discriminatory legislation at the municipal and state levels. For instance, one of the articles of the second constitution of California, ratified in 1879, specified
that no corporation was allowed to employ directly or indirectly any
Chinese or Mongolian. It was stipulated that "no Chinese shall be employed on any state, county, municipal, or other public work, except
in punishment for crime." The United States Circuit Court in California, in the case of *Tiburcio Parrott vs. Ah Chong,* later declared this article unconstitutional. [2]

With the help of sympathetic white employers the Chinese went to
court time and again to challenge the constitutionality of these discriminatory laws. State and federal courts, for several years, consistently struck down anti-Chinese municipal and state laws. The courts
ruled that such laws were contrary to the Fifth Amendment, which required "due process" and "equal protection under the law." Second,
the laws ran counter to the Civil Rights Act of 1870, which prohibited
discrimination against any person and barred the imposition of immigration taxes on a particular group of nonresidents. Third, they were
contrary to the Sino-American treaties, which provided for the most-
favored-nation treatment for the Chinese. And finally they breached
the Burlingame treaty, which gave the Chinese the rights of free immigration. [3] The Supreme Court, on a few occasions, also suggested
that the United States Congress alone had the authority to pass legislation for the limitation of alien immigration.

But by the late 1870s pressure was mounting to exclude Chinese
labor from California. Battle lines were drawn between employers
who wanted to use Chinese labor and the workers and independent
small farmers who opposed them. The press on the West Coast de-

bated the issue in its columns. On April 3, 1876, the California legislature appointed a special committee to investigate the social, moral, and political effects of Chinese immigration. While the committee was holding its hearings, a mass rally sponsored by anti-Chinese partisans was held in the Union Hall of San Francisco. The meeting passed a resolution demanding an end to Chinese immigration and authorized a memorial to the United States Congress to be presented personally by distinguished citizens. Bowing to the California "lobby" and pressure from other Western states, in July, 1876, Congress appointed a joint special committee to investigate Chinese immigration and to provide a conspicuous forum in which all views could be elaborated and brought to the public eye.

The committee consisted of two members from each house, Senators Oliver P. Morton of Indiana (chairman) and Edwin R. Meader of New York, and Congressmen Aaron A. Sargent and W. F. Piper of California. Since Morton was critically ill, Sargent was named acting chairman and actually prepared the final report for the committee. On October 21, 1876, the committee began its lengthy hearings in San Francisco. Numerous witnesses of all types were called to testify, but the few Chinese witnesses who appeared in the sessions were handicapped by language problems and a lack of knowledge of American culture. The attitude of landowners, manufacturers, and big employers toward Chinese immigration was stated with great clarity and frankness in the testimony of Colonel William W. Hollister, a very large California landowner. Hollister believed that the country would be greatly enriched by Chinese labor. When asked whether any legal limitation should be placed upon Chinese immigration, Hollister replied; "No, sir, I would open the door and let everybody come who wants to come . . . I say, fully, freely, and emphatically, that the Chinese should be allowed to come until you get enough here to reduce the price of labor to such a point as that its cheapness will stop their coming."[4] But lowering the cost of labor was not the only reason Hollister favored unlimited Chinese immigration; he was apparently impressed with Chinese workmanship. He believed the Chinese laborers were superior to any other immigrant group. He found them willing, intelligent, accurate, prompt, and skillful in their work.[5] Other landowners and employers shared Hollister's views, either wholly or in part. In addition to people who owned land, gasworks, factories, and railroads, many religious leaders opposed any move to restrict the immigration of the Chinese to America. For instance, the Reverend Otis Gibson testified that the presence of Chinese among the whites imposed a duty on Americans and gave an opportunity for Christianizing the Chinese.

On the other hand, white laboring people and artisans opposed the influx of Chinese as contributing to unemployment. These witnesses tended to exaggerate the number of Chinese who had reached American shores and loudly declared that the presence of large numbers of Chinese laborers had deterred the entry of more highly skilled white laborers from Europe. Other hostile witnesses included lawyers, doctors, small proprietors, judges, and newspaper reporters. Most acknowledged that Chinese immigration had invariably enhanced the material prosperity of the West Coast but they maintained that such gains were deceptive and unwholesome, and indeed a threat to America's free institutions. Typical was the testimony of James N. Bassett, editor of the *Los Angeles Herald:* "My observation has been that the labor of the Chinese who are here now and are coming here tends to make the rich richer and the poor poorer . . . Chinese labor, undoubtedly, has been beneficial to a few people and injurious to the masses."[6]

During the hearings, the Congressional committee examined 103 witnesses; the testimony was published in a 1,200 page report. Since the committee was dominated by Californians and its report was principally drafted by the biased Sargent, the committee recommended that "measures be taken by the Executive toward a modification of the existing treaty with China, confining it to strictly commerical purposes; and that Congress legislate to restrain the great influx of Asiatics to this country."[7] Scarcely had the joint committee submitted its report before several bills were introduced into the forty-fifth Congress (1878-79) calling for termination of Chinese immigration. The chairman of the Committee on Education and Labor, Albert S. Willis, a Democrat from Kentucky, combined the proposals into the so-called Fifteen Passenger Bill.

The bill crystallized public debate on Chinese immigration in the 1870s. Briefly stated, it provided that no vessel should take on board at any point in China, or elsewhere, more than 15 Chinese passengers with the intention of bringing them to the United States. Violation of this provision was made a misdemeanor, punishable by a fine of $100 for each passenger and imprisonment for six months. A shipmaster was required, under like penalties, to report on his arrival a certified list of all Chinese passengers. The penalty for failure included a lien upon the vessel.[8] Opponents of the bill declared that it was in violation of the Burlingame treaty, a revival of Know-nothingism, a complete capitulation to the demands of Denis Kearney and his Workingmen's Party. They reasserted that the Chinese were not coolies nor were they unassimilable. Supporters of the bill, on the other hand, argued that "the Chinese had no regard for the family, did not recognize the relationship of husband and wife, did not observe the tie of parent and child, and were laborers under a mortgage."[9] The bill passed the House by a vote of 155 to 72. The Democrats voted 104 yeas and 16 nays, while the Repubicans voted 51 yeas and 56 nays. In the Senate, the Chinese immigration became more or less a sectional issue, with the West and the South supporting restriction and the East opposing. The bill passed by a small majority.

While Congress was still debating the bill, the newly arrived Chinese ministers, Chen Lanpin and Yung Wing, visited Secretary of State William Evarts and expressed strong opposition to the bill. They informed the secretary that they were as much shocked by the tenor and style of the debate as they were by the insulting bill. With good reason, the Chinese diplomats complained that the language Americans politicians used was "offensive and opprobrious" and similar to that of "common people of inferior characters."[10] American merchants and missionaries who had lived and worked in China also made protests against the bill. S. Wells Williams, who was a missionary and diplomat in China before returning to teach Chinese history at Yale, believed that the bill was not in the best interest of the United States. Williams urged President Rutherford B. Hayes to veto the bill, fearing it could cause the Chinese government to abrogate the principle of extraterritoriality and expose Americans living in China to the consequences of a sudden abrogation of treaty protection. Apparently, this line of reasoning convinced the President because on March 1, 1879, Hayes sent a long veto message to Congress.[11]

With this action the President had successfully avoided a potential international crisis. Nevertheless, Hayes was concerned about the political consequences of his veto on the Pacific coast, and he noted in his diary that the "Chinese labor invasion was pernicious and should be discouraged."[12] Therefore, the President sought out a competent and well-qualified man to undertake a mission of treaty revision in Peking. The man chosen was James B. Angell, a distinguished jurist and historian who was then president of the University of Michigan. To make a more balanced commission, John F. Swift of California, a well-known Sinophobe, and William H. Trescot of South Carolina, an ex-Confederate diplomat, were also appointed delegates.[13]

After two months' preparation, which included consultation with Dr. Peter Parker, an old China hand, S. Wells Williams, historian George Bancroft, and Governor Frederick Low of California, the commission members left for China on June 19, 1880, aboard the ship *Oceanic*. They arrived in Peking on August 9 and, within a week, the Chinese government appointed Bao-yun and Li Hongzao to conduct negotiations with the Americans.[14] Both Bao-yun and Li were of high rank and had great influence in the Qing court, being grand councilors and concurrent member ministers of the Zongli Yamen, a prototype foreign ministry. During the course of negotiations, Swift posed some minor but resolvable problems because of his rigid California view of the immigration issue; Li, a staunch Confucianist and a known xenophobe, was also uncompromising. But thanks to the leadership and persuasive abilities of Angell and Bao-yun, the negotiations were successfully concluded on November 8, 1880. In addition to a migration treaty, they also concluded a commercial treaty; both of which were signed on November 17.[15] European diplomats in Peking were astonished to learn that after forty-eight days of negotiation, the Americans had secured two treaties. German and Russian diplomats had labored two years to conclude a single treaty.

The migration treaty, known also as Angell's treaty, was brief but contained four provocative articles. The first two read:

    I. Whenever in the opinion of the Government of the United States, the coming of Chinese laborers to the United States, or their residence therein, affects or threatens to affect the interests of that country . . . the Government of China agrees that the Government of the United States may regulate, limit, or suspend such coming or residence, but may not absolutely prohibit it.

   II. Chinese subjects, whether proceeding to the United States as teachers, students, merchants or from curiosity, together with their body and household servants, and Chinese laborers who are now in the United States shall be allowed to go and come of their own free will and accord, and shall be accorded all the rights, privileges, immunities and exemptions which are accorded to the citizens and subjects of the most favored nation.[16]

Article III assured that the United States would exert all its power to provide for the protection of the Chinese in this country. Article IV provided that whenever the United States government adopted legislative measures regulating or limiting Chinese immigration, the Chinese government should be informed and that the latter could bring to the attention of the former any phase of the legislation that might work hardships on the Chinese immigrants.

The treaty as a whole satisfied American interests. As Swift said: "It has untied the hands of Congress and the matter of Chinese immigration is in the control of our government."[17] In the years that followed there were countless disputes between the signatories over the exact provisions of the treaty. In practically every clash, the policies of the United States governement prevailed, no matter how eloquently and skillfully the Chinese argued their cases. Whether the treaty was needed has been hotly debated. Anti-Chinese partisans naturally argued that it was definitely necessary as a measure to alleviate unemployment and economic distress in California. But as historian Ping Chiu correctly points out, Chinese labor was not a liability to the California economy but an asset. After thoroughly analyzing a remarkable amount of data on Chinese laborers in the gold mines, in railway construction, in agriculture, and in other manufacturing and service industries, Ping Chiu concludes that the Chinese should not be blamed for California's economic depression in the 1870s.[18] However, in the depression period, when the competition for jobs was keen, economic distress nonetheless led to antiracial outbursts, particularly because the American people had such a negative "national image" of the Chinese.[19] At any rate, Angell's treaty marked the end of the free Chinese immigration guaranteed by the Burlingame treaty, and the United States Congress immediately began consideration of its first exclusion law against the Chinese.

2. The Exclusion Acts of 1882 and 1884

Scarcely had the first session of the Forty-seventh Congress convened in 1882—which happened to be a year of state elections in California—when Senator John F. Miller, Republican of California, introduced a bill to suspend the immigration of Chinese laborers. The bill provided that starting 60 days after passage of the bill and for 20 years thereafter, the immigration of skilled and unskilled Chinese laborers was to be suspended. The bill also provided for an elaborate system of registration, certification, and identification of Chinese residing in the United States, with imprisonment and deportation as penalities for violation and fraud.[20] The Senate debate on the bill lasted for eight days and Miller received support from all of his Western colleagues and most of the Southern Democrats. Republican Henry M. Teller of Colorado and Democrats James Z. George of Mississippi, Wilkinson Call of Florida, and John T. Morgan of Alabama were among the most outspoken supporters of Miller's bill.[21]

On the other side, Republicans George F. Hoar and Henry L. Dawes of Massachusetts, Orville H. Platt and Joseph R. Hawley of Connecticut, John Sherman of Ohio, and George Edmunds of Vermont opposed both the content and the timing of such a bill. During the heated debate, virtually all the old arguments on the positive and negative effects of Chinese immigration were repeated. Opponents of the bill did gain one small concession, extending the period before the act should go into effect from 60 days to 90 days. The bill passed the Senate by a vote of 29 to 15.[22] When the bill was sent to the House, 11 amendments were offered but all were defeated at the hands of the

Democrats and the Californians. When it passed the House, the tally stood 167 for, 66 against, with 55 members not voting.[23]

While Congress was debating the Exclusion Bill, China was busy dealing with both domestic upheavals and external threats to her peripheral regions, in particular, Moslem rebellions along the Russian border in the Northwest, French aggression in Vietnam, and Japanese occupation of the Ryukyu Islands (Okinawa). The Chinese migration issue was thereby a low priority on the Qing diplomatic agenda. Consequently, in spite of Peking's sympathy for the overseas Chinese in America, it was unwilling to take strenuous measures to oppose the exclusion law. A study of the Zongli Yamen documents makes it clear that the Qing dynasty had tried hard to win American friendship. Even before Angell's mission to China, Prince Gong, Director of the Zongli Yamen, had told American minister George Seward that his government was willing to devise measures to prohibit undesirable Chinese from going to America.[24] When ex-President Ulysses S. Grant visited China during the summer of 1879, Governor-General Li Hongzhang of Zhili led him to believe that if the United States government could help China force the Japanese out of the Ryukyu Islands, China would make a concession on the Chinese migration problem.[25]

It is evident that in the mind of Governor-General Li Hongzhang, the dispute with the United States over Chinese immigration was not nearly so important as the territorial dispute with Japan. Of course, a statesman like Li, who was a practitioner of *realpolitik,* was ruthless at times and was ready to trade off a minor diplomatic loss for more important strategic gain. Li and his colleagues were forced under the circumstances to "use barbarians for the control of barbarians." In this case, he wanted to enlist the support of a potential ally—the United States—against China's major adversary, Japan. Consequently, Li Hongzhang recommended to the throne that his right-hand man Zheng Zaoru, who had met Angell earlier in Tianjin and had executed Li's policies for years, be the second Chinese minister to be accredited to Washington, D.C. Minister Zheng's instructions on the immigration issue were, therefore, to agree to a reasonable exclusion law while simultaneously seeing to it that such a law would not cause too much hardship to the Chinese immigrants.

Shortly after Miller's bill passed Congress, the assiduous Zheng Zaoru visited Secretary of State Frederick T. Frelinghuysen and told the secretary that the time fixed in the bill, 20 years, was unreasonable and clearly a violation of the meaning and intent of Angell's treaty. Quoting Angell's words, the Chinese minister suggested to Frelinghuysen that "a period of five years" for suspension would be a reasonable one for Congress to fix by way of experimentation.[26] Zheng asked for clarification of the term "skilled labor." The inclusion of the term in the bill, he complained, would operate harshly upon a class of Chinese merchants, such as shoe-makers, cigar-merchants, laundry-men, merchant-tailors, among others, who were entitled to admission to the United States under the terms of Angell's treaty. Zheng also opposed the registration and passport certification requirements, charging they were "discriminatory" and a violation of the most-favored-nation clause. Finally, he warned Frelinghuysen that if the bill, as it stood, became law, it would leave the impression in China that the United States government was violating the spirit of Angell's treaty and consequently would prejudice sensible Chinese against the United States.[27]

Zheng Zaoru's effort apparently paid off. Three days after his interview with the secretary of state, President Chester A. Arthur vetoed the bill. The President objected to the bill on the grounds that 20 years, nearly a generation, was too long, that provisions requiring personal registration were in violation of the most-favored-nation guarantee, and that the bill would have a tendency to cause ill feeling toward the United States among Asian nations and drive their trade and commerce toward friendlier lands.[28] Congress failed to override the President's veto, but immediately drew up a new bill with changes designed to meet the President's objections. The revised bill quickly passed and on May 6, 1882, President Arthur signed the historic bill into law. The main provisions of the Exclusion Act of 1882 were as follows:

1. The entry of Chinese laborers to the United States was to be suspended for 10 years.
2. Any shipmaster landing a Chinese laborer from any foreign port was subject to either a fine not to exceed $500 or one year in prison for each such person landed.
3. The preceding sections were not to apply to Chinese laborers in the United States on November 17, 1880, or to those who might come within 90 days after the approval of the act.
4. Any Chinese included in the first part of the preceding section who desired to leave the country by ship was to be registered by the collector of the port, with full identification, and a copy of such identification was to be given to the Chinese as evidence of his right to come and go of his own accord.
5. The same provision was to apply to those leaving by land.
6. Chinese other than laborers were to be identified by a certificate from the Chinese government.
7. The penalty for any falsification was to be a fine of up to $1,000 or imprisonment up to 5 years.

8. The collector of the port was to board ships before the landing of Chinese passengers and compare certificates.
9. Any Chinese entering by land without proper certificate was to be returned to the place from which he came.
10. State and Federal courts were forbidden to naturalize Chinese.
11. The term "Chinese laborers" was to include both skilled and unskilled.[29]

The major difference between the approved bill and the vetoed one was the reduction of the period of suspension from 20 to 10 years. Chinese officials pointed out in their memoranda to the State Department that 10 years was still too long and was in fact a violation of the spirit of Angell's treaty. They also complained that the provisions requiring a type of certificate not imposed on European immigrants and the denial for Chinese naturalization were clearly discriminatory and would inevitably cause the Chinese great hardship.[30]

That the Chinese Exclusion Act was racially motivated is no longer seriously doubted by scholars. In 1882 only 39,579 Chinese entered the United States while 102,991 immigrants from Great Britain and 250,630 from Germany were admitted.[31] Nevertheless, for decades the harshest racist realities were not clearly exposed. Chinese scholars in China, preoccupied with their traditional dynastic histories and disdainful of those who left their ancestral lands, did not bother to investigate problems of this nature. The Chinese minority who chose to stay in America were intimidated into silence. Not until the 1960s, when ethnically conscious young college students began to search for their roots, has the act been fully exposed. In recent years the growth of research into Chinese immigration to the United States, reflected in the establishment of several Asian-American Studies programs, has expanded interest greatly. For Chinese Americans, the Exclusion Act of 1882 has become their ethnic Pearl Harbor. But as infamous as the act was, it was only the first of a series of increasingly stringent laws against the Chinese.

In the execution of the exclusion act, the Arthur administration was, at the outset, willing to soften its effects on the Chinese. For example, the government agreed to the Chinese suggestion that laborers who wished to visit China but subsequently wished to return to America could do so by obtaining certificates from the Chinese consul-general with the counter-signature of the Collector of Customs of the United States. In December, 1882, Attorney General B. H. Brewster ruled that a Chinese laborer merely passing through the country could not be considered as within the prohibition of the exclusion law. The Treasury Department then issued a ruling in July, 1883, governing such visits in transit.[32] But certificate registration and the transit system created many problems for the Treasury Department officials, and there were frequent charges of evasion of the law by the Chinese. Specifically, the Chinese officials were accused of issuing certificates in large numbers to laborers as "students," "teachers," and "traders," the so-called exempt classes. It was also charged that the transient Chinese allegedly took advantage of the loopholes and attempted to find jobs in the United States. Soon the courts were filled with cases growing out of these provisions.

In response the United States Congress decided, in 1884, to adopt a more restrictive bill to stop the alleged abuses and frauds. The Exclusion Law of 1884 suspended for 10 years the entry of Chinese laborers from any foreign place and authorized the collector of the port to secure from every departing Chinese the individual, family, and tribal names, besides the data for identification required in the 1882 Act. It also specified that any Chinese not included under the classification "laborer" had to secure from the government of which he was a subject a certificate in English setting forth his status, profession, occupation, and so on. Under this law, the term "merchant" was so defined as to exclude hucksters, peddlers, and dealers in fish. It required that the destination and financial standing of travelers be reported on their certificates. Moreover, penalties were provided for any substitution or falsification of certificates, including the deportation of any Chinese found to be in the United States illegally.[33]

Nevertheless, 10 exempt classes of Chinese, who were not considered a threat to the employment of white Americans, were given admission to the United States. These included: (1) teachers, ministers, missionaries of religious denominations, newspaper editors, and other public instructors; (2) students; (3) travelers for curiosity or pleasure; (4) merchants and their lawful wives and minor children; (5) government officials, their families, attendants, servants, and employees; (6) Chinese previously lawfully and permanently admitted to the United States returning from temporary visits abroad; (7) Chinese in continuous transit; (8) Chinese born in this country and their children; (9) Chinese citizens lawfully admitted to the United States who later went in transit from one part of the United States to another through foreign contiguous territory; and (10) bona fide seamen.[34]

One effect of the Exclusion Acts was a steady decline of the Chinese population in the United States. As the federal census indicates, during the ten-year span after the passage of the 1882 Exclusion Act, the Chinese population decreased by a total of 81,973[35] (see Appendix 3). The attendant effect of the population change was the continued withdrawal of the Chinese from the majority society. The Chinese tended to congregate in the Chinese quarters of metropolitan cities and avoided work contacts with labor organizations by becoming small, independent entrepreneurs, such as laundrymen, grocers, and restaurateurs. They socialized primarily with their kinsmen and rarely participated in local and state affairs. They became an invisible minority.

3. Outrages against the Chinese

The debate over and the passage of the vexatious exclusion acts fueled anti-Chinese campaigns all over the West. While white hostility toward the Chinese existed from an early date, it did not reach serious proportions until the early 1880s. Relatively few whites were responsible for the attacks, but unemployed laborers, frequently led by young labor unions such as the Knights of Labor, committed numerous outrages against the Chinese. Chinese were attacked in 34 California communities, harassed or expelled from 9 Washington localities and tormented in 3 Oregon and 4 Nevada towns. Millions of dollars worth of their property was damaged and burned in mining towns in Colorado, Alaska, South Dakota, and elsewhere. Notable atrocities against the Chinese took place in the California towns of Eureka (1885), Redlands (1893), and Chico (1894), and in Juneau, Alaska (1886). But the most serious incidents occurred in Los Angeles, Denver, Rock Springs in Wyoming, on the Snake River, and in Tacoma and Seattle in Washington.

As inflammatory news increased in the San Francisco press, Los Angeles papers seemed to emphasize the issue and created in Southern California a climate of hostility toward the Chinese. In 1870, the total Chinese population of Los Angeles was 172. Almost half of the Chinese in Los Angeles lived in the block just south of the Plaza, known as Negro Alley, an area that remained a Chinese quarter until most of it was demolished in 1950. It was in Negro Alley that a mob of several hundred whites shot, hanged, and stabbed 19 Chinese to death on October 24, 1871. The massacre occurred after a white man was killed accidentally when he tried to stop a shooting duel between two Chinese rivals. Six years after the massacre, several Chinese buildings in Negro Alley were razed by arsonists, who went unpunished. The notorious Los Angeles prostitutes' "cribs" (housing primarily Caucasian girls) were immediately adjacent to the Chinatown, and white ruffians and hoodlums, many involved in the prostitution racket, were a constant menace to the Chinese in the city. Several contemporary writers confirm the constant harassment and the siege mentality it produced in the Chinese community.[36]

Map III. Anti-Chinese Riots in Western States

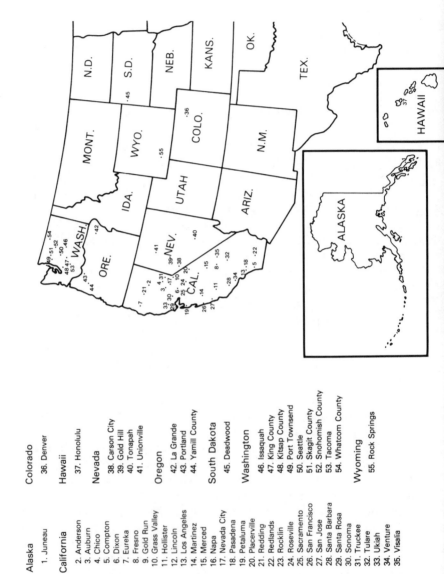

Alaska
1. Juneau

California
2. Anderson
3. Auburn
4. Chico
5. Compton
6. Dixon
7. Eureka
8. Fresno
9. Gold Run
10. Grass Valley
11. Hollister
12. Lincoln
13. Los Angeles
14. Martinez
15. Merced
16. Napa
17. Nevada City
18. Pasadena
19. Petaluma
20. Placerville
21. Redding
22. Redlands
23. Rocklin
24. Roseville
25. Sacramento
26. San Francisco
27. San Jose
28. Santa Barbara
29. Santa Rosa
30. Sonoma
31. Truckee
32. Tulare
33. Ukiah
34. Venture
35. Visalia

Colorado
36. Denver

Hawaii
37. Honolulu

Nevada
38. Carson City
39. Gold Hill
40. Tonapah
41. Unionville

Oregon
42. La Grande
43. Portland
44. Yamill County

South Dakota
45. Deadwood

Washington
46. Issaquah
47. King County
48. Kitsap County
49. Port Townsend
50. Seattle
51. Skagit County
52. Snohomish County
53. Tacoma
54. Whatcom County

Wyoming
55. Rock Springs

The next major outbreak against the Chinese took place on October 13, 1880, when some 3,000 white men surrounded houses occupied by about 400 Chinese on Blake Street in downtown Denver. Again, the outbreak was spawned largely by the sensational and inflammatory reporting of the area newspapers and the presence of large numbers of unhappy white laborers who had migrated from the South and mid-West to Denver. At the outset, the rioters broke in the windows and doors of Chinese dwellings, reportedly cursing and yelling: "Kill the Chinese! Kill the damned heathens! Burn their houses! Give them hell! Run them out; shoot them, hang them!"[37] The mob rampaged through Denver's Chinese quarters from 2 P.M. until 10 P.M. A Chinese named Look Young, employed at the Sing Lee Laundry, was killed. Many other Chinese were brutally beaten, and property damage was estimated at $53,655.69. Finally, the police used water hoses to disperse the mob and took all the Chinese to the city jail for safety. During the three days the Chinese remained in jail, Denver authorities did not protect Chinese property; lawless elements continued to loot in the Chinese section.[38] When the riot was over, the Chinese legation sent Colonel Frederick A. Bee, a San Francisco lawyer employed by the Chinese consulate, to make an investigation. The Chinese minister later presented Bee's reports to the State Department and pressed the United States government for compensation for the Chinese victims.

The Chinese minister, Chen Lanpin, was not well acquainted with the constitutional principles of the United States; he insisted to the Secretary of State William M. Evarts that the matter should be a question of intercourse between China and the United States. Evarts replied that the federal government could not interfere in local affairs and that his government had no obligation to compensate the Chinese who had suffered from the lawlessness of the mob. Diplomatic discussion of the Denver riot continued until James A. Garfield assumed the presidency. His Sinophobic Secretary of State, James G. Blaine, bluntly told Minister Chen not to pursue the matter. The Denver case actually touched upon a range of diplomatic and legal issues. Did an international treaty, such as the Burlingame treaty, make the United States liable for any Chinese losses in this country? Did treaties form a part of the supreme law of the United States equal to the Constitution? To both questions Secretary Blaine answered "no." He argued that treaties, no less than statute law, must be made in conformity with the Constitution. Should a provision in either a treaty or a law be found to contravene the principles of the Constitution, such provisions must give way to the superior force of the Constitution.[39] Nevertheless, the question of the liability of the United States for Chinese losses would be raised again as anti-Chinese outrages continued.

During the three to four years after the Denver riot, ill will toward the Chinese increased rapidly. The so-called "Chinese question" was discussed in numerous public meetings. Large parades and demonstrations were held on the West Coast. Particularly galling to American labor was the increasing use of Chinese as strikebreakers. It was this tension that triggered the next major violence. In 1875, during a strike of white miners, the Union Pacific Railroad Company introduced 150 Chinese workers into its mines in Rock Springs, Wyoming Territory. The move created much bitterness against the Union Pacific, and an increasing hostility grew among the white miners toward the Chinese. By September, 1885, there were 150 white and 331 Chinese employed in the Rock Springs mines. On September 2, in broad daylight, a band of about 150 armed white men suddenly attacked their Chinese coworkers. Twenty-eight Chinese miners were killed, 15 others were wounded, and several hundred Chinese were chased out of town. Chinese property valued at more than $147,000 was damaged.[40]

Wyoming authorities appointed a team to investigate the massacre, but it was dominated by members of the Knights of Labor. Honest witnesses of the Rock Springs affair were intimidated, and the grand jury brought in no indictments.[41] As in the case of the Denver riot, the Chinese legation in Washington sent its own fact-finding team and collected evidence for a diplomatic settlement. With the assistance of John W. Foster, legal counsel to the Chinese legation, Minister Zheng Zaoru, on November 30, 1885, presented to Secretary of State Thomas Bayard an eloquent, logical, and persuasive letter of claim. Bayard insisted that the United States was not liable for the tragic and outrageous outbreak; nevertheless, he was able to persuade President Grover Cleveland to compensate the Chinese "solely from a sentiment of generosity and pity" toward an innocent body of men, but not under "obligation of treaty or principle of international law."[42] On March 2, 1886, Cleveland sent to Congress a special message, requesting authorization to award an aggregate amount not exceeding $150,000 for the Chinese losses. After about a year Congress passed the indemnity legislation but the debates were filled with renewed pressure from West Coast representatives to expel the Chinese.

The Rock Springs massacre inflamed anti-Chinese sentiment in the coal mines of Washington Territory. On the night of September 11, 1885, a small band of armed masked men raided a Chinese settlement of coal miners at Coal Creek. The Chinese were assaulted and their quarters and clothing burned. Eight days later, a group of white miners drove Chinese miners out of the Black Diamond area and injured

9 of them. Throughout the towns and small communities north of the Columbia and west of the Cascades, public meetings were held to discuss the Chinese issue; many applauded the violence perpetrated against the Chinese.[43] In Tacoma sentiment against the Chinese was strong; the lawless elements were openly supported by the mayor and other officials of Pierce County. In Seattle, anti-Chinese activists organized an "Anti-Chinese Congress" on September 28 to frighten the Chinese. The Chinese community in Seattle was burned down during the night of October 24, 1885. In Tacoma on November 3, a mob about 300 strong went to the Chinese quarters and demanded that its residents leave the city, forcing them to evacuate their homes. Chinese belongings were dumped from wagons and the evicted Chinese were left all night in rain and cold. Following this, the mob went to the smaller towns of Pierce, King, Kitsap, Snohomish, Skagit, and Whatcom counties to expel the Chinese. The rioters published anti-Chinese proclamations which demanded that all Chinese leave Washington within a day lest they be forcibly evicted.[44]

In this volatile situation, Governor C. Squire finally requested federal assistance. He also publicly announced that the persons accused of killing three Chinese and burning Chinese property would be tried for first-degree murder.[45] At this juncture, President Cleveland decided, on November 7, to send federal troops into Tacoma and Seattle to maintain law and order. With the troops stationed at strategic points, the riots were suppressed by noon of November 8. [46] Cleveland's action was the first use of federal troops to protect Chinese settlers. It was impossible, of course, for federal troops to continuously provide security for the widely scattered Chinese settlers. The Snake River massacre in 1887 in remote eastern Oregon best illustrated this problem.

In June, 1887, a gang of seven white ruffians attacked a Chinese mining camp at Log Cabin Bar near the Snake River and killed ten Chinese miners in the most brutal manner. They took between $5,000 and $10,000 in gold dust from the dead bodies before throwing them into the Snake River. For several months, Oregon authorities were unable to locate the murderers because they had left the state and no federal funds were available to pay for a search for the runaway criminals. To show its concern and indignation, the Chinese consulate-general at San Francisco offered a reward for the apprehension of those responsible for the murder and grand theft, while the Sam Yup Company, to which the victims belonged, employed two agents to discover the whereabouts of the ringleaders, who were later caught by the Oregon authorities. Finally, on May 15, 1888, the first trial of the criminals took place in Baker, Oregon. Of the seven accused murderers, one died in jail, three were found not guilty, and three remained at large and their warrants were never served.[47]

4. Chinese Immigration and Sino-American Relations

The series of violent outbreaks against the Chinese in America ultimately alarmed the Qing government. Peking characterized the immigration issue "a Gordian knot" of Sino-American relations; its officials who had served in America were irritated by the numerous migration-related problems. As a result, the Chinese government began to work out a self-prohibitory policy by which Chinese laborers would not be permitted to leave the country for America but at the same time those sojourning Chinese already in the United States could receive better treatment. The person chosen to negotiate such a treaty was Zhang Yinhuan, another confidant of Li Hongzhang and also a native of Guangdong. Zhang's counterpart in the negotiations was the Democrat Thomas Bayard whom President Cleveland selected as secretary of state.

The negotiation began in January, 1887, with political clouds hanging over the horizon. American politicians were already mapping out strategy for the 1888 presidential campaign while the Peking authorities had become quite sensitive to Chinese public opinion. Initially, the United States pressed for a 30-year suspension of Chinese immigration, but the Chinese countered with a proposal which would give the Chinese government the discretionary power to control its emigrants. The Chinese also demanded that more adequate protection and additional indemnity payments for future outrages against the Chinese be included in the treaty as matters of prime importance.[48] Because of the huge gap between the two proposals, the negotiation broke down, seemingly leaving no hope of reaching an agreement. Meanwhile, endless complaints of illegal Chinese entry into the United States were heard from the West Coast, and President Cleveland was concerned about the political consequences of the Chinese problem. In the previous presidential election the Democrats had lost California, Colorado, Nevada, and Oregon, with a total of 17 electoral votes, by relatively close margins. As the 1888 presidential election drew nearer, Cleveland ordered the resumption of negotiations. Both parties exhibited a new earnestness and were able to work out a compromise. Bayard and Zhang signed a draft-treaty on March 12, 1888. The new treaty prohibited the migration of Chinese laborers to the United States for a period of 20 years, but did not apply to the return of any Chinese laborers who had "a lawful wife, child, or parent in the

United States, or property of the value of $1,000 or debt of like amount due him."[49]

The Bayard-Zhang treaty immediately met with objections from both sides of the Pacific. The Republicans, who had a slim majority in the Senate, made several amendments to obstruct the treaty, while angry Cantonese held demonstrations and mobbed Minister Zhang's home in Canton. Under such circumstances, the Qing government decided to delay ratification of the treaty. Because of the delay, the London *Times,* on September 1, 1888, reported a rumor that the Peking high authorities had rejected the treaty. By this time the treaty had been amended in every article by the U.S. Senate. Without waiting for official Chinese reaction, William L. Scott, Chairman of the National Democratic Campaign Committee and an intimate friend of President Cleveland's, hastily drafted an anti-Chinese bill and introduced it into the House of Representatives on September 3, only two days after the *Times* had reported the unfounded rumor. The Scott bill provided that Chinese laborers who left the United States should not be permitted to return, and that all certificates of identity for temporary visits abroad should be declared null and void.[50]

The bill passed Congress on September 18 and became law when Cleveland signed it on October 1. However, the Qing government never recognized the Scott Act as a law in compliance with international proceedings, arguing that Cleveland had not renounced the unratified Bayard-Zhang treaty even though he endorsed the legislation against the Chinese immigration.

The Scott Act was devastating to the Chinese community, since at least 20,000 who left the United States for temporary visits in China with proper certificates in their possession were now denied reentry in this country and about 600 persons, who were already on their way to America, were forbidden to land upon arrival.[51] One of these, Chae Chanping, had resided in the United States from 1875 to 1887 and returned from China with a certificate soon after the Scott Act went into effect. Upon his arrival in San Francisco, the immigration authorities prohibited him from landing. The Six Companies raised about $100,000 to test the constitutionality of the Scott Act on Chae's behalf. In the subsequent proceedings, which were settled in 1889, both the United States Circuit Court in California and the United States Supreme Court held that the Scott Act was constitutional. The Circuit Court ruled that a treaty was subject at any time to modification or change by Congress. The Supreme Court decided that the Act of 1888 was in contravention of the express stipulation of both the Burlingame treaty and the Angell treaty, but that because it was the exercise of a sovereign power vested in Congress it ought to be re-

spected and obeyed as the supreme law of the land. Justice Stephen
Field, who was a Californian, wrote the majority opinion: "If there be
any just ground of complaint on the part of China, it must be made to
the political department of [the United States] government, which is
alone competent to act upon the subject."[52]

The Supreme Court ruling gave the United States Immigration Bureau a green light to devise measures by which restrictive laws could
be effectively enforced. Henceforth, all Chinese ship passengers arriving in San Francisco were detained in a two-story shed at the Pacific
Steamship Company wharf until immigration officials could examine
their papers. The detention station was a wretched facility and frequently as many as 500 people were confined there. The Reverend Ira
M. Condit, who visited the place on several occasions, described the
situation:

> Merchants, laborers, are all alike penned up, like a flock of sheep, in
> a wharf-shed, for many days, and often weeks, at their own expense,
> and are denied all communication with their own people while the in-
> vestigation of their cases moves its slow length along.[53]

Newspaper reporters described the treatment of the Chinese
confined at the detention station as "worse than for jailed prisoners."[54]

While the Chinese were still protesting the Scott Act, Congressional hearings were once again held in 1891, this time to determine
whether the Chinese exclusion law of 1882 should be repealed, al-
tered, or extended. The climate of public opinion had so changed
that the need for cheap labor, which had been proclaimed in 1876, was
now asserted with much less assurance. The record of the 1891 hearings was but a pale imitation of the analysis of California society
spread before the public in the 1870s. The same patterns of divergent
thought were still there, but the pros and cons debate was less fully
elaborated than when expressed by Colonel Hollister and Frank Pixley in the 1870s. In reality, by the early 1890s, everyone knew that the
question of Chinese immigration had been closed.[55]

Soon after the hearings were concluded, Thomas J. Geary, a Democratic Congressman from California, introduced a bill into the House
calling for sterner enforcement of the Exclusion Act of 1882 and for its
extension for another 10 years, to be effective on May 5, 1892. The
Geary Act added a number of new anti-Chinese provisions including
the denial of bail to Chinese in habeas corpus proceedings. More important, it required that all Chinese in the United States apply for a
certificate of residence within one year. These certificates were to

contain necessary data for identification, and duplicates were to be filed in the office of the Collector of Internal Revenue Service. Those without certificates were liable to deportation. These provisions were strengthened in 1893 by the passage of the McCreary Amendments which appropriated sufficient funds for the Geary Act's expensive enforcement. The McCreary Amendments provided for an addition of six months time for registration but rigidly defined the term "merchant" so that Chinese engaged in mining, fishing, huckstering, and laundering were clearly in the "labor" category.[56]

The Chinese community responded as it had to the Scott Act; it raised a large sum of money and hired three prominent American attorneys, Joseph H. Choate, J. Hubley Ashton, and Maxwell Evarts, to test the constitutionality of the Geary Act in the case of *Fong Yueting, Lee Joe and Wong Quan vs. U.S. A.* Once again, the Chinese lost their legal battle. The Supreme Court, on May 15, 1893, ruled that Congress had the right to exclude or expel aliens, either absolutely or upon conditions, and that it had the right to provide a system of registration and identification for aliens within the country.[57] At this juncture the Chinese government was totally occupied with the threatening crises in Korea, and its leaders, such as Li Hongzhang, wanted to enlist the support of the United States. Consequently, Chinese officials in the United States persuaded their compatriots to comply with the Geary Act and the McCreary Amendments and to register with the Internal Revenue Service. Meanwhile, Peking instructed its new minister to Washington, Yang Ru, to negotiate a workable and honorable migration treaty so as to end the antagonism.[58] Grover Cleveland, who was in his second term as President, was equally eager to find a permanent solution to the festering problem.

Under these conditions negotiations were once again opened, this time between Secretary of State Walter Q. Gresham and Minister Yang Ru. The talks went smoothly and a new treaty, known as the Gresham-Yang treaty, was signed on March 17, 1894; both the Chinese and the United States governments promptly ratified it. In general, the terms of the Gresham-Yang treaty were similar to those of the unratified Bayard-Zhang treaty of 1888. Consisting of six articles, it stipulated that Chinese laborers be prohibited from coming to the United States for a period of ten years and that the Chinese government accept the Geary Act and McCreary Amendments. The Scott Act was made null and void. Although the treaty also guaranteed that the Chinese in the United States would be given the privileges of the most favored nation, "excepting the right to become naturalized citizens," it gave the United States government undefined powers of "necessary regulation" to which the Chinese pledged not to object.[59]

This last provision, whether due to Yang Ru's ignorance of international law or not, was a blank check which made it possible for the United States government to adopt harsh measures against both labor and nonlabor classes of Chinese. It also allowed Immigration Bureau officials broad powers to harass the Chinese who passed through the U.S. Customs House.

The Gresham-Yang treaty did not end altogether the antagonism which the presence of the Chinese had given rise to in America. As the United States pushed its territory beyond the continent, it also carried the exclusion policy into its newly annexed dominions. Under acts passed on July 7, 1898, and April 30, 1900, Chinese in the Hawaiian Islands were required to register and obtain certificates of residence within one year. In the spring of 1902, Congress again passed, and President Theodore Roosevelt signed, a bill to prohibit the entry and to regulate the residence of Chinese persons and persons of Chinese descent within the United States, its territories, and all possessions under its jurisdiction. This law and its subsequent amendments adversely affected the Chinese population in the Pacific Islands under American administration. The Chinese in Hawaii and the Philippines, in particular, were embittered by the law. The excuse for the suspension of Chinese immigration to the continental United States was that such immigration was detrimental to white labor. But in the Pacific Islands there had been no such complaint. On the contrary, the enforcement of the exclusion laws against the Chinese in Hawaii and the Philippines was contrary to the nearly unanimous wishes of the natives, because the Hawaiian and Filipino natives needed the Chinese in their economic life.

The exclusion law of 1902 represented a new stage in the campaign against the Chinese. This law, coupled with an anti-Chinese policy developed largely by the U.S. commissioner-general of immigration, Terence V. Powderly, formerly a powerful labor leader, was designed to drive out resident Chinese as well as to bar new arrivals. Furthermore, in 1903, the Roosevelt administration placed the Immigration Bureau under control of the Department of Commerce and Labor, which was headed by Victor H. Metcalf, a well-known Sinophobic Californian.[60] Although Powderly was forced to resign in 1902 because of unethical dealings with New York immigration officials, the new commissioner-general of immigration, Frank P. Sargent, was also a friend of organized labor. During his tenure from 1902 to 1908, Sargent established a draconian administration for enforcement of the Chinese exclusion laws. Indeed, the Chinese grew more fearful of him than of his predecessors; he had built the notorious Angel Island Detention Center to crack down on fraudulent Chinese immigrants.

5. Chinese Reaction to American Exclusion

Historian Delber McKee holds that this extreme period of anti-Chinese enforcement policy was the immediate cause of the 1905 anti-American boycott.[61] Other American scholars generally maintain that the aim of the boycott, which was intended to injure American commerce and trade in China, was to bring pressure to bear upon the United States and on the Qing government for a modification of the Gresham-Yang treaty. This interpretation should be taken seriously because Article VI of the treaty said that, "if six months before the expiration of the treaty neither government shall have formally given notice of its final termination to the other, the treaty shall remain in full force for another ten years."[62] But most Chinese historians believe that the 1905 anti-American boycott was in fact the result of a growing Chinese national consciousness. Chinese humiliation and anger, defeats and frustration at the hands of foreigners, during the second half of the nineteenth century, worked to bring about this emotional outburst. The boycott literature also indicates that, by the turn of the century, the wealth and influence of the overseas Chinese had become increasingly important to China's treaty-port economy. Overseas Chinese had established intricate financial ties with bankers and merchants in Shanghai, Canton, and Amoy. Chinese merchants in America did not openly advocate the boycott against American goods, but through their constant contacts and exchanges with the Chinese bourgeois class in China they made it clear that American injustices could best be countered by economic pressure. It is highly possible that the Chinese in Hawaii, the Philippines, and San Francisco were the most important boycott advocates.[63] Their brothers in Chinese treaty ports only acted to echo their wishes.

The Chinese boycotters objected not just to the provisions of the American exclusion laws; they were especially annoyed by the manner in which Chinese exempt classes were treated. During Frank Sargent's administration as immigration commissioner, numerous abuses and harassments against Chinese residents were reported. For example, on October 11, 1902, Boston immigration officers raided a Chinese party without warrants and arrested 250 Chinese, of whom only five were later proven to be unlawful residents.[64] One of the victims of the Boston raid was Feng Xiawei, who felt so distressed that he wrote a book deploring his unhappy experience in America. Feng later returned to China and committed suicide near the American consulate office in Shanghai as an act of protest. Feng's book and martyrdom fed a growing anti-American atmosphere in China. Thousands of Chinese across the country, particularly in Guangdong, joined demonstrations in Feng's memory.[65] In the meantime, reports of the ill treatment Chinese received in America continued to pour in and aroused Chinese resentment against American discrimination. Most offensive of all were reports that even the Qing officials were sometimes mistreated. In 1903, a military attaché of the Chinese legation named Tan Jinyong was badly beaten by two San Francisco policemen, his queue was tied to a fence, and he was handcuffed and taken to the police station. The attaché believed that he had brought disgrace to his people and chose to take his own life. During Tan's funeral, thousands of Chinese, who felt personally outraged, marched to his grave.[66] Instances such as these could only fuel the already existing sense of humiliation and anger felt by many Chinese. The time was right for an expression of their indignation when the United States government asked to renew the Gresham-Yang treaty for another ten-year term.

The boycott began May 10, 1905, in the Shanghai Chamber of Commerce, a nerve center which not only controlled China's mercantile activities but encompassed an overseas Chinese financial network. The leader of the boycott was a Fukienese merchant named Zeng Shaojing, who sounded the slogan of the campaign: "When our government proves itself unable to act, then the people must rise up to do so."[67] Zeng sent telegrams to the chambers of commerce of 22 other treaty ports and urged them to join the boycott movement until the United States modified its immigration policy and improved its treatment of the Chinese people. In less than a month, the first anti-American boycott spread from Shanghai to practically every major city of China. The people involved in the movement included teachers, students, urban professionals, laborers, women and, of course, overseas Chinese in America, Hong Kong, Japan, and Southeast Asia.

At the height of the boycott, many doctors in Shanghai, Canton, Peking, and cities across China refused to purchase American medicine. Chinese cigarette smokers in Canton bought Chinese manufactured cigarettes instead of American brands. During the traditional Chinese moon festival, Chinese women in Guangdong province decided to make rice cakes in place of the usual moon cake, which required American flour. The boatmen of Canton resolved not to ferry American goods across the Pearl River.[68] All major Chinese newspapers carried articles about these antiexclusion activities and expressed support for the boycott. Students demonstrated in major cities and conducted emotional meetings in support of the campaign. Antiexclusion songs were composed and sung, pamphlets describing the nationwide boycott activities were printed, and samples of American products to be boycotted were displayed. The exact loss to American trade is difficult to ascertain. However, the agency of the Standard Oil

Company in Canton reported that its sales steadily decreased after establishment of the boycott in May, 1905.[69]

When the boycott started, the Qing government tried to use the expression of public opinion to advantage in negotiations with the United States. Between August 12, 1904, and January 25, 1905, the Chinese minister to Washington, Liang Cheng, submitted two different drafts to the Roosevelt administration to replace the expired Gresham-Yang treaty, but both were turned down. Meanwhile, the boycott activities were escalating and becoming more violent. The Qing government then realized that potentially the boycott could develop into another Boxer Rebellion. Consequently, it changed its stand and took measures to suppress the boycott, but its countermeasures were mostly limited to cautious and mild proclamations.

On the other side of the Pacific, President Roosevelt publicly expressed his disapproval of abuses in the administering of the exclusion laws. Secretary of State John Hay, who was pushing for an "Open Door Policy" in China, believed that the exclusion laws against the Chinese had become a major barrier to the extension of trade and cultural ties between the two countries and that they undermined his China policy. In June, 1905, in his diary, Hay confided that he wanted President Roosevelt to "put a stop to the barbarous methods of the Immigration Bureau."[70] Five days later, Roosevelt issued an Executive Order to the Department of State and Department of Commerce and Labor, ordering American consuls to be courteous in their treatment of all nonlabor Chinese immigrants, such as merchants, teachers, students, and travelers. Dismissal was threatened for any Immigration Bureau officials who mistreated Chinese who had proper documents.[71] Roosevelt's words and actions soothed some Chinese and, by early 1906, the boycott demonstrations began to abate in the Chinese cities. The emotionally charged boycott movement died a natural death near the end of 1906. Although the Qing government refused to renew the Gresham-Yang treaty, the United States unilaterally extended and reenacted all of the anti-Chinese exclusion laws, dictating the course of Chinese immigration until their repeal in December, 1943.

In recounting the stories of American exclusion, hostility, and violence against the Chinese, one would undoubtedly categorize them as a shabby chapter of American history. Certainly, the Chinese were never a threat; at the peak of their immigration, they numbered about one percent of California's population. But why were they barred from participation in American political processes and deprived of the basic privileges of liberty and democracy? Why were they treated worse than blacks and American Indians, who at least were accorded United States citizenship? Were these discriminations caused mainly by racial antagonisms, by the poor American images of the Chinese, and by politicians and demagogues? Or were there other significant factors that previous studies have not fully explored?

Any attempt to answer these difficult questions must keep in mind the extent to which the Qing officials were involved in conflicts created by Chinese immigration. It is a well-known fact that, through the Chinese legation in Washington, D.C., and its consulates, the Qing government hoped to acquire not only the loyalty of the Chinese in America but also financial contributions and other support for China's modernization, famine relief, and defense fund. The Qing officials were active in promoting Chinese culture and education, keeping the Chinese in America informed of events in China. Another important function of the legation was raising funds from the Chinese community in America through the sales of Qing titles. Chinatown leaders were often found serving on these fund-raising committees. United States authorities were concerned that the Chinese in America could be an easy prey of the Qing officials. With the demand of the Qing government for political loyalty, and the extraction of money and services from the Chinese in America, the United States government at times regarded the Chinese consulates as operating outside normal diplomatic functions. It is clear that the strong influence of the Qing officials over the life of their compatriots reinforced the sojourner's mentality and inspired the Chinese to resist acculturation.

The Chinese in America responded most positively to the call of the Qing government by not only maintaining their Chinese identity in terms of cultural performance but also by their interest in events in China, particularly its modernization and political reform. However, so long as the Chinese proclaimed that their political loyalty and future lay with China, they would naturally perceive themselves as aliens, and were so treated by the white Americans. Indeed, the nineteenth- and early twentieth-century Chinese in America did not behave differently from their Cantonese brothers in China. Both by self-definition and in the perception of others, these sojourners were "truly Chinese." Furthermore, the fact that Chinese Americans remained in close contact with their native land through trade and return visits made the preservation of Chinese culture a business necessity in America's Chinatowns.

Unfortunately for these Chinese sojourners, the political health of the Qing government began to weaken during the decades following their landing in the New World. By the late nineteenth century, Qing officials had lost much of their bargaining power with the American authorities. As a result, many Chinese who suffered from wanton outrages or flagrant discriminations cursed the Qing government for being too weak to protect them; some swore to take revenge upon the hapless and helpless Qing officials. By the turn of the twentieth century, the Qing officials had lost the respect of and leadership over the Chinese community. Reformers and revolutionaries increasingly offended Qing officials by appealing to the Chinese in America. With this development, the loyalty of the Chinese was further divided, leading to a new phase in the history of the Chinese in the United States. Ironically, it was because of the political turmoil in China and the divided loyalties it created that the Chinese in America gradually shook off the sojourner's mentality and began to identify themselves more with America than with China. As they went through a period of transition from sojourners to immigrants to settlers, becoming more American and less Chinese, they reaped many rewards but also endured unexpected pain. Such was to be the price of acculturation.

1. Chinese on board the steamship *Alaska*, bound for the Gold Mountain. Courtesy The Bancroft Library, University of California, Berkeley.

2. Chinese coming off the ship in an American port. Courtesy Bancroft Library.

3. Nineteenth-century Chinese woman and child. Courtesy Bancroft Library.

4. Chinese Freemasons in Fourth of July parade, Oakland, 1907. Courtesy Bancroft Library.

5. Anti-Chinese riot in Seattle, Washington Territory, reported in *Harper's Weekly*, March 6, 1886. Courtesy Bancroft Library.

6. Chinese schoolchildren in an American public school, about 1890. Courtesy Bancroft Library.

7. Chinese workers completing a railroad trestle. Courtesy Southern Pacific Railroad Co.

8. First issue (March 10, 1904) of *Chinese Reform News,* the oldest Chinese newspaper in New York.

9. Chinese troops on maneuver at Eagle Rock, California, about 1900. Courtesy Eagle Rock Valley Historical Society of California.

10. Gateway to San Francisco's Chinatown

11. A market in Chinatown

12. Officials of the Chinese Association of Arkansas, June, 1943

13. Model Grandmothers of the Year, San Francisco, 1983

IV

LIVING IN THE
SHADOW OF EXCLUSION

> He who rides in the chair is a man; he who
> carries the chair is also a man.
>
> —Chinese proverb
>
> If you do not ask their help, all men are
> good-natured.
>
> —Chinese proverb

1. Chinese Political Activities in America

The anti-American boycott of 1905 clearly demonstrated the nature and extent of the frustration and anger of Chinese nationalists. However, in the mind of powerful Qing officials, American exclusion was a minor diplomatic problem, hence they would not allow it to undermine cordial Sino-American relations. To be sure, American exclusion touched upon China's national prestige and pride, but it had no direct effect upon her territorial integrity. During the years between 1882 and 1905 China lost prestige to Japan and suffered the humiliating Boxer catastrophe, while the major imperialistic powers were nibbling away at the outer edges of the Chinese Empire. The United States, by comparison, seemed less aggressive and dangerous; with its Open Door policy, it seemed to offer some potential as an ally. Before and during the Sino-Japanese War of 1894–95 the United States tendered its good offices to help China. After the Boxer Rebellion, the United States was the first country to return to China the excess Boxer Indemnity, a sum totalling $27,920,000, for educational use. Many of the students who benefited from the funds, after completing their education in America, returned to China to become leading citizens.[1] In sum, in spite of the troublesome exclusion issue, it was generally to China's advantage to maintain good relations with the United States.

In America, the failure of the boycott and the inequities in the treaty revisions convinced many Chinese immigrants that any real improvement in their status required the support of a strong and independent China. Some of them, therefore, supported the reform and revolutionary movements which threatened China's conservative Manchu ruling class by the end of the nineteenth century. An unsuccessful but bloody coup d'etat was staged in September, 1898, by the reformists, and the revolutionaries stepped up subversive activities in the late 1890s. Editorials in the Chinese-language newspapers published in New York, Hawaii, and San Francisco repeatedly called for constitutionalism and progressive social and economic reform. They argued that China's stature in the international community and the Chinese immigrants' status in America were intimately related. The Qing government increasingly feared that the overseas Chinese secret societies might become the principal haven for an antidynastic movement. Their fear and suspicion were soon confirmed by Chinese political activities in America.

At the turn of the century the two major political movements vying for support of the Chinese people in America and in China were the reformist Baohuanghui (Imperial Reform Party) and the revolutionary Tongmenghui (United League). The reformers wanted to use Western techniques to supplement Chinese tradition and proposed a program whereby the modernization of China could be accomplished within the framework of the imperial administration. They differed among themselves on the degree to which they would dilute Confucianism and accept Western values. The most important leader of this movement was Kang Youwei, who in the summer of 1898 launched the famed but abortive "One Hundred Days' Reform." As a result, his patron, the Emperor Guangxu, was imprisoned by the Empress Dowager and he and his supporters were forced to flee the country. The revolutionaries, who were anti-Manchu and antitradition, wanted more drastic changes. Politically, they were nationalists and proponents of a system of government based more broadly on the will of the people. Sun Yat-sen, who was Cantonese, as was Kang Youwei, and had turned against the dynasty as early as 1885, emerged as one of their outstanding spokesmen.

The reformers and the revolutionaries became bitter rivals in China as early as 1895 but their struggle in North America started with the founding of the reform party in British Vancouver in the spring of 1899. In the early stage, the reform party had widespread support among the Chinese residents in Chinatowns, and Kang Youwei was looked upon as the hope of the future. But with the failure of the reform efforts to bring about any significant changes in China and with the death of the Emperor Guangxu in 1908, the pendulum began to swing to Sun and his revolutionary cause. In general, the scholarly reformers felt both condescending and distrustful toward the Western-oriented and Western-educated revolutionaries. Kang in particular came to despise Sun Yat-sen as an illiterate, because he was not a classical scholar nor a degree-holder in the civil service examination system, in spite of the fact that Sun had earned a degree from the Medical School of Alice Memorial Hospital in British Hong Kong. Indeed, Kang and Sun differed on almost everything; and so deep was the gulf that an active hostility arose between the two movements in America.[2]

This acrimony was intensified in America when Liang Qichao, the theoretician of the reform movement and the premier disciple of Kang Youwei, visited North America from March until November, 1903. During this tour, Liang expanded the reform organization to include a total of 103 branches. He jubilantly reported to Kang that 25 Oregon towns had a reform party organization, as did 12 towns in western Montana.[3] Liang gave hundreds of speeches, held countless interviews and busily raised funds among his Cantonese compatriots. Later, when Sun learned that Liang had collected hundreds of thousands of dollars in America from people who thought they were contributing to the overthrow of the hated Manchus, he levelled a blistering attack at Liang. He charged that Liang had abased himself by supporting the ruler of an alien race and by making the Han Chinese forever the slaves of the Manchus.[4]

During his visit to America, Liang also set up a commercial corporation which sold several hundred thousand dollars worth of stock to party members. Beginning with assets of nearly $600,000, the corporation invested its money in banking, book publishing, restaurants, real estate, and other businesses. For instance, it transferred $60,880 to the Compania Bancaria Chino y Mexico (Hua-Mo Yinhang) in Mexico, which in turn invested in land, buildings, and streetcar line businesses. A sum of $58,813 was transferred to the New York branch of Hua Yi Bank, and a restaurant in Chicago called King Joy Low absorbed $61,000.[5] Profits from the commercial corporation were channeled to other party programs, such as education, military training, and newspaper propaganda. Party sponsored newspapers in America included: *The New China Daily,* published in Honolulu (1899) with Chen Jiyan as its editor; the *Wenxing Bao* (Literary Renaissance) (1892), located in San Francisco and edited by Ou Jujia; *The Chinese Reform News* (1904) in New York; and *The Chinese Times* (1900) known locally as *Sun Bo,* in Vancouver, B.C.

In Honolulu as early as 1903 the editor of the *New China Daily* began organizing Chinese boys into a youth club to practice military drills and to study Chinese history and language. This developed into the Minglun school in 1907. In the mainland United States, military schools called Gancheng Xuexiao (The Vanguards) were established in New York, St. Louis, Oakland, and other major American cities. Other schools named Aiguo Xuexiao (Patriotic Schools) were also founded by the reform leaders. By 1905 there were 22 such paramilitary schools throughout the United States funded and operated by the reform party or its subsidized organizations. Kang Youwei wrote the school songs for these schools, and retired army officers were employed to drill the Chinese youths.[6]

However, the reform party was basically an elitist organization and remained politically and intellectually remote from the masses. Furthermore, there were reported charges against the party leaders for embezzling funds. After the death of the Emperor Guangxu, many reformist leaders in America came to view the Manchu leaders as too corrupt and reactionary, and began to shift their allegiance to Sun Yat-sen's nationalistic revolutionary cause. The success of the Double-Tenth revolt in 1911 ultimately dealt a severe blow to the reform movement. In Portland, Oregon, and Stockton, California, gangs of militant Chinese smashed the offices of the reform party and tore down the signboards because of their objection to the word "imperial." Other branches in North America suffered from attacks and denunciations at the hands of Sun Yat-sen's supporters.

Sun Yat-sen's rise to predominance among Chinese Americans was not smooth, however. Sun organized his first revolutionary society, the Xingzhonghui (Revive China Society) in Honolulu in the winter of 1894. Initial members of this small group were exclusively Cantonese men living in Hawaii and, for several years, the society was ineffective and unable to raise any funds to support Sun's revolutionary ambitions. Later, Sun joined the Ket On Society in order to befriend its leaders and enlist their support. A historical accident which occurred in the spring of 1904 cemented the fates of Sun and the San Franciscan Chee Kung Tong. As Sun was trying to gain entry into the United States with a forged passport, a common practice for exiled revolutionaries, he was detained in a wooden shed near the San Francisco wharf and, after a lengthy interrogation, received a deportation notice. It was apparent that his enemies had informed the U.S. immigration authorities and that Sun, if he were expatriated to China, would be tried for treason and put to death. At this critical moment, he spotted the address of the *Chung Sai Yat Po,* a progressive Chinese language newspaper published by Dr. Ng Poon Chew (Wu Panzhao), and asked an American newspaper boy to deliver a terse note to the publisher. Ng immediately transmitted the urgent message to the

Chee Kung Tong, which hired an attorney and raised the necessary money to post bail for Sun. Sun finally gained entry to the country by claiming to have been born in Hawaii.[7]

Sun's rescue created a sensation in the Chinese community. He was as controversial as he was heroic; the reform party denounced his ideas while the secret society members stood behind him. With the backing of a powerful secret society chief named Wong Sam Ark (Huang Sande), Sun began to gain supporters among the exclusive Chinese organizations in San Francisco. A few days after his release Sun announced a meeting at San Francisco's Chinese Presbyterian Church on Stockton Street and made his first public speech before a huge crowd. The enthusiastic audience purchased $2,700 worth of revolutionary bonds issued with Sun's personal seal. Nevertheless, the more conservative and wealthier Chinese immigrants continued to keep their distance; most of them still supported the Qing government or the more moderate reform movement. Against these odds, Sun tried to transform the Chee Kung Tong from a Triad mutual aid club into a tightly organized revolutionary party. The Chee Kung Tong leadership finally accepted Sun's suggestion that a new constitution be drafted and that every member be required to register.[8]

After personally drafting the constitution for the Chee Kung Tong, Sun began a nationwide campaign for new membership. Between May 24 and December 4, 1904, Sun, accompanied by the tong chief Wong Sam Ark, visited more than 25 American cities. He used a traveling opera troupe to attract crowds wherever he appeared. The theme of the opera was designed to arouse discontent over injustice and inequality, and to preach the need for revenge. During the performances' intermissions, Sun and Wong lectured on the importance of a republican revolution and on the future reconstruction of a strong and independent China. They admonished their audiences not only to seek wealth but also to maintain an interest in the welfare of their mother country. In Baltimore the Triad Lodge sponsored three showings of the opera, and in New York City large crowds attended the lectures. Nevertheless, the result was not so fruitful as Sun had anticipated. Only a small number of Chinese registered with Sun's newly organized Chee Kung Tong.[9]

But Sun was a persistent man with a strong will. Leaving America, he went on his second world tour, arriving in Japan in the summer of 1905. There he made contact with several Chinese political activists of various ideological persuasions and founded the Tongmenghui, marking a new epoch in the history of the Chinese revolution. With the establishment of the Tongmenghui, Sun had the organizational tool he needed to develop a following. Among his important new converts was a U.S.-born Chinese, Lee See Nam (Li Gongxia), who in 1907 joined the Tongmenghui in Hong Kong and, two years later, founded the Young China Association in San Francisco to serve as a front for Sun's revolutionary organization. Branches of the association were subsequently formed among Chinese students in Berkeley and Chicago; some of them later held responsible positions in China. The association's organ, the *Youth,* originally published weekly, was expanded in 1910 into a daily newspaper, *Young China.*[10] Nationalistic and revolutionary propaganda was stepped up during Sun Yat-sen's third visit to America (1909–1911). Chapters of the Tongmenghui were established in New York, San Francisco, Chicago, Sacramento, St. Paul, Milwaukee, Boston, Portland (Oregon), Seattle, and several Canadian cities. Fund raising to support the revolution was much more successful than during Sun's previous trips. For instance, in 1910, the U.S. Chee Kung Tong raised more than $7,000 to support an abortive armed uprising in Canton.[11]

The climax of Sun's revolutionary movement came in the early summer of 1911 when he successfully merged the Tongmenghui and Chee Kung Tong into one organization. It was estimated that one thousand Chinese attended the ceremony in San Francisco where Sun officiated at the union of the two groups. Immediately following the ceremony, Sun established the so-called Triad Subscription Bureau (Hongmen Chouxiang Ju) to function as the financial arm of the revolutionary union.[12] The Triad Subscription Bureau was located on the second floor of the Chee Kung Tong and began to channel substantial amounts of money to revolutionary groups in China. With this merger Sun's movement had already surpassed the reform party; ahead of him lay the more foreboding task of toppling the Manchu regime in Peking.

Chinese history, like Sun's revolutionary activities, is filled with unexpected twists and turns; the events that led to the downfall of the dynasty surprised the Qing ruling clique as much as they did Sun Yat-sen. Angered by the government's plan to nationalize the railroads, the people of Sichuan province staged a strike against the local government in 1911; this incident led to an attack by a Tongmenghui group on the Qing military stronghold in Central China. Due to a mishandling of explosives, a bomb went off and a handful of Tongmenghui members were forced to begin their attack prematurely on the night of October 9, at Wuchang. Unlikely as it seemed, this event eventually led to the successful revolution that ended more than 2,000 years of dynastic government in China.

2. Building a New Image

The Chinese in America greeted the successful revolution as the dawning of a new era. Many of the more ambitious Chinese returned to China, bringing with them new ideas, needed skills, and capital. They wanted to be a part of a new China that needed reconstruction educationally, economically, and socially. A few activists wanted to be part of the political transformation of China; some got what they wanted, but others quickly became disillusioned. Wong Sam Ark, for example, soon became embittered, feeling that the new Republican government ignored his organization; others of Sun Yat-sen's followers were disappointed because they were waiting for rewards that Sun could not deliver. Although many were disappointed, the returned patriots did introduce into China American concepts of technology and government. Furthermore, those who remained in the United States contributed large sums of money for the improvement of their native districts in Guangdong.

The creation and existence of the new Republic also had a profound impact on life within the Chinese American community. Chinese American leaders tried to build a new image of the Chinese as a modern and progressive people. Most Chinese men cut off their queues, which increasingly were considered embarrassing, and adopted Western dress in place of traditional Chinese garb. By the 1920s, with the exception of the few older immigrants, Chinese men no longer wore Chinese clothing in public, although community leaders occasionally donned Chinese attire with silk top hat and mandarin gowns and shoes during funeral services or Qingming festivals. Public practice of Chinese religions and festivals gradually diminished; Taoist temples and priests became less important to Chinese social and religious needs. Ancestor worship, which required that dutiful children burn incense and serve food in front of the household's wooden tablets, also diminished among the native-born. Second-generation Chinese Americans not only ignored the old traditions, they increasingly began to go to Sunday schools and mission classes which taught them Christianity and Western culture.

Symptoms of Americanization in the nation's Chinatowns were pervasive. In San Francisco the Chinese established a YMCA in 1912, a boy scout troop in 1914, and a YWCA in 1916. Even in San Rafael, a small California town, there was a Chinese YMCA. In addition to activities undertaken by the American YMCA, the Chinese groups gave free English lessons. By 1921, there were five Chinese YMCA's and three YWCA's in the United States. The Chinese also began to understand and celebrate Independence Day, Thanksgiving, and Christmas and became more familiar with the meaning and significance of American history and institutions. The fact that Chinese families held baby and bridal showers evidenced their slow melting in the great American pot. The Chinese also took measures to wipe out the old vices associated with Chinatowns, working to make their sections as clean, safe, and decent as possible. Prominent Hawaiian Chinese formed an Anti-Opium League to assist the authorities in apprehending opium smokers. The League also raised money and purchased medicine from China to help Chinese opium addicts break their habits.[13] When the 1906 earthquake and fire burned down San Francisco's old rookeries, Chinatown came to include new buildings. The Chinese built a dispensary in 1900 and a modern hospital named "Donghua" (East China) in 1925. The Hawaiian Chinese, on the other hand, raised enough money in 1920 for construction of the Palolo Home to house their elderly countrymen.

In the three decades that followed establishment of the Republic, the spearhead of the Americanization movement was the Chinese American Citizens Alliance (CACA), an organization which evolved from the Native Sons of the Golden State. The CACA was mainly educational, aiding members to become better citizens and to exercise their franchise intelligently. Those familiar with the American form of government lectured to fellow members on American laws, politics, economics, and social topics. After World War I Chinese Americans became increasingly conscious that their vote was their primary protection against discrimination. On a number of occasions during those years they successfully defeated anti-Chinese politicians, most notably California state Senator Camminetti, who attempted to disfranchise the Chinese. In 1932, Chinese Americans organized a New York Chinese American Voting League and conducted a highly successful campaign to turn out the vote for Franklin D. Roosevelt. In 1936, Roosevelt polled a huge majority in the New York Chinese community, receiving the votes of approximately three out of every four eligible Chinese voters.[14] In both elections, the CACA was active in educating Chinese voters.

One of the reasons for the CACA's success was the increasing number of native-born Chinese in America. According to the United States census, in 1900 they accounted for only 10 percent of the total Chinese population. This figure increased to 21 percent in 1910, 30 percent in 1920, 41 percent in 1930; and by 1940, there were more native-born Chinese (52 percent) than foreign-born. In the period of 1890–1940, the number of foreign-born Chinese had dropped from 100,000 to 40,000. By World War II the former laboring sojourners had become mostly older people.[15]

After its inception in 1905, the CACA grew rapidly in membership. Branches were formed in New York and Chicago in 1916, and, by the early 1910s, chapters of the CACA were also found in Portland, Pittsburgh, Detroit, and Boston. Later, native-born Chinese in Helena (Montana), Houston, San Antonio, Albuquerque, Washington, D.C., Tucson, and Phoenix joined the umbrella organization of the CACA.

As a result of this growth, the CACA built an elegant headquarters in San Francisco, established a life insurance fund, promulgated a constitution and, most important, published a newspaper, the *Chinese Times.* By 1981, the organization had held 36 biennial national conventions and had continued to fight for racial equality as well as serving as an important charity and community-service organization. Recently, however, the CACA has become increasingly elitist and Republican-oriented. Its leaders are too politically and socially inexperienced in democratic group processes to accommodate a wide variety of opinions and ideas with much ideological resilience. Its inability to gain a wider constituency has led to not only its gradual decline but the rise of the Chinese-American Democratic Club, which was formed in 1954 and has since helped to erode the CACA strength.[16] In the end, the Chinese failed to develop a national organization comparable to the Japanese American Citizen League or the National Association for the Advancement of Colored People in its communitarian scope and programs.

As male Chinese-American citizens were slowly breaking the racial barrier in American society, the role of the female also changed dramatically during these years. Gone were the days when Chinese baby girls trembled at the sight of small bound feet. Gone also were the Confucian traditions which required that women stay home and remain subservient to their mothers-in-law and husbands. Although the ratio of Chinese males to females remained lop-sided (93.5 percent vs. 6.5 percent in 1910; 87.4 percent vs. 12.6 percent in 1920; 79.8 percent vs. 20.2 percent in 1930; 74.1 percent vs. 25.9 percent in 1940), Chinese women in America were increasingly treated with dignity and respect. Many of them, like their American counterparts, began to take jobs outside the home. Most of the school-age girls received American as well as Chinese educations, much like their brothers. Tye Leung, an interpreter for the U.S. Immigration Station in San Francisco, became in 1912 the first Chinese woman to vote in an American presidential election. Other Chinese women became dentists, pharmacists, and bank managers. During World War II, several Chinese women's organizations appeared. They played an active role in supporting the Chinese resistance war against Japan. Madame Chiang Kai-shek's 1943 visit to America greatly inspired Chinese women to follow a modern and progressive path.[17]

The brief history of the Chinese Republic inspired Chinese Americans but it also disappointed them, for a strong and prosperous China did not emerge as early as the overseas Chinese had expected. On the contrary, China was plagued by the turmoil of warlordism, the invasion by Japan, and the bitter rivalry between Nationalists and Communists. The Chinese people, inside and outside of China, were once again faced with complicated schisms that opened bitter rifts in the Chinese-American community. And while the Chinese in America were at a loss as to how to react to the constant political chaos in China, their relatives in Guangdong were suffering from economic disasters and social instability as a result of incessant wars. Many Cantonese once again looked upon the United States as a haven and a land of abundance and peace. Consequently, in spite of strict enforcement of the exclusion laws, many struggled to enter the United States at all costs.

One common and dangerous method of illegal entry was by smuggling across the Canadian or Mexican borders. Halifax in the north and Tucson in the south became relatively easy points of illegal entry. A report of the House Committee on Immigration in 1901 indicated that Chinese were being smuggled into the United States at a rate of 20,000 per year. Another source reported that in 1932 and 1933 alone, a total of 4,953 Chinese were caught illegally crossing the Mexican border into Arizona.[18] Investigations revealed scores of efforts to gain entry illegally. The United States Immigration Bureau discovered that for several years the Canadian Pacific Railroad had worked in collusion with American officials at Malone, New York, to smuggle Chinese into this country. The *New York Herald* charged that many Chinese landed in New York from Cuba, falsely claiming to be merchants or giving their destination as some point in Canada. They were permitted to land under a bond of $200. This bond, once given, allowed the Chinese to roam about the city at will for 20 days. During this time, the reporter revealed, the Chinese made arrangements for permanent stays in the United States.[19] Many others jumped ships at the harbors of Seattle, Portland, San Francisco, and New York.

The most sophisticated illegal-entry scheme was called the "slot racket." During visits to China, an American citizen of Chinese extraction, who was eligible for reentry to this country, would report the birth of children, usually male, when there had been no such event. He thereby created a "slot," which was sold to someone who had no relatives to sponsor his entry into the United States. Unscrupulous merchants worked as brokers for such illicit deals. The fictitious offspring of American citizens who entered the United States in this manner were often called "paper sons."

3. The Angel Island Stories

Responding to these frauds and deceptions, the United States Immigration Bureau adopted several equally notorious measures to halt illegal practices. The most famous, most controversial, and most effective was the building of an immigration station on wild Angel Island in the middle of San Francisco Bay. Unfortunately, hundreds of thousands of honest and lawful Chinese immigrants were victimized when, for reasons beyond their control, they failed to satisfy the inquiries of the usually hostile immigration inspectors. Essentially a brainchild of the U.S. Immigration Commissioner General Frank P. Sargent, Angel Island was designed to detain questionable new Chinese arrivals until such time as they could be interrogated and their papers thoroughly scrutinized. The procedure could take a few days or a few weeks, but several cases lasted for months and even years. Pending the examination hearings, the detainees lived in filthy and hazardous facilities. The confinement complex was a conglomeration of ramshackle buildings that were firetraps. Even the United States immigration officials admitted that "if a private individual had such an establishment he would be arrested by the local health authorities."[20] However, in spite of its deplorable conditions and strong protests from the Chinese community, Angel Island remained the detention quarters for Asiatic immigrants, primarily Chinese, from 1910 until 1940. During its 30 years of existence, it processed more than 175,000 Chinese entries and deported about ten percent of the Chinese detainees.

The Chinese detained at Angel Island resented not only the long, boring confinements but also the poor quality of food provided by competitive contractors. In 1911 an American firm bid 12 cents per meal and in 1916 the average cost per meal had fallen to a mere 8 cents.[21] On several occasions, Chinese community leaders and the Chinese consul-general in San Francisco brought this problem to the attention of the United States authorities. However, no measurable improvement was made until 1919, when a protest riot broke out. After troops had restored order, immigration authorities instituted fuller menus. But meals remained a troublesome issue. In March, 1925, when officials decided, because of crowded conditions, to let new arrivals dine first, another riot occurred. Then, on June 30 of the same year, when a white waiter served detainees stale bread, he and a guard were attacked. Spontaneously, the Chinese began breaking dishes and destroying furniture. Again troops with fixed bayonets were called in from a nearby army camp.[22] The frequency of the outbreaks indicated the high level of frustration and anxiety created by the detention. One poet detainee wrote: "This is called an island of immortals, but as a matter of fact, the mountain wilderness is a prison."[23]

The majority of the Chinese detainees at Angel Island applied for entry claiming citizenship by birth or by "derivation." Most of the citizens in the earlier years were "native sons" but, by the late 1920s, more and more sons of immigrants and even grandsons began to apply for admission. The United States authorities found it very difficult to verify claims of the Chinese applicants because the San Francisco earthquake and fire of 1906 had destroyed countless documents. Moreover, birth certificates were not commonly issued in Chinese villages at that time. In order to screen out applicants with fraudulent credentials, immigration authorities institutionalized a harsh inquiry system. Primary inspection began with an inspector who, if satisfied with the applicant's interview, could admit him without further examination unless detained by officers of the U.S. Public Health Service. When there was dissatisfaction with the applicant's interview, the primary inspector could hold the Chinese for a hearing before the Board of Special Inquiry, normally consisting of a chairman and two other members. Hearings on citizenship applications were slow, frustrating, and humiliating. The applicant, regardless of the validity of his claim, would face a lengthy interrogation that required the recollection of minute details and the support of witnesses who might not be readily available. The questions asked were probing and often highly personal. For instance: How many times a year were letters received from the applicant's father? How did the applicant's father send the money to travel to America? How many steps were there at the front door of the applicant's house? How many cousins did the applicant have? What was the location of the kitchen rice bin? Who lived next to the applicant's house? Of what material was the flooring in the bedroom of the applicant's house?[24]

Since the immigrant's success in passing the hearing hurdle determined whether he would be granted admission or sent back to China, many began to study so-called "coaching papers" even before they boarded their ships. This was particularly necessary for the "paper son" as he had to memorize every fact about his fictitious father and relatives and their home lives. The Reverend Edward Lee, who worked for thirteen years as an interpreter for the immigration service, recalled a case involving two young men seeking admission as the sons of a merchant.

> They [the inspectors] ask the first applicant if there was a dog in the house. He said, "Yes." Later they ask the second if there was a dog in the house. He said, "No, no dog." The first applicant was recalled, and that question was put to him. He said, "Yes, well we had a dog, but we knew we were coming to the United States, so we ate the dog."[25]

A substantial number of the "paper sons" were debarred by this means, but many who had valid claims were also denied entry because they failed to answer the questions put to them by unfriendly immigration officials. From 1892 to 1925, a total of 6,327 Chinese were prohibited from landing. Nevertheless, if the applicant disagreed with the judgment of the board of inquiry, his family could still appeal to the higher immigration authorities in Washington, D.C., or take their case to the courts.

Even before establishment of the Angel Island detention center, the Chinese had learned to utilize courts to prove they belonged to the exempt classes or were true offspring of American citizens and therefore qualified to gain admission to the United States. In the San Francisco federal archives there is a body of court cases containing such information as dockets, minutes, orders, final records, subpoenas, briefs, pleadings, depositions, and other court records. In 1898, in the case of *United States vs. Wong Kim Ark,* the Supreme Court ruled that a person born in the United States of Chinese parents was an American citizen by birth, and therefore, was eligible for reentry to America after visiting China. Two years later, the court ruled in the case of *United States vs. Mrs. Cue Lim* that the wives and children of Chinese merchants were entitled to come to the United States as exempt classes.

However, in subsequent court decisions, Chinese rights were restricted. For example, the United States Supreme Court ruled in 1924, in the case of *Chang Chan et al. vs. John D. Nagle,* that Chinese wives of American citizens were not entitled to come to the United States, upholding the 1924 Immigration Act. In the 1927 case of *Weedin vs. Chin Bow,* the Supreme Court declared that a person born abroad of an American parent or parents who had never resided in the United States was not of American nationality. Though Chin Bow was the son of an American citizen of Chinese extraction, he had never lived in this country and, therefore, was not qualified for admittance. In 1928, in the case of *Lam Mow vs. Nagle,* the Supreme Court decided that a child born of Chinese parents aboard an American ship on the high seas was not born in the United States, and should not be considered a citizen of the United States or allowed to enter the country.[26]

For many Chinese, then, life under detention was miserable and monotonous as they waited weeks for hearings or months for court decisions. They daydreamed, worried, and grew discouraged or angry; all of these emotions were captured in poems scribbled on the walls of the detention building.[27]

> Everybody says journey to North America is easy and a pleasure,
> But I suffered misery on the ship and worry in the wooden enclosure,
> Several interrogations I have been through, but still feel in chain,
> I sigh for my brethren who are being detained.
>
> The three-beams low building can barely shelter my body,
> Discussing experiences on the Island slopes only makes me moody.

Wait till the day I become famous and fulfill my wishes,
I will not speak of humanity when I level these bases.

These poems, of which 135 have survived, have recently been translated by the Chinese Culture Foundation of San Francisco. The Chinese community has also secured permission to create a museum in
the decaying barracks. Like better-known Ellis Island in New York
Harbor, where millions of Europeans first saw America, Angel Island
was the historical stop for Asian immigrants. While some European
immigrants suffered on Ellis Island, the Angel Island experience was
probably much worse. Many Chinese still harbor bitter memories of
their encounter.

In addition to a center to detect illegal immigrants, Angel Island
was also used as a quarantine station to prevent health hazards that
might be caused by immigrants infected with the communicable diseases prevalent among aliens from Asian countries. In fact, near the
detention center was a modern hospital. It included surgical facilities
as well as a dispensary, nurses' and doctors' quarters, and separate
wards for the Chinese, Japanese, and other groups. The list of diseases which were classified as "loathsome and dangerously contagious" included trachoma in 1903, hookworm and filariasis in 1910,
clonorchiasis or liver fluke in 1908, and lunacy in 1926. The Chinese
community believed that these health regulations were specifically set
up as barriers against the Chinese immigrants, and its leaders were as
determined to have the list amended as they were to improve the Chinese image in America. In the winter of 1910, they delegated King H.
Kwan, a British-trained doctor from China, to lobby in Washington,
D.C. Dr. Kwan's reputation and his scientific presentation finally convinced United States health authorities that parasitic filariasis, on
which account over a thousand Chinese were denied entry, was not a
dangerously contagious disease and that Chinese patients should be
permitted to stay in America for medical treatment.[28]

In 1921, the Chinese community also waged battle against the liver
fluke regulation after learning that 53 Chinese detainees on Angel Island were pronounced unfit for admittance because of this disease.
The Six Companies, on behalf of the detainees, petitioned the United
States immigration and health authorities to reverse the judgment
and successfully persuaded them to allow 32 Chinese to come to San
Francisco under bond. In the meantime, Chinese applicants in Seattle
encountered the same problem; 63 were detained by Seattle immigration officials in 1924. The Seattle "China Club" later asked several doctors in Peking to give affidavits to corroborate its contention that liver
fluke was not contagious. Finally, in 1927, the Chinese Chambers of
Commerce of Honolulu and San Francisco dispatched Dr. Fred Lam

of Honolulu to Washington, D.C. to argue against this particular regulation. Lam successfully proved to American health officials that liver fluke was not a contagious disease and, as a result, it was removed from the list.[29] The successful efforts to remove these diseases from the health list were major symbolic victories. Chinese Americans were anxious to escape the negative image of being "the sick men from the East."

4. Abnormal Lives during Normalcy

Between the two World Wars, as the United States was developing into a world power and as the American people were occupied with several pressing domestic and foreign issues, the Chinese immigration problem was no longer a matter for such emotional debate as it once had been. Furthermore, circumstances now dictated that the Japanese become the focus of America's irrational, racist passions. After 1900 almost all anti-Asian hatred was directed against the more numerous and, from the white point of view, more threatening Japanese. During this period, the attitudes of the white society toward the Chinese vacillated between approval and disapproval. Americans were still disturbed by the unlawful entry of Chinese immigrants and the engagement of a few in illegal occupations, but they were impressed by the order maintained in the Chinese community and by the methods of mutual aid extended through huiguan and family/clan solidarity. Chinese Americans rarely sought relief nor did they become disruptive to the mainstream society. Unlike the Japanese and the Filipinos, the Chinese produced only a handful of local labor leaders, but no radical intellectuals or prominent left-wing politicians. Even in Hawaii, where the Chinese were prospering in business, they stood on the political sidelines while the other Asian groups battled the white establishment.

In spite of these relatively pacific relations, the anti-Japanese exclusion law of 1924 also had a significant effect on Chinese residents in the United States.[30] The Immigration Act of May 26, 1924, was essentially designed to prevent an influx of Japanese picture brides and other illegal Oriental immigrants disguised as students. But in accordance with its provisions, the authorities took measures that were radical departures from the then existing interpretations of the Chinese exclusion laws. These provisions included: (1) the inadmissibility of the wives and children of Chinese merchants; (2) the inadmissibility of the Chinese wives of American citizens of Chinese descent; and (3) young Chinese students were required to be accepted by an accredited institution of higher education; primary and secondary students were excluded. Students also had to prove to the satisfaction of American officials that they had adequate financial support to maintain their stay in America. Finally, they must regularly attend an accredited institution, carry a minimum number of credit hours, and must leave the country at the completion of study or the expiration of visa. Aside from the 1924 Act, no new anti-Chinese legislation was passed. The Chinese were left alone in a period of benighted neglect.

Within the Chinese community, a notable change was taking place during these interim years, namely, the redistribution of the Chinese population. The decade of the 1920s saw an increase of 21.6 percent of Chinese population, from 61,639 to 74,954, 64 percent of them residing in major cities. In the decade of the 1930s, Chinese population increased 3.4 percent, reaching a total of 77,504, 71 percent of them living in major American cities.[31] As Western frontier towns closed their mines or shut down their mills, the Chinese population disappeared because these communities offered limited possibilities for occupations and businesses customarily engaged in by the Chinese. Of course, until 1943 Chinese immigrants were barred from seeking citizenship and consequently could not homestead; they seldom owned real property. In the metropolitan areas, on the other hand, they could engage in occupations that would not compete with or threaten the white population. Laundries, restaurants, curio shops, grocery stores, and cocktail lounges were among their preferences. Usually all members of the family were expected to make some contribution to the family business. Young children carried packages for customers or unloaded goods while older brothers and sisters served as clerks or cashiers.

According to the 1920 U.S. census, of the 45,614 Chinese in the labor force, 5,049 worked in various kinds of farming, only 150 still worked in mines, 4,256 were employed in manufacturing and mechanical trades, 790 were employed in transportation, 7,479 were sales and clerical workers, 186 were in public service, 462 had joined the professional and managerial ranks, 794 worked in printing and publishing, but a striking majority of 26,488 worked for laundries and restaurants.[32] In New York City, almost one-third of the Chinese were engaged in hand laundering. On the West Coast, in the Midwest and on the Atlantic Coast, more than 30 percent of the Chinese worked for chop suey restaurants. And as late as the 1930s, more than 60 percent of all Chinese workers made their living as domestics, laundrymen, cooks, and waiters.

In Hawaii the picture was brighter. There the Chinese fared much better than their brothers and sisters in the mainland United States, partly because of fewer racial barriers and partly because of a faster pace of acculturation in the Hawaiian Chinese community. In the

1920s affluent Chinese merchants began to live outside Chinatown in suburban homes much like those of the white majority. In 1930, 21 out of the 24 suburban and urban Hawaiian areas examined by sociologist Clarence Glick had at least 200 Chinese residents.[33] When the 1940 census was completed, it showed that the Hawaiian Chinese not only were actively participating in governmental and community affairs but also were becoming an influential socio-economic group. Many Chinese held government and white-collar jobs and a substantial number of them dominated several economic areas, particularly banking, real estate, livestock, and the tourist industry.

Redistribution of the Chinese population on the U.S. mainland naturally resulted in a decline of some Chinatowns and an explosive growth in others. For example, the Butte, Montana, Chinese population had dwindled to 88; only 110 Chinese were left in Denver; Salt Lake City's Chinatown had virtually vanished; Boise, Idaho, had no Chinese in 1930; and the once sizable Chinatown in Rock Springs, Wyoming, had ceased to exist. On the other hand, Boston, Los Angeles, New York, and San Francisco gained substantial numbers of Chinese.

Chinese population in Boston grew from 200 in 1890 to 1,000 in 1920 and 1,300 in 1940. Between 1905 and 1925, the Chinese settlement in Boston spread from the South Railway Station to the traffic artery of Kneeland Street. The Chinese took over several blocks of homes formerly occupied by Arabs and turned them into restaurants, grocery stores, trading associations, and art stores, as well as family dwellings.[34] Chinese also shared in the rapid growth of Los Angeles.The 1920s and 1930s saw a sharp increase of Chinese population in Los Angeles as the city was developing into a metropolitan giant. By 1930, it had a total of about 3,000 Chinese, by 1940, 4,736. Los Angeles's Chinatown also underwent a change in locale when more than half of its buildings were torn down to make way for the Union Station. The New Chinatown, which was built on North Broadway, was first occupied in 1938. A portion of the old Chinese settlement opposite the Plaza lingered on for another decade, but that area was finally leveled to make way for a park.[35] New York counted a total of over 11,000 Chinese by 1930. The New York Chinatown was bounded on the North by Canal Street, on the West by Mulberry Street and on the East and South by the Bowery and Park Row.[36] Finally, San Francisco, which had its ups and downs, also benefited from redistribution of the Chinese population. Although its Chinese population had dropped from 30,000 in 1878 to 7,744 in 1920, it rebounded to 17,782 in 1940. As the largest Chinese city in the Western Hemisphere, San Francisco doubled its Chinatown area during this period. However, that city's Chinatown remained a crowded and expensive place in which to live.[37] In 1940, before the Chinese were greatly affected by World War II, the

28 American cities with established Chinatowns reported the population figures shown in Table 4.[38]

TABLE 4

City	Population Native	Chinese
San Francisco, Ca.	534,536	17,782
New York, N.Y.	7,454,995	11,051
Los Angeles, Ca.	1,504,277	4,736
Oakland, Ca.	302,163	3,201
Chicago, Ill.	3,396,808	2,013
Seattle, Wash.	368,302	1,781
Portland, Ore.	305,394	1,569
Sacramento, Ca.	105,958	1,508
Boston, Mass.	770,816	1,383
Brooklyn, N.Y.	2,698,285	1,251
Stockton, Ca.	54,714	1,052
Philadelphia, Pa.	1,931,334	922
Fresno, Ca.	60,685	790
Washington, D.C.	603,091	656
Detroit, Mich.	1,623,452	583
San Antonio, Tx.	253,854	471
Phoenix, Ariz.	65,414	431
Baltimore, Md.	859,100	379
Cleveland, Ohio	876,336	308
Minneapolis, Minn.	492,370	304
Newark, N.J.	429,760	259
New Orleans, La.	494,537	230
El Paso, Tx.	96,810	210
San Jose, Ca.	68,457	176
Pittsburgh, Pa.	671,659	141
Jersey City, N.J.	301,173	112
Denver, Colo.	322,412	110
Butte, Mont.	37,081	88
Total	26,683,463	53,497

5. The Great Depression Hits Chinatowns

Before the Great Depression, a number of Chinese in America tried to build major businesses. Unfortunately, their limited capital and inability to compete with large American companies doomed most to failure. The China Mail Steamship Company, organized in San Francisco in 1915, lost more than 1.7 million dollars in eight years; the Canton Bank, founded in San Francisco in 1907, filed for bankruptcy after only eleven years of operation. Other West Coast companies that had short lives included the Western Canning Company of Oakland, the Chinese American Shipping Company, and the National Packing of Isleton, which, after an initial success in fruit and vegetable canning, also had to cease its operation.

A handful of talented Chinese merchants did manage to survive amid the fierce competition of the American free enterprise system. In New York, the most important example was the Wah Chang Trading Corporation. In Stockton, California, the symbol of success was Chin Lung, nicknamed the "Chinese Potato King." But the most prominent Chinese-American businessman was Joe Shoong who founded the China Toggery in San Francisco in 1907. By 1928, he had expanded his small business into the famed National Dollar Stores. Later his business developed into a chain with over 40 outlets in the major cities of California, Utah, Arizona, and Hawaii. It employed more than 600 people and grossed over 13 million dollars each year in the 1930s. The only other Chinese in the Western Hemisphere whose wealth rivalled that of Joe Shoong was C. Q. Yee Hop of Honolulu, who began with a modest meat business in 1887 but eventually came to own a variety of enterprises in Hawaii.

The economic foundation of the Chinatowns was built on shaky ground, however, since the chief contributors to their prosperity, the bachelor laborers, were gradually disappearing. When the Depression hit the American economy, Chinese small proprietors, like many of their white counterparts, often went bankrupt. Between 1929 and 1935 many stores in Chinatowns were closed and their owners thrown into the swollen ranks of the unemployed. Many Chinese merchants lost their savings in the bank failures. The Chinatown community was so economically close-knit that the depression had a snowballing effect. As Chinese restaurants closed they invariably destroyed Chinese grocery stores. By 1931, about 25 percent of the Chinese in the United States were jobless. New York's Chinatown was the hardest hit; approximately 3,000 Chinese in the city had lost their jobs by 1932.[39]

The Chinese Six Companies and other private charity organizations quickly assumed their traditional relief responsibilities, distributing food and clothing to the needy and the desperate. In San Francisco, the Donghua Hospital established a temporary shelter for the sick and the elderly who had no other means to provide for themselves. In New York, the Chinese Merchants Association filed a petition in the New York Supreme Court in 1931, asking permission to mortgage its clubhouse property at 41 Mott Street for $45,000 to be spent in the relief of the needy.[40] In general, the Chinese did not turn to federal relief agencies for help; most relied on self-help and community benevolence. In the depth of the depression a few Chinese accepted direct relief but most were too proud; it appears that many preferred starvation to the indignity of accepting a government dole. In 1943 Congressman Warren Magnuson of Washington recalled: "During the trying days of the depression as a matter of curiosity one time I did check the W.P.A. roll in King County, in the State of Washington, and there was one lone Chinese on that roll."[41]

But the Great Depression did foster an acute labor-management struggle in the Chinese community as Chinese working men became more militant and opened contact with American labor organizations. Previously, a few old-fashioned trade guilds existed in Chinatowns, mostly dominated by the employers. A few small independent trade unions existed, including the Mon Sang Association, formed by Chicago Chinese waiters in 1918, and the Unionist Guild, formed by San Francisco garment workers in 1919. None of these, however, reached a substantial membership, nor did they receive support from American unions. But the concept of labor solidarity lingered on and, in the mid-1920s, a Chinese workers' club was organized in San Francisco, partly to find jobs for unemployed Chinese. In early 1929, Chinese laundry workers staged a strike against their employers in the Bay Area, forcing a compromise settlement.[42] But these early efforts were sporadic and without lasting effect.

The Chinese labor movement in America was begun in Alaska by a group of Chinese salmon-cannery workers. Before World War II, the Alaska Packers Association, the biggest salmon cannery company in Alaska, annually recruited 400 to 500 Chinese from San Francisco to work in its factories for about four months, during April and July. Working hours ranged from 12 to 16 hours daily and the job was strenuous. Furthermore, the work was seasonal and demanded a long journey for the workers. These circumstances, combined with low wages, finally led the workers to strike in 1936. So successful was this confrontation that the Chinese cannery workers, after returning to San Francisco, organized the Chinese Workers Mutual Aid Association (CWMAA) in September of 1937. Until its demise in 1951, the CWMAA spearheaded the drive to organize Chinese workers and championed their crusade for better working conditions.[43]

In the second half of the 1930s, Chinese picketers were visible in a number of national strikes. For example, Chinese workers participated in the 1936 San Francisco waterfront strike and also in the 1937 San Francisco hotel strike. In New York, during the National Maritime Union strike of 1936–37, approximately 3,000 Chinese seamen participated in the walkout. The most publicized strike of Chinese labor came in early 1938 when the Chinese Ladies Garment Workers' Union selected San Francisco National Dollar Stores as its target. At the time of this strike, the National Dollar Stores paid its Chinese garment workers between $4 and $16 per week; union wages for the same work ranged from $19 to $30 per week.[44] In November, 1937, the workers presented their demands for better pay to the owner, but to no avail. Disgruntled by the intransigence of the owners, the workers organized the International Ladies Garment Workers' Union (ILGWU)Local 341, known as the Chinese Ladies Garment Union. When further negotiations produced no compromise, the 108 Chinese workers walked out on February 26, 1938. With the moral as well as financial backing of the ILGWU, the strikers were able to sustain 13 weeks of picketing and won some concessions from their employer. The agreement signed on June 10 guaranteed a 5 percent increase in weekly wages, a $14 per week minimum wage, and paid holidays.[45]

In spite of these successes, when compared with other ethnic minorities the Chinese made little headway in unionizing their labor force. Membership for the Chinese labor unions remained small, their leadership weak, and their activities limited. Once again, Chinese cultural background retarded unionization. Other contributing factors were that there were relatively few Chinese workers in heavy industries and that there was a general fear of deportation, particularly among those who entered the United States illegally. Furthermore, Chinese laborers still suffered from latent American racism. Although the CIO movement had by the 1930s accepted Chinese unskilled labor organizations, such as the Laundry Workers' Union, Elevator Union, the Culinary and Miscellaneous Workers' Union, and the Apartment and Hotel Union, the AFL continued to exclude Chinese until after World War II. Chinese butchers, carpenters, plumbers, electricians, chauffeurs, and other skilled workers were still excluded by the craft union movement.[46]

6. Linkage with Wartime China

The world economy in the post–World War I era had become increasingly interdependent. The American Great Depression had global repercussions. One of its victims was Japan, where a paucity of natural resources provided growing justification for an invasion of Manchuria in 1931. For China the Manchurian Incident was the beginning of World War II, and for the Chinese in America it was a time to express their patriotism. When Secretary of State Henry L. Stimson declared, on January 7, 1932, his doctrine of nonrecognition of territorial changes by forcible means in northeast China, the Chinese of America fully supported and applauded the secretary's policy. On January 28, 1932, the Japanese extended the war, assaulting Shanghai by air and sea bombardment and by a massive land attack. While the

Japanese enjoyed a superiority in military strength, they met a gallant and unexpectedly fierce Chinese resistance. In defiance of an appeasing government and without reinforcements, the Chinese 19th Route Army, commanded by General Tsai Tingkai, held off the Japanese at Shanghai for 34 days. Under heavy international pressure and because the Nanjing government promised to demilitarize Shanghai, the Japanese withdrew. But the hero of this military triumph, General Tsai, who was constantly at odds with China's strong man Chiang Kai-shek, was afterwards dismissed on charges of insubordination. The deposed General Tsai then visited the United States, bringing the pressing problems of China closer to Chinese Americans. Tsai's 1934 American tour was, therefore, a good barometer by which the linkage between the Chinese in America and their motherland could be measured and analyzed.

Tsai, who was a native of Guangdong, arrived in New York City with a company of supporters on August 28, 1934. They were greeted by about 3,000 Chinese and a huge American welcoming crowd. That evening, Tsai addressed a large Chinese audience and expounded his goal of "defending China and resisting Japan." Tsai stayed in New York's Waldorf-Astoria Hotel and received a constant stream of American reporters, frequently blasting Chiang Kai-shek's "appeasement" policy toward Japan. During his visit in New York, Tsai also reviewed a Chinese parade in Chinatown, addressed a Chinese school audience and, of course, was feted by several Chinese groups.[47] Tsai's next stop was in Boston where, according to his travel journal, hundreds of thousands of people welcomed him, including many of the Chinese residents in New England. The mayor of Boston and the governor of Massachusetts awarded him medals in honor of his bravery against the Japanese.[48]

Tsai visited a number of other major American cities, including Philadelphia, Washington, D.C., Cleveland, Detroit, San Antonio, St. Louis, Kansas City, Los Angeles, San Diego, and San José, everywhere receiving a hero's welcome, not only from Chinese but also from Americans. When Tsai arrived at the San Francisco train station, he was greeted by more than 4,000 people, including the mayor and other local officials. As his motorcade slowly entered Chinatown, students from the Chinese Public School, Nom Kue School, Baptists' School, and St. Mary's School, resplendent in their uniforms, lined up along Grand Avenue to pay their respect. On November 3, six Chinatown restaurants hosted a banquet reception. While the party was in full swing, the crackling of firecrackers could be heard throughout Chinatown. That evening all Chinese shops in San Francisco were illuminated to show their appreciation of the general's valor.[49]

Not until Madame Chiang Kai-shek's celebrated American tour of

1943 did another Chinese citizen receive such a magnificent reception in the United States. Tsai was a perfect hero—courageous, modest, and seemingly devoid of personal ambition. Chinese Americans adored him and made him into a Charles Lindbergh-type figure. In a weakening China, where defeat, retreat, and concession had become commonplace, and where selfish warlords scrambled for personal wealth and power, Tsai's simple life-style, unbending will, and above all, his exceptional performance in Shanghai were, to the Chinese in America, refreshing and encouraging. Many American Chinese hoped he would take up the mantle of Sun Yat-sen, but that did not happen as Tsai never had a chance to command his own army during World War II. As a matter of fact, his decision to collaborate with the Communists in 1949 has made him a controversial figure in modern Chinese history.

Tsai's reception was, however, symbolic of the growing Chinese-American support for national reform in China. Even before Tsai's visit, a number of young Chinese had returned to China to encourage the thrust for modernization. For example, Fong Joe Guey, who had gained fame as the first Chinese aviator in the world by piloting his small homemade plane over Oakland, started the Guangdong Aviation Company in 1911; Tom Gunn, another Chinese pilot who received his license in America in 1912, went to work in China; and J. K. Choy of Honolulu departed for the land of his parents when he was only 17 years old, and later became president of a large navigation company in China. One study of the period 1927–1932 discovered that 741 United States citizens of Chinese ancestry from Hawaii chose to live in China. Over 100 Chinese returned from America to teach in universities and colleges in China, in particular at Lingnan University, St. John's Shanghai University, Peking Union Medical College, and Yanjing University.[50]

A full-scale war between China and Japan finally broke out July 7, 1937, and the Chinese community in America immediately made financial and other contributions to help resist Japanese aggression. Popular sympathy in the United States was wholly with the Chinese. The war greatly stimulated American interest in the life, philosophy, social traditions, and history of the Chinese, which made Lin Yutang's *My Country and My People* and *The Importance of Living* best sellers in the United States. Atrocities committed by Japanese soldiers in China, such as the Rape of Nanjing, were often headlined in major American newspapers. Achievements of individual Chinese, ranging from Hiram Fong's election to the legislature of the Territory of Hawaii in 1938 to Kingman Dong's painting exhibitions and Anna May Wong's Hollywood films, received growing recognition in the American press.

Before the United States entered World War II, some young Chinese Americans made their way into the battle against fascism. A group of 33 youthful Chinese pilots from Portland, Oregon, joined Chiang Kai-shek's air force long before Pearl Harbor. On August 21, 1937, under the prodding of the Chinese consulate-general in San Francisco, the Six Companies called an emergency meeting to which 91 Chinese organizations throughout America sent representatives. The meeting resulted in the founding of the China War Relief Association of America, which ultimately included 47 chapters in the western hemisphere. The most urgent business of the association was to raise money for the financially troubled Nationalist government, which had been forced to withdraw to the isolation of Chongqing in October, 1938. But the association also encouraged a boycott against Japanese merchants and organized demonstrations against Japan. Joined by Koreans, the association twice held anti-Japanese parades in New York in 1938 and picketed the shipyards of Los Angeles (January, 1939), Everett, Washington (January, 1939) and Astoria, Oregon (March, 1939). By means of such demonstrations, the Chinese attempted to stop Japanese ships from carrying scrap iron and other forms of raw materials out of American harbors.[51]

No sooner had Japan bombed Pearl Harbor on December 7, 1941, than the United States and China became allies in the Pacific War. The Chinese in America intensified their support of China's resistance with the fervent encouragement of the American government. The Chinese in America bought large quantities of wartime bonds issued directly by the Central Bank of China. The bonds were in several denominations, ranging from $5 to $5,000, each carrying a flashy and patriotic name such as Liberty Bond or Victory Bond. Some of these bonds were afterwards redeemed by the Nationalist government to Chinese subscribers, some were used to build classrooms in America's Chinatowns. But most of the bonds are still locked in the attics or basements of many Chinese families in the United States.[52] In addition to buying war bonds, the Chinese in America contributed millions of dollars to alleviate the suffering of China's war refugees, to help flood victims, and to buy uniforms, tanks, and airplanes. During the eight years of war against Japan, the Chinese in the United States gave approximately $25 million dollars to the Chinese government. The most significant donations and bond subscriptions came from San Francisco ($5 million), New York (about $3 million), Chicago ($2.4 million), Los Angeles ($2.2 million), New England ($2.1 million), Sacramento ($800,000), Stockton (over $400,000), Seattle ($400,000), San Antonio ($373,000), Fresno ($360,000), Portland, Oregon ($310,000), Washington, D.C. ($300,000), Detroit ($300,000), St. Louis ($280,000), Rhode Island ($180,000), Pittsburgh ($170,000), Milwaukee ($170,000), Columbus, Ohio ($70,000), Cincinnati ($60,000), Houston ($57,000), New Orleans ($52,500), and Arkansas ($16,800).[53]

Throughout World War II, the government of the United States tried to stimulate the Chinese war effort. President Franklin D. Roosevelt insisted that China be treated as a major power, and with this in mind he invited Madame Chiang Kai-shek to visit the United States in 1943. Educated in America as a teenager, Madame Chiang spoke very good English. Beautiful and gracious, she proved to be an exceptional "good-will ambassador." During the months of February, March, and April of 1943, Madame Chiang became one of the most popular and familiar figures in America; her tour received extensive coverage in the press. During her one-week visit to San Francisco, the *Chronicle* published no fewer than 20 articles and editorials about Madame Chiang. Coverage by other major U. S. newspapers, such as the *New York Times,* the *Chicago Tribune,* the *San Francisco Examiner,* and the *Los Angeles Times,* was as favorable as it was extensive. Her electrifying speech to a joint session of Congress on February 18, a gigantic rally at New York's Madison Square Garden, and large receptions in Chicago, San Francisco, and Los Angeles not only greatly aroused American sympathy for the plight of China but also presented a new image of the Chinese people to the American public.

Favorable news coverage of Madame Chiang did much to improve the public image of America's Chinatowns and their inhabitants. By implication, the focus on the New China also reflected favorably upon the Chinese in the United States. Chinese Americans, now equated with Madame Chiang, were portrayed as modern, intelligent, proud, tolerant, and Christian.[54] Though Madame Chiang was probably the most important public figure in changing the Chinese image in the war years, other notable figures also contributed. For example, in May, 1943, the Copernican Quadricentennial National Committee selected Dr. James Y. C. Yen, a pioneer in the Chinese Mass Movement, as one of its ten recipients for the Copernican Citation. Yen's name was printed in every American newspaper alongside those of such prominent Americans as Albert Einstein, John Dewey, Henry Ford, Orville Wright, and Walt Disney, as one who, like Copernicus, had revolutionized the channels of thought.[55]

7. World War II and the Chinese of America

America's admiration for Madame Chiang Kai-shek and China as a wartime ally, combined with the practical need to counter Japanese propaganda that the United States had treated the Chinese as an inferior minority, led to the repeal of all Chinese exclusion laws. Immediately after Madame Chiang's visit to Capitol Hill in February, the Committee of Immigration and Naturalization began hearings on various bills designed to repeal the Chinese exclusion laws and to place the Chinese on a quota basis. On October 7, 1943, the committee favorably reported H.R. 3070 to accomplish that purpose. This bill was to change a policy of 60 years standing which 30 Congresses had not seen fit to alter.[56] Four days later, President Roosevelt sent a brief message to the House of Representatives supporting the legislation. He considered the act essential to the war effort and to establishing a secure peace in Asia. Roosevelt admitted that nations, like individuals, make mistakes, and then added:

> We must be big enough to acknowledge our mistakes of the past and to correct them. By the repeal of the Chinese exclusion laws, we can correct a historic mistake and silence the distorted Japanese propaganda. The enactment of legislation now pending before Congress would put Chinese immigrants on a parity with those from other countries. . . . While it would give the Chinese a preferred status over a certain Oriental people, their great contribution to the cause of decency and freedom entitled them to such preference.[57]

During debate of the bill, Warren Magnuson of Washington, Edward Gossett of Texas, and Walter Judd of Minnesota led the overwhelming majority of the lawmakers who supported it, while John B. Bennett of Michigan and a handful of others opposed it. The minority opponents argued that the impetus of such legislation lay in foreign-policy considerations rather than racial equality and that the Chinese and the whole world would soon learn that it was largely a charade. They also pointed out that the bill would be of no material benefit to China and that it amounted to nothing more than a feeble gesture to do a futile thing at the expense of a sound and long-established rule of immigration.[58] Proponents of the bill answered the assertion by quoting from a Chinese government radio broadcast from Chongqing which said in part: "The repeal of the acts as recommended by President Roosevelt will be exceedingly welcomed here and will be considered as further cementing the traditional friendship between the United States and China."[59]

The bill was introduced under extraordinary wartime circumstances, so its passage was actually a foregone conclusion even before debate began. Only ten days after President Roosevelt sent his message, the House passed the so-called Magnuson bill, and a month later the Senate gave its approval. Roosevelt signed it into law December 17, 1943, and a new chapter in the history of the Chinese relation to America had begun. Under this bill a yearly quota of 105 Chinese immigrants would be allowed into the United States, regardless of their place of birth. Although highly discriminatory when compared with European quotas, under the circumstances the formula was perhaps the best compromise, for it neutralized the position taken by labor and veterans' organizations, which feared a vast influx of cheap labor. But the quota did nothing to aid those Chinese born in Latin America, Hong Kong, and elsewhere who wished to emigrate under other national quotas. Furthermore, repeal of the exclusion laws did not bring about an end to legal discrimination against the Chinese. Miscegenation laws still existed in at least 18 states of the Union, Chinese schoolchildren were segregated throughout the country, and Chinese workers were not allowed to hold public employment.[60]

Most of the Chinese, however, did not view this legislation as symbolic or an empty gesture because, when the bill went into effect, more than half of the Chinese in America, about 40,000, were foreign-born, and as a result of the legislation became eligible for U.S. citizenship.[61] Furthermore, after 1944 an increasing number of nonquota Chinese immigrants were admitted into the country. For example, an average of 137 Chinese scholars came to teach in the United States each year, as compared to 10 per year before passage of the bill. The War Bride Act of December 28, 1945, made it possible for wives and children of American citizens of Chinese extraction to apply as nonquota immigrants.[62] Perhaps most important of all, for the approximately 12,000 Chinese who were drafted or enlisted in the United States armed services, the repeal legislation was a morale booster. And for the thousands of Chinese who worked at assembly lines to produce weapons for global warfare, the bill was a patriotic incentive.

The Japanese surprise strike at Pearl Harbor ushered in a series of massive changes in American society. The United States again opened its doors to job opportunities that had been previously closed to the Chinese. Because of the wartime manpower shortage, Chinese found work in defense industries, frequently in technical and scientific positions which offered good wages. The removal of restrictions in the U.S. Navy and Naval Reserve resulted in recruitment of 500 Chinese as apprentice seamen. The Richmond Shipyard and the Moore Shipyard in California paid a minimum wage of 95 cents per hour to Chinese workers. In 1943 Chinese made up some 15 percent of the shipyard work force in the San Francisco Bay Area. Even Chinese women shared in emergency war-production efforts, as many of them worked for the Toyad Company of Los Angeles. Outside of California, Chinese also benefited from wartime employment opportunities. The Seattle-Tacoma Shipbuilding Corporation and the Bechtel Price Callahan Company in Alaska, which manufactured war materials, put

Chinese on their payrolls. Other Chinese found work in the shipyards of Delaware and Mississippi, in arsenal plants of New Jersey, and in airplane factories on Long Island and in Texas. Generally, the Chinese in America still found themselves shunted off to menial jobs, but growing numbers were hired as technicians and engineers. The income gap between whites and Chinese, though still considerable, was somewhat reduced during the war years. The war indeed gave a new economic beginning to Chinese-American society.

Nowhere was the new Chinese-American role better exemplified than in the armed services. As soon as the United States entered the conflict, Chinese community leaders urged young Chinese to enlist in the armed forces of the United States as a demonstration of their loyalty to the American cause. The New York Chinatown cheered itself hoarse when the first draft numbers included Chinese Americans. Of the only 11 Chinese of draft age in Butte, Montana, all enlisted before being drafted. On the battlefields of Europe and Asia, Chinese soldiers fought side by side with white comrades whose grandfathers had tried to expel their ancestors. Of the 59,803 Chinese adult males in the United States, including citizens, residents and students, over 20 percent were drafted or enlisted in the U.S. army. In addition, a smaller number served in the navy and the air force[63] (see Appendix 4).

As nineteenth-century Chinese had given their lives constructing railroads across the American continent, twentieth-century Chinese died to safeguard American liberty. Two hundred fourteen Chinese died in World War II combat. That number was small when compared to the national average, but it nevertheless showed the patriotism of a people long discriminated against in the United States. The struggle for equality was by no means over but the war had brought changes. Many young Chinese veterans used the G.I. Bill to go to college and begin a pursuit of the American dream. And the inroads Chinese had made into the American labor force were never reversed.

Equally important gains had been made on political, legal, and social fronts. American xenophobia against Japan before and during World War II benefited the Chinese by comparison; with repeal both of the exclusion laws and of the naturalization prohibition, more and more Chinese could and did build normal lives in America. The old sojourner's bachelor society was being replaced by a highly structured social order and family system that was to become a mainstay of Chinese stability and distinctiveness. American attitudes toward the Chinese also changed. Chinese achievements in education and occupational skills, together with low delinquency and crime rates and rare recourse to social welfare, had convinced many whites that the Chinese were, and could be, valuable members of United States society. World War II had unmistakably changed American images of the Chinese as well as the Chinese self-perception, from the Yin (negative) pendulum to that of the Yang (positive).

Nowhere was there better proof of these changes than in Chinese education, language, and behavior. In 1920, when psychologists began to test Chinese children, these children scored at much the same level as Caucasians in performance, nonverbal, and number tests, though substantially lower on verbal ones.[64] As more Chinese youngsters went to white schools and more interaction occurred between the Chinese and white adults, the English-language proficiency of the Chinese population also dramatically improved. By 1950 about one-third of the Chinese in San Francisco habitually used Chinese, one-third English, and the rest used both.[65] It is to be assumed that outside of San Francisco and New York City, a much higher percentage of Chinese began habitually using English for social and business communications. As the Chinese population slowly and progressively went through the acculturation processes, the question increasingly became one of how to preserve an old heritage and still adapt to a culture so jarringly different.

Naturally, there were wide family and individual differences in degree of acculturation, but in general Chinese-Americans were accepting many American traits while discarding traditional Chinese ones. Chinese men became more aggressive and brash, more active in political and legal action, while becoming less authoritarian in dealings with their wives and children. They also tended to discard such traditions as filial piety, ancestor worship, and expensive wedding and religious ceremonies. But they continued to hold such Chinese values as reverence for family, respect for education and hard work, cultivation of propriety and patience, and restrictiveness in upbringing of children. They still ate rice as their staple diet, and felt guilty if they went against the wishes of their parents and elders. They increasingly led dual lives that were filled with feelings of ambivalence. They were neither truly Chinese nor truly Americans. They were Chinese Americans!

V

THE CHINESE-AMERICAN COMMUNITY IN TRANSITION
THE POST—WORLD WAR II ERA

The people turn to a humane ruler as
water flows downward or beasts take to
wilderness.

—Mencius

By nature men are pretty much alike; it is
learning and practice that set them apart.

—Confucius

1. The Stranded Chinese Students

World War II left the United States a confident, powerful, and relatively unified nation, but China's economy was ravaged, its social inequalities widened, and its people ripe for civil war. The Nationalist government's currency depreciated in a vicious spiral. The chaotic postwar reoccupation of Japanese-held territory unexpectedly turned a great number of Chinese, particularly in Manchuria, northern China, and Taiwan, against the Nationalists, who were increasingly viewed as corrupt and self-serving. Meanwhile the Communists, under the ruthless leadership of Mao Zedong, had fought the Japanese bravely and had created a dynamic centrally-controlled movement in China's Northwest. By 1945 they were attracting great numbers of poor peasants and disillusioned intellectuals. From 1946 to 1949 China suffered through one of the bloodiest civil wars of modern times. The United States, now the leader of the Western democratic alliance, was inevitably drawn into the Chinese political struggle. The Truman administration's efforts to help reconstruct China after the war was frustrated by the growing internal rivalry in China. America's "China Tangle," a topic which has been thoroughly examined by scholars, ultimately proved to be expensive and futile.[1] Many Americans, including Secretary of State George C. Marshall, came to conclude that the billions of dollars in aid granted to the Nationalist government were being squandered. The ultimate collapse of the Nationalist government was nonetheless a stunning surprise to America, and once again the status of the Chinese in the United States was dramatically changed.

When the Communists gained control of the mainland some 5,000 foreign-born Chinese who had been admitted to the United States for the pursuit of specific objectives since World War II were stranded. These people were nonimmigrants, including students, tourists, businessmen, government officials, journalists, priests, and other temporary visitors. Immigration officials later grouped them all in a student classification because of their uncertain legal status. While the great majority, probably 4,000, were students, some were highly trained professionals in such fields as education, science, technology, medicine, and agriculture. In addition, a number of former Chinese officials from the Nationalist government sought asylum in America. Some Nationalist Chinese consular officials also chose to remain in the United States after the termination of their duties. Finally, there was a small group of very wealthy Chinese who fled the mainland with personal fortunes, in some instances embezzled government funds, and moved to America to start new lives or to rejoin their families.[2] These diverse groups were treated by immigration authorities as "stranded students," a category which had evolved out of the Chinese immigrant experience.

Since the first Chinese student, Yung Wing, graduated from Yale in 1854, the flow of Chinese students had never ceased, in spite of the exclusion laws against Chinese laboring immigrants. At the turn of the century, the number of Chinese students in America began to increase, partly because of China's westernization movement and partly because of the Boxer Indemnity Fellowship. After establishment of the Republic of China in 1912, there were increasing demands in China for men and women trained in Western ideas. Various organizations and individuals in China vied with each other in giving encouragement and providing means for promising youths to go abroad. Principal among them were the provincial governments, industrial and business organizations, and Christian missions, both Protestant and Catholic. In addition, the majority who came to America did so at their own expense or were supported by their families.

By 1942, before the Japanese invaders occupied China's major cities and cut communication lines, over 1,500 Chinese students were studying in American universities and colleges.[3] Fearing that the Japanese might gain access to Chinese funds in the United States, the Chinese government, in July of 1941, asked the United States to freeze all Chinese assets until further notice. As a result, Chinese students lost their sources of financial support and, with the United States entry into the war, other means of remittances from the Pacific were also suspended. In this emergency the China Institute in America, which was headquartered in New York and was in charge of administering the Boxer Indemnity and other fellowships, appealed to the United States government for assistance. In April, 1942, the State Department Bureau of Education and Cultural Affairs set up a "China Program" and began sending monthly allowance checks of $75 to selected Chinese graduate students throughout the United States. Meanwhile, the Chinese Nationalist government, through its embassy in Washington, D.C., also extended financial assistance to worthy Chinese students who would otherwise be forced to drop out of school. Other public and private agencies also helped Chinese students to find jobs in America's wartime industries.[4]

As the war turned in the Allies' favor in 1944, the Chinese government in Chongqing began formulating plans for massive postwar reconstruction. Among other steps, the government hoped to send a large group of professionals and students to the United States after the war. Young professionals who had had basic training during the war and had shown ability and promise were encouraged to apply for advanced study in America. College presidents, professors, and the administrators of various government agencies were asked to recommend bright young Chinese for such a program. The Foreign Economic Administration of the United States, which had a budget of $4.8 million as part of the 1945 lend-lease to China appropriation, was to administer the program. Accordingly, between 1945 and 1947 a total of 1,200 Chinese railway engineers, health officials, finance experts, teachers, and technicians were sent to the United States via India. In addition, the Chinese government and the Nations' Relief and Rehabilitation Administration of the United States offered fellowships for students who wished to pursue advanced study in engineering and technology in America. The U.S. State Department granted funds to the China Institute in America to recruit bright liberal arts and social sciences students for two years of training in America.[5] Other Chinese came on private funds or as members of groups sponsored by American religious and business organizations. For instance, the International Harvester Company of Chicago offered scholarships to 20 Chinese students in one year. For ambitious Chinese students, this was indeed both the worst of times and the best of times. With so many opportunities for financial aid, the number of Chinese students in the United States steadily climbed. (see Table 5).[6]

TABLE 5

Academic year	Total number of Chinese students
1943–44	706
1944–45	823
1945–46	1,298
1946–47	1,678
1947–48	2,310
1948–49	3,914

Like the nineteenth-century Chinese who came seeking jobs in America, the great majority of these students were men between 20 and 40 years old. The ratio of male to female students was 5 to 1 at most colleges, and often as lopsided as 20 to 1.[7] But unlike their illiterate and generally despised laboring countrymen who preceded them, these newcomers shared a strong sense of pride and responsibility for the future of China. They knew they represented the highest echelon of Chinese society and came to the United States to prepare themselves for an important mission. Everywhere they went they generally commanded respect and won affection from their American professors, associates, and acquaintances. The crumbling of the Nationalist government in 1948 and 1949 suddenly destroyed their future, causing emotional and financial problems for them. Fortunately, the United States government quickly stepped in and provided relief. On June 25, 1948, Congress passed the Displaced Persons Act, allowing the Chinese already in the United States to change their legal status, enabling them to stay and to work. On June 16, 1950, a second act gave the Chinese an opportunity to further adjust their status under stipulated conditions. Furthermore, from 1949 to 1955, the State Department spent $7,899,879 for tuition, transportation, living expenses, and medical care for the Chinese students.[8]

These Chinese students also received aid from private sources. Henry R. Luce, American publishing magnate, donated his New York home, now called "China House," to Chinese students. The China Institute in America established branches in New Jersey and Indiana and at Berkeley, California. The Sino-American Amity, a Catholic educational, cultural, and social-service organization founded in 1943 by Cardinal Yu Bin in Washington, D.C., also responded to the relief call. In 1952 the group established a branch office in New York, assisting more than 4,000 students in the next two decades.[9]

In spite of these relief programs, the stranded Chinese, like most Chinese in America during the Cold War era, were deeply disturbed by the continued strife in China. Soon after Mao Zedong pronounced the establishment of the People's Republic on October 1, 1949, the United States government published a white paper recognizing Taiwan as part of mainland China and declaring American neutrality even if the Chinese Communists sought to take the island by force. The coming of the Korean War drastically revised America's strategic policy in East Asia. When Mao sent Chinese "volunteers" to aid the North Koreans, the Truman administration retaliated with a trade embargo on the People's Republic and simultaneously canceled its policy of neutrality in the Chinese civil war. Once again the Nationalist Chinese became allies of the United States. This period of changes in Chinese government and American policy created serious difficulties for the "stranded students."

On August 5, 1954, the United States government issued an order restraining Chinese nationals with technical knowledge that might be beneficial to the Communist regime from leaving the United States.[10] A number of Chinese scientists and engineers suspected of sympathizing with the Communist regime were placed under FBI surveillance. One such person, who drew national as well as international attention, was Dr. Qian Xueshen, a renowned expert in aeronautical engineering and jet propulsion. In 1935 he had received a Qinghua University scholarship, and came to America to study with the famed Hungarian-born rocket expert Theodore von Karman at the California Institute of Technology. In 1945, Qian headed a U.S. scientific delegation to study German rocket development, and upon his return to America became the youngest professor ever to teach at Massachusetts Institute of Technology. In August, 1950, Qian tried to return to mainland China. He was stopped in Honolulu, and truckloads of books and research notes that he had shipped ahead were seized. They later proved to contain no sensitive information. Qian was detained for 15 days for interrogation by the U.S. Immigration Bureau and later freed on $15,000 bond. He remained under security surveillance until September, 1955, when he and 75 other Chinese intellectuals were allowed to leave for China after negotiations between Washington and Peking representatives at Geneva. Since his return to China, Qian has directed China's nuclear-missile propulsion program.[11]

Few of the "stranded students" chose to return to Communist China; however, some went to work in Hong Kong and Taiwan. The vast majority opted to stay in the United States and, although clinging to their Chinese heritage, ultimately joined the great American melting pot. Of those who remained, a significant number became distinguished Chinese Americans, including acclaimed philosopher Wang Hao of Rockefeller University, the Nobel Prize-winning physicists Chen-ning Yang and Tsung-dao Lee, and computer wizard An Wang. According to a survey made by the China Institute in America, in the year 1954, over 60 of these students had become teachers of Chinese history, language, or culture in major American universities. Many others secured responsible positions in America's research laboratories. What had begun as an effort to train an elite Chinese intelligentsia for work in their native land ended as a major infusion of talent into the American educational and industrial system.

These few thousand highly skilled and talented Chinese professionals constituted only a small percentage of the Chinese population in the United States, which by 1950 had reached a total of 150,005.[12] But their achievements in America not only helped to instill in the native-born Chinese a sense of national pride and ethnic consciousness but also created a more favorable Chinese image among the American people. These "stranded students" settled mostly in seven metropolitan areas—San Francisco, Oakland, Los Angeles, Chicago, Boston, Manhattan and Brooklyn, and Seattle. They were attracted to these areas not only by the employment opportunities but also because of the presence of strong Chinese communities in each city. For instance, the Chinese population in the Chicago metropolitan area had increased about 50 percent between 1940 and 1950. These new professionals in America's Chinese community represented the first wave of student-immigrants who were to exhibit characteristics of cultural pluralism, that is, they generally maintained their Chinese heritage while selectively adopting the dominant culture. They were fluent in English but spoke Chinese at home. They worked for and with whites but regularly socialized with other Chinese. They were more interested in public affairs than their sojourner predecessors, yet few became members of non-Chinese voluntary organizations. Although a significant number of this group regularly attended church, their exogamy rates remained very low. Their slower cultural assimilation and acquisition of American values brought about a different experience from that of the American-born Chinese.

2. Chinese Cultural and Educational Activities

As the student-immigrants emphasized the persistence of ethnic cultural traits, some of them became part-time editors of Chinatown newspapers. Others accepted teaching jobs in Chinese-language schools. Such schools in America dated back to 1908, when the Qing

government sent an official, Liang Qinggui, to promote cultural activities in the North American Chinese community. Near the entrance of New York's Chinatown, the Chinese built their first such
center, naming it the Chinese Public School. Under the auspices of
the Chinese Consolidated Benevolent Association, this school grew
from 20 students to more than 100 by 1933. In 1940 there were about
200 Chinese youngsters attending the school in late afternoons, after
their regular grade schools were closed. Each student paid only $3 a
month, which was insufficient to support the institution. The association subsidized the effort and eventually came to own and maintain
the property. After World War II the school board was reorganized
and the institution expanded rapidly to accommodate six elementary
and two high-school classes.

During the 1950s and 1960s, the Chinese population in New York
grew rapidly. So did the student body in the Chinese Public School,
reaching the 1,000 mark in 1964, and by 1975 total enrollment was
3,250 during the regular session and 500 more for summer classes. In
the mid-1980s, this oldest Chinese-language school in America was financially stable, had a faculty and staff of over 130 persons, and was by
far the largest and most successful such institution in North America.
Since World War II four more Chinese-language schools have been
founded, one subsidized by private funds and three others supported
by church organizations.[13] Students in these schools were taught Chinese history, Chinese language, geography, abacus, civics, and intro-
ductory courses in the sciences and mathematics. After their regular
classes in American schools, they attended the Chinese sessions from
4:00 to 7:00 P.M. Mondays through Fridays and from 9:00 to 12:00
A.M. on Saturdays.

The Chinese-language school in San Francisco was started in 1909
and for several years the president of the Six Companies also served as
president of the school. Known as the San Francisco Chinese Public
School, the institution accepted its first female students in 1920. In the
1930s and 1940s enrollment stayed between 300 and 400 pupils, then
grew to a peak figure of 560 in 1956. Chinese-language education in
San Francisco, however, was not so centrally structured as that in New
York. Several small schools, some of them no more than tutorial
classes, were set up by different clan/regional associations and religious groups. In 1968 the San Francisco Chinese Public School registered only 482 students.[14] Ironically, as bilingual education and
affirmative-action policies were introduced into American public
schools in the 1970s, fewer and fewer Chinatown children attended
Chinese language classes.

Almost all Chinese communities of any size in America founded
Chinese-language schools in the early twentieth century. In Oakland,

at least ten tutorial-type Chinese language programs have been founded since 1908, but most of them were short-lived. Two years after World War II ended, the Oakland Chinese began construction of the Chinese Community Center. Its completion in 1953 was the source of great pride in the community; by 1960 the center housed a Chinese school with 600 students. A variety of Chinese cultural and language schools could also be found in practically every Chinese community in California, some of them dating back to the first decade of the century. For example, such schools were founded in Sacramento in 1908; Fresno, 1910; Stockton, 1912; San Diego, 1914; Los Angeles, six such schools, with the earliest one founded in 1916; Watsonville, 1917; Vallejo, 1921; San Jose, 1922; Isleton, 1932; Salinas, 1925; Marysville, 1932; and Palo Alto, 1961.[15] Outside of California, Hawaiian Chinese enrolled their children in a number of Chinese-language schools when the reform party was most active there at the turn of the century. By 1934 a total of 20 Chinese-language schools with 3,372 students operated in the Territory of Hawaii. Approximately 40 percent of the Chinese schoolchildren in Hawaii were thus studying some form of Chinese history, culture, and language.[16] Chinese-language and arts schools were also established in Chicago in 1910 (three more were founded in 1928, 1932 and 1959); Boston, 1916; Phoenix, 1919; Detroit, 1920; San Antonio, 1922; Cleveland, 1928; Pittsburgh, 1919; Washington, 1930; New Orleans, 1931; Minneapolis, 1932; Philadelphia, 1932; El Paso, 1939; Tucson, 1957; St. Louis, 1957; and Miami, 1960.

Many Chinese communities grew and expanded in the years after World War II, but other Chinatowns were devastated by postwar population shifts and Americanization of the Chinese. In the decade from 1940 to 1950, twelve Chinatowns disappeared. Many others lost substantial population and could no longer sustain institutions for the study of Chinese culture.[17] Typical was the fate of the Chinese school in Arkansas. Before the United States entered World War II, the approximately 400 Chinese in Arkansas set up a Chinese-language school at McGehee, about 45 miles south of Pine Bluff on Highway 65. By early 1940 the school's steering committee had gathered donations to supply the necessary books, chairs, desks, teaching aids, and even lunch money. Mrs. Yaoming Wu, who had recently emigrated from China, was appointed headmistress of the school and three volunteer teachers from Arkansas later joined the faculty. The students, who at once numbered forty-five, traveled from 30 to 150 miles every Sunday to attend Chinese classes. Commuting such long distances, however, created serious problems. After Pearl Harbor, gasoline rationing made it very difficult to continue the trip every week. Furthermore, when the United States declared war on Japan, several of the 45 students enlisted in the U.S. armed forces. The McGehee Chinese school of Arkansas was forced to close permanently after operating for less than two years.[18]

A similar institution was established in Cleveland, Mississippi. Founded in 1943, the school's enrollment for several years remained very low, sometimes including as few as eight pupils. But the isolated Chinese living in the Delta tried hard to keep their school open. The school issue was particularly pressing to the Chinese in the South because they suffered from racial discrimination which had been upheld in the U.S. Supreme Court case of *Gung Lum vs. Rice* in 1927. Gung Lum was an affluent Christian merchant in Rosedale, Mississippi. His daughter, Martha, was American-born but when she attempted to enroll in the white high school in October, 1924, she was refused admittance. Her father filed a writ of mandamus on her behalf, demanding that trustees of the school board and the State Superintendent of Education cease discrimination against Martha and admit her to the high school. Mississippi officials ordered Martha to attend a Negro high school that was not in her district.

The state court ruled that the school board had acted lawfully since Mississippi statutes required a separation of students into whites and colored. The United States Supreme Court, in a unanimous opinion, held that the Mississippi state law did not violate any constitutional guarantee, even though Gung Lum was a taxpayer and his daughter an American citizen; the separation of races in schools was within the discretion of the state and did not conflict with the Fourteenth Amendment. In keeping with the precedent established in *Plessy vs. Ferguson* in 1896, the court further stated that a state might separate the races in public and private educational institutions provided that the races were accorded equal facilities.[19] Of course, the role of "separate but equal facilities" was only a legal fiction. The nine justices who sat on the bench knew that wherever segregation was practiced, the white students were afforded facilities far superior to those provided for the nonwhite students. Thousands of Chinese families across the country shared with Gung Lum the bitterness of flagrant discrimination, and many sent their children to China for advanced education. The Lum family soon left Mississippi so that Martha could attend a nonsegregated school in Elaine, Arkansas.

Mississippi was not the only state that excluded Chinese children from white schools. As late as 1926 the state of California enforced a code which read: "When separate schools are established, Chinese or Mongolian children must not be admitted into any other school."[20] Although admittance of Chinese students into white schools gained wide acceptance during and after World War II, segregated schools were not outlawed until 1954. Confronted by such educational discrimination, the Chinese community became obsessed with education, and Chinese families emphasized the need for their children to become high achievers.

Chinese parents invested a great deal of parental pride and expectation in their children. Under parental control and subtle pressure to excel, most Chinese youngsters did well as students. Many of them won academic honors; they received advanced degrees far in excess of their proportion of the population. Families often pooled their resources to send the eldest son to college, believing in the Chinese tradition that to be well educated brought status and prestige not only to the Chinese boy but to the whole family or clan. This strong motivation contributed to the success of Chinese-language schools. A generation of young Chinese students tried to complete their assignments in the public schools and spent the afternoons, Saturdays, Sundays, and their summers studying Chinese culture and language. Consequently, many Chinese youths in the larger centers were able to speak and write Chinese.

Objections were raised by assimilationists against such schools as retarding the process of acculturation. But cultural pluralists argued that, inasmuch as Chinese courses were given in U.S. colleges and universities to prepare American intellectuals and businessmen for the Asian field, the Chinese children in America who had the opportunity to learn Chinese culture would be particularly equipped for such careers. Such courses were comparable to those of other ethnic groups, including Germans and Jews, in the study of their languages and cultures. Moreover, Chinese bilingual and bicultural education never expected or received support from public funds. While the debate over the values of cultural pluralism versus assimilation will surely continue, there seems little doubt that a knowledge of Chinese language and culture has greatly enriched Chinese Americans.

3. Chinese Language Newspapers in America

One indication that a substantial bilingual Chinese population persisted in America was the fact that by the end of World War II there were 14 Chinese dailies among the 95 foreign-language newspapers in the United States.[21] Some of these papers were founded at the turn of the century by competing political groups; others came into existence during or after World War II. Chinese-language newspapers in America date back to 1854 when the *Golden Hills News* (Kim Shan Jit San Luk) first appeared in San Francisco. In the mid-nineteenth century, the Chinese also published several other papers, most notably the San Francisco *Oriental,* the Sacramento *Chinese Daily News,* New York's *Chinese Reform News,* and San Francisco's *Chinese Free Press,* the last an organ of the secret society Chee Kung Tong. None of these, however, survived for a long period. They were plagued by poor management, limited circulation, and the declining Chinese population that resulted from exclusion.

A few papers did survive, however, and exerted significant influence on the Chinese American community.[22] One of them was the *Chinese World* of San Francisco, the first bilingual daily printed in both Chinese and English. Founded in 1891, the *Chinese World* served for several years as the organ of Kang Youwei's Reform Party, which was renamed the Constitutionalist Party in 1906. Known for its political conservatism and cultural traditionalism, the paper enjoyed patronage and support from the landlord class and many warlords in China and the upper echelons of Chinese society in America. But between 1927 and 1945, as the Kuomintang emerged to become the dominant power in China as well as in America's Chinatowns, the Constitutionalist Party and the *Chinese World* declined in influence. When Dai Ming Lee, a leader of the Constitutionalist Party and a follower of the Kang-Liang Reform Movement, became the paper's editor-in-chief in 1945, he unleashed a series of slanderous and vitriolic attacks on the Kuomintang.

Shortly after establishment of the People's Republic of China, Lee made contact with Chairman Mao Zedong of the Chinese Communist Party. On at least one occasion, pro-Kuomintang elements disrupted Lee's office and threatened to kill him if his paper continued to smear the character of Chiang Kai-shek. The *Chinese World,* despite such harassment, seized the new political tension in China as an opportunity to regain influence in America's Chinatowns. In a short span, its subscription increased to more than 4,000 and for several years it had the largest circulation of any Chinese-language daily in the United States. Under Lee's direction, the *Chinese World* inaugurated an English-language section and launched a New York edition in 1957, but it was not a success. In the 1950s, the paper continued to criticize the Kuomintang government on Taiwan but also came to oppose the Chinese Communists on the mainland. Finally, with increasing competition from a growing number of Chinese language newspapers, its popularity began to dwindle in the 1960s. Financial difficulties and internal dissension, which plagued the paper after Lee's death in 1961, finally caused its demise in 1969.[23]

A second significant Chinese newspaper was the *Chung Sai Yat Po* (China-West Daily) which printed its first issue February 16, 1900, in San Francisco. Its founder, Dr. Ng Poon-chew, was an eminent Christian scholar and an active community leader. During the early years of the paper's existence, Ng enlisted the invaluable assistance of John Fryer, a pioneer Sinologist and University of California professor. Because of its Christian influence, the publication consistently called for reform and progressivism in the Chinese community. *Chung Sai Yat Po* loudly denounced such Chinese customs as polygamy, opium-smoking, queue-wearing, foot-binding, and other practices. It persistently emphasized education, modernization, and integration with the larger white society. Politically, the paper tried to remain neutral, although it once applauded Kang Youwei's reform program and even supported Sun Yat-sen's revolution and republicanism. When Dr. Ng died in 1931, his heir took over management of the paper and was able to remain a major public opinion maker in the Chinese American community throughout the 1930s and 1940s. With the coming of World War II, the paper lined up squarely behind the war effort of the Allies. Its editorials constantly urged the Chinese to enlist in the U.S. armed forces and to purchase war bonds. In 1949 the paper was sold to a group of businessmen who supported the People's Republic. When the Korean War broke out in the summer of 1950, many readers were frightened by the paper's pro-Peking editorials, and circulation declined. Debts slowly piled up, and the paper was forced to declare bankruptcy on January 1, 1951.[24]

The oldest surviving Chinese newspaper in America is the *Young China Morning Paper,* founded in San Francisco by Sun Yat-sen's partisans in 1910. As it evolved into a major commercial press, its relationship with the Kuomintang followed an unsteady course. After Sun Yat-sen was driven out of China in 1914, the paper temporarily suspended publication, because of the loss of financial support from wealthy Chinese backers. In the late 1920s the Kuomintang in China was divided into a left-wing faction represented by Wang Jingwei and a right-wing faction dominated by Chiang Kai-shek. A similarly faction-ridden leadership also plagued the *Young China* until 1927 when Chiang's supporters finally gained control of the paper. During the war against Japan, *Young China* enjoyed a tremendous popularity among the Chinese in America because it not only presented the official stance of the Nationalist government, which was an ally of the U.S. government, but it also became a vehicle whereby Chinese in the United States could express their nationalism and patriotism. The collapse of the Nationalist government in 1949, however, seriously hampered the paper, and for the next decade it was plagued by low circulation and internal discord. In 1964 the beleaguered paper was bought by a real-estate tycoon, Feng Yuming, but he was unable to reverse its decline. For a while it appeared that *Young China* was doomed to follow the fate of its competitors, but on August 1, 1970, the Kuomintang government on Taiwan paid $150,000 to purchase it.[25] Once again, *Young China* became the partisan organ of the Nationalist government in America.

While *Young China* represented the right wing of the Chinese news media in America, New York's *China Daily News* became the organ of the left. Published first in the spring of 1940, the paper experienced severe financial and managerial problems at its beginning. But within a decade it had grown and expanded into a respectable daily in the Chinese community. When the Communists seized power in China in 1949 the paper quickly threw in its lot with the new socialist government. The *China Daily News*, though not Communist-controlled, slanted its editorials and news reports in favor of Mao's regime. It frequently urged the Chinese in America to give moral as well as material support to the People's Republic at a time when the new China was perceived by the United States government as an extension of Soviet power. Consequently, the paper became a thorn in the side of the Kuomintang establishment and, beginning in January, 1951, it drew a barrage of attacks from such pro-Kuomintang papers as the *Chinese Journal* and the *Chinese Nationalist Daily*. The *China Daily News* was labeled the "Russian Daily News," "anti-American," and "pro-Communist."[26]

The *China Daily News* soon became a target for the McCarthyites during the anti-Communist hysteria of the 1950s. Several times during the months of September and October, 1951, U.S. Treasury Department officials visited the offices of the *China Daily News* and inspected the books and records of the paper. Early in March, 1952, Eugene Moy, editor and president of the paper, and a number of responsible staff members were summoned to appear before the grand jury of the Southern District of New York on a charge of alleged violation of the Trading with the Enemy Act of December 17, 1950. After about six weeks of investigation and testimony, the grand jury handed down an indictment containing 53 charges, ranging from illegally publishing advertisements for Communist banks and reporting false news to blackmailing Chinese Americans into sending millions of dollars to mainland China. Eugene Moy publicly declared that the indictment was the climax of a relentless drive by the combined forces of the Kuomintang clique, the China lobby, and certain forces in the United States government. Moy also proclaimed that his paper was the only Chinese-language newspaper in the United States that had consistently supported peaceful solutions to all outstanding problems in the Far East.[27]

Despite Moy's impassioned testimony, he and his paper were found guilty by a New York federal court. Almost immediately after the verdict was read, his supporters formed a "Committee to Support the *China Daily News*" and began to receive contributions and pledges of support from both Chinese and American sympathizers. The committee later put forth a tremendous effort to raise funds to defray the costs of an appeal. The drama ended when the United States Supreme Court upheld the lower court decision, sentencing Moy to a one-year jail term and fining the paper $25,000. Nevertheless, the *China Daily News* survived under the most difficult circumstances, although it was published only irregularly at times. Its publication continued to be closely scrutinized by the United States government until 1972 when President Richard M. Nixon visited Peking. Since that historic visit, the political atmosphere has drastically changed and the *China Daily News* circulation has grown dramatically in recent years.[28]

In addition to these major papers, a number of Chinese dailies and weeklies with smaller circulation were published in such cities as San Francisco, Seattle, New York, Chicago, and Los Angeles. They represented different socioeconomic interests and reflected different shades of political opinions, each having its own network of support. Many of them, unfortunately, could not survive because of meager subscriptions and long-term financial losses, and were forced to close down or merge with a major paper. The 1950s saw a trend toward the merging of minor papers with bigger papers. By the end of 1960 the number of Chinese-language newspapers had been reduced to 11, out of some 65 foreign-language dailies still publishing in the United States.

In the 1960s and 1970s, as an increasing number of new immigrants arrived from Taiwan and Hong Kong, Chinese readership in America witnessed quantitative and qualitative changes. The number of Chinese daily newspapers in New York, for example, had increased to six by 1972: *The Chinese Journal*, the *United Journal*, *The China Tribune*, *The China Times*, *Sing Tao Jih Pao*, and the *China Post*. The Chinese in several major cities also published a number of weeklies, biweeklies, monthlies, and periodicals. With a highly educated population, Chinese readers became more demanding and more sophisticated; indeed, many of them preferred daily newspapers published in the Far East. In recent years the *Central Daily* of Taiwan and the *Ming Bao* of Hong Kong have enjoyed popularity among the Chinese in America. And beginning in the mid-1970s the Chinese in metropolitan areas could also enjoy Chinese-language radio and television programs produced in Taiwan and Hong Kong.

4. Internal Strife in Post–World War II Chinese-American Communities

The diversity of Chinese-language newspapers clearly indicated that the Chinese-American community was as politically fragmented during the post–World War II era as it was at the turn of the century when the reformist Kang Youwei and the revolutionary Sun Yat-sen were wooing Chinese support. Momentous political changes in China necessarily had powerful repercussions in America. On the eve of the Kuomintang defeat, the approximately 77,500 Chinese in America (this figure does not include Hawaiian Chinese) were faced with very difficult decisions about their loyalties. Some of them, represented mainly by the conservative Six Companies, shared traditional values taught through generations, and identified themselves with the Kuomintang government in Taiwan. Others, alienated by Kuomintang politics and heartened by dreams of a powerful China under socialist government, voiced support for the Communists. But during the Cold War era, when Washington assumed Communist China to be a Soviet subsidiary and therefore a new instrument in the monolithic Communist plan of world conquest, all supporters and sympathizers of the Peking regime were subject to attacks and harassment from the Kuomintang and United States authorities. Consequently, pro-Communist groups served only as a pale shadow in the Chinese community, with Chinatowns totally dominated by the Kuomintang in the 1950s and 1960s.

Of the "old left" organizations in America's Chinatowns, the New York Chinese Hand Laundry Alliance was, at one time, a strong voice. Founded in 1933, it was formed to improve working conditions for the Chinese laundry workers. During the Korean War, however, it was suspected by the Six Companies of supporting Mao's revolution. Many of the alliance's frightened members were caught in a quandary, and dropped out of the organization.[29] Scarcely less known was the Chinese Workers' Mutual Aid Association (CWMAA), founded in San Francisco in 1937. On October 9, 1949, when CWMAA was holding its 12th anniversary meeting in San Francisco Chinatown, a scuffle broke out between Kuomintang partisans and pro-Mao elements. The event drew the attention of the NBC network, and the left-wing Chinese organization was made known for the first time to the American public. As a result, cautious Chinese avoided any connection, even social, with the organization. Its membership dwindled sharply, and in 1954 it was forced to dissolve.[30]

Other anti-Kuomintang groups included the Chinese Youth League on the West Coast and the Overseas Chinese League for Peace and Democracy on the East Coast. The former, after World War II, changed its name to the Chinese American Democratic Youth League of San Francisco, locally known as Min Qing. It sponsored a biweekly publication in Chinese, presented periodic cultural programs in the Bay Area, and promoted romanization of Chinese-language characters. According to the late historian Liu Boji, the FBI, beginning in 1956, started a technical surveillance of the Min

Qing, covertly taking pictures of every person who came to the youth league's office, then located on Stockton Street.[31] As in the case of CWMAA, the league was disbanded in 1959, but some of its members persevered and continued their antiestablishment activities. The Overseas Chinese League for Peace and Democracy was founded by General Feng Yuxiang. During the Resistance War he had been allied with Chiang Kai-shek. They made a political odd couple and were ridiculed for that at the time. The unpredictable Feng was bitter about Chiang's treatment of him, so when Feng visited America in 1946 and 1947 he organized one of his several anti-Chiang alliances. Membership never exceeded 200, even though it set up branches in Washington, D.C., Minnesota, and San Francisco.[32] All these dissident voices, however, had little impact on Chinese community attitudes as a whole or individual behavior.

It is clear that a substantial number of Chinese in America regarded with pride the growing power of their homeland, although they had no direct contact with Peking. Most Chinese in the United States were reluctant to appear a disloyal ethnic minority in American society, remembering quite well what had happened to the Japanese in America during World War II. Chiang's supporters succeeded in creating a climate in America that equated criticism of Chiang with treason against the United States. Such fears were magnified when Eisenhower, in his first State of the Union message, disavowed Truman's policy to neutralize the Taiwan Straits and thereby opened the way for Chiang Kai-shek to try to reconquer mainland China. Eisenhower's hard line toward Communist China culminated in 1955, when the United States and the Nationalist government on Taiwan signed a mutual security pact. Domestically, the Internal Security Act of 1950 and the Communist Control Act of 1954 greatly broadened the powers of the U.S. Attorney General to suppress Communist activities and Communist-front groups within the United States. Between 1951 and 1957, the House Committee on Un-American Activities held numerous hearings in major U.S. cities and subpoenaed hundreds of witnesses, including a number of Chinese, to testify in open and closed sessions. These international developments, and domestic pressures in the 1950s, froze most Chinese in America into a posture of grim nonrecognition of the People's Republic.

The most important organizational expression of this mood was the formation of the Anti-Communist Committee for Free China in New York in June, 1951. Affiliated with the Chinese Benevolent Association of New York, this anti-Communist group had broad support from 60 Chinese civic, business, cultural, and social organizations. It proposed to follow the ethical teachings of Confucius and to uphold the principles of American democracy. The Committee opposed communism on the grounds that it undermined Chinese civilization, destroyed the family system, uprooted Chinese culture, and was the international enemy of the United States. Charging that Chinese Communist leaders were the puppets of Stalin, the organization pledged its unequivocal loyalty to the United States.[33] The Anti-Communist Committee for Free China became the means for many Chinese to prove their patriotism and loyalty to their adopted country.

Encouraged by the Koumintang and the Chinese Consolidated Benevolent Association, a variety of anti-Communist organizations appeared in the 1950s in Chinatowns from Portland to Tucson and from Oakland to Houston. As the Korean War drew to a close, pro-Kuomintang elements stepped up their anti-Communist activities. They were encouraged by the fact that over 14,000 Chinese Communist prisoners of war in Korea chose not to return to mainland China but requested expatriation to Taiwan. Five of these prisoners of war addressed the representatives of some 79 Chinese community organizations on September 20, 1954, when the All-American Overseas Chinese Anti-Communist League held its first meeting in New York City.[34] The purposes of the Anti-Communist League, as stated in its charter, were to "let the American people know that the Chinese are not Communists, and to rally all overseas Chinese people against Communism and to the support of the Republic of China."[35] The organization was founded as a lobbying and propaganda agency. It sponsored an annual memorial service for Chinese killed by the communists on the mainland, lobbied American Congressmen against recognition of the People's Republic, and tried to reassure the American public that Chinatowns supported Chiang Kai-shek's government. But, more important, these organizations aimed at easing official suspicions of un-American activities.

In the long run, perhaps the most important accomplishment of the Chinese anti-Communist organizations was that they successfully headed off mass deportation of Chinese who had entered this country illegally. The danger of mass prosecution of the Chinese arose in 1955 when the United States Consul in Hong Kong, Everett F. Drumwright, charged that the People's Republic had used American passports as a means of moving subversive agents and spies into the United States. Immediately, federal authorities began investigating thousands of Chinese residents who allegedly had used false naturalization papers and birth certificates to obtain U.S. passports. A number of the Chinese in America were successfully prosecuted for such fraud. For example, a New York Chinese named Eng Wing-on, who was a part-time interpreter for the Immigration and Naturalization Service, was charged in 1956 on five counts of conspiracy and passport fraud in connection with five cases of false passport applications made in Hong Kong.[36] Other Chinese brokers allegedly involved in the buying and selling of fictitious passports were also prosecuted, and some of them were scheduled for deportation.

When such prosecutions and deportations were publicized, fears permeated Chinatowns. At this juncture, the leadership of the Six Companies called a national emergency meeting. It resulted in the formation of a new organization named the National Chinese Welfare Council which was able to make a "deal" with the federal authorities. The deal was called "Confession Program." Chinese residents who had gained entry into America by fraudulent means were encouraged to come forward and confess their guilt to the U.S. immigration authorities. If the authorities were convinced that no subversion was involved, the Chinese immigrants were given legal status. This lengthy and fearful confession program served not only to rectify many long-standing immigration irregularities but it also successfully screened out a group of disaffected leftists who had pronounced affinities for Red China. A few Communist sympathizers, including Chen Tienmin, who held a doctorate in political science from the University of California at Berkeley, were rounded up, denaturalized, and eventually deported. Ninety-nine percent of the illegal Chinese aliens, however, were allowed to stay in America. A San Francisco authoritative source estimated that the Immigration and Naturalization Service Office in San Francisco alone processed and accepted more than 10,000 such confessions.[37]

5. New Controversies over the Six Companies

As the "Confession Program" effectively stifled left-wing forces and caused Chinese Americans to sever ties with mainland China, it drove the conservative Kuomintang elite and Chinatowns' anachronistic Six Companies together. With the emergence of a new Chinese middle class, the once powerful Six Companies could no longer keep Chinatowns isolated and beholden to their dictates during the late 1940s and early 1950s. But anti-Communism was the overriding issue of the 1950s, so the declining Six Companies allied itself with the Kuomintang government to revitalize its power bases in Chinatowns. It supported overseas Chinese attachment to Nationalist China, encouraging this by promoting Chinese language and cultural traditions. Its close link with Taiwan enhanced its power and increased its prestige with many Chinese residents who were culturally loyal to a traditionalist Chinese society. Several Six Companies leaders, such as the powerful Wong Yen Doon of San Francisco, were made National Policy Advisors to Chiang Kai-shek and were appointed members of the legislative branch of the Nationalist government.[38] These circumstances made it possible for the Six Companies to restore its historical role as the "official representatives association of Chinese in America," a role it had played well in the late 1800s.

The nineteenth-century Six Companies had shielded Chinese laborers from racism, argued in the courts against legislative discriminations, and provided social services for the Chinese community. The post–World War II Six Companies opposed school busing, fought off an AFL-CIO effort to unionize Chinatown restaurant workers and seamstresses, and rebuffed the federal antipoverty program in Chinatowns. Unfortunately, times had changed, but the mentality of the Six Companies leadership had not changed fast enough to face new problems and new challenges. For example, in its early years the Six Companies provided services for the poor, the aged, and the newly arrived immigrants; these services were no longer needed by third- and fourth-generation Chinese Americans. When services were needed, they were provided by government agencies and grassroots organizations. In the nineteenth century, when most Chinese could not vote, the Six Companies often played the role of power broker between the Chinese community and the white authorities in city hall. In more recent years, the Chinese have become more politically conscious and have shown their understanding of voting power. In San Francisco about 7,000 Chinese names were on the voting rolls in 1959, but in 1969 the number had increased to 14,000. Two years later the figure was 17,000 and by the presidential election of 1972, approximately 20,000 Chinese cast votes. Election returns in the San Francisco Chinatown have illustrated that the Chinese did not automatically vote for candidates backed by the Six Companies.[39]

The Six Companies remained a controversial organization in the 1960s and 1970s, as it had been in the nineteenth century. Liberal and progressive elements among Chinese Americans believed that the Six Companies was a stumbling block to reform in Chinese communities because its leadership was too old and too mercantile-oriented. This view was highlighted by a series of articles in the *San Francisco Examiner* in mid-August of 1967, criticizing the deteriorating economic and social conditions of San Francisco's Chinatown. The paper described the Chinese quarters as a feudal enclave for immigrants where suspicion, fear, and hostility reigned; a ghetto where men, women, and children worked for pittances and lived in the deepest deprivation, beset by poverty, gambling, oppression, disease, crime, and fear; the articles charged that Chinatown had changed little since the late nineteenth century. The articles were written by Mrs. Jane E. Conant, a staff member of the paper. She documented a number of specific cases of deprivation. For example, she found children less than a year old who had already contracted tuberculosis and babies with all their primary teeth rotted away from poor nutrition. Many families at poverty level lived in tenements and worked for low pay, where properties were owned by wealthy merchants and the Six Companies.[40] The paper also deplored the poor working conditions in the sweatshops, where the garment workers' union claimed that the workers were underpaid and overworked in violation of state and federal laws. Chinese seamstresses were paid 55 cents an hour, far below the minimum wage, and they dared not speak out for fear of losing their jobs. Furthermore, the sweatshops, which were generally located in basements, were universally dirty, poorly lighted and ventilated, and generally unsanitary. Chinatown of the 1960s, according to the *Examiner*, was a sad and dangerous ghetto where new "coolie" laborers from Hong Kong were being exploited by Chinese bosses.[41]

A few weeks after these damaging articles were printed, the Six Companies called a press conference. It dismissed the articles as "a blanket indictment of the entire segment of the Chinese people of San Francisco," and, at the same time, offered evidence to refute the charges and clarify misunderstandings.[42] The rebuttal was given by Dr. Kalfred Dip Lum, a retired professor of political science and a highly respected Chinatown figure. In his lengthy "Refutation of Misunderstanding about San Francisco Chinatown," Lum called the *Examiner's* articles "slanderous and erroneous" and accused Mrs. Conant of seeing "one side of the scene" and hearing "one side of the story." Lum pointed out that the San Francisco Chinatown had, in fact, made progress in the past generation and had become a mecca of tourism, with thousands pouring in every day for sightseeing. He attributed development and progress of Chinatown to the unselfish efforts, charitable spirit, and generous contributions of the older leaders who were schooled in the traditional Chinese morals, ethics, and virtues. As to the charges about low wages and long working hours, Lum dismissed them as "a typical characteristic of the Chinese people living in Chinatown because the situation is unique and family-like."[43]

The contradictory assessments of a liberal American newspaper reporter and an old traditionalist Chinese scholar once again highlighted the significant cultural barrier between East and West. It is true that cultural misunderstandings persist. Recently, for example, the Los Angeles health authorities fined Irwin Lai, the owner of a Chinese restaurant serving Peking Duck, for leaving raw ducks at room temperature. The authorities claimed that the raw duck must be refrigerated. The Chinese owner insisted that if the duck were refrigerated it would lose its delicacy and taste and would become American duck.[44] In a sense, the same cultural clash contributed to the conflicting perceptions of San Francisco Chinatown. Certainly, when new immigrants arrived from Hong Kong they preferred to stay closer to their relatives and friends who could provide moral as well as material support. Thus, new immigrants continued to choose California, New York, and Hawaii as their residential areas. Of the total number of Chinese in America in 1960, California had about 40 percent, New York and Hawaii each had 16 percent, and the other 28 percent was spread over the remaining 47 states. Moreover, the new arrivals tended to congregate in only a few American cities, notably San Francisco-Oakland, where Chinese population rose from 21,000 in 1940 to more than 50,000 in 1960, and New York, which saw its Chinese population increase from 12,753 in 1940 to 36,500 in 1960.[45] It was this influx of newcomers crowded into America's Chinatowns that intensified existing social, economic, health, and educational problems and shocked many outside observers.

The coming of new, unskilled immigrants was made possible by two Congressional acts. The Immigration and Nationality Law, known also as the McCarran-Walter Act of 1952, provided for family reunification, set national origin quotas, and permitted unrestricted numerical immigration from Western Hemisphere countries. It also removed the inequality against Chinese women, who were previously not entitled to the same privileges under nonquota status as Chinese men. This resulted in a more balanced ratio between Chinese males and females in the United States, as shown in Table 6 and Table 7. The Refugee Relief Act of 1953, which was amended and expired at the end of 1956, apportioned 2,000 for Chinese out of a total of 205,000 nonquota immigrants. In spite of the fact that both these acts were still discriminatory against the Chinese, between the enactment of the McCarran-Walter Act on December 24, 1952, and the end of 1960, a total of 27,502 Chinese immigrants were admitted to the United States. The vast majority of them chose to settle in or near ten metropolitan areas, where relatives and friends could find jobs and provide shelters for them. Tables 6 and 7 give population figures by city in 1960 and 1970 respectively.[46]

6. Art and Literature

Steady urbanization of the Chinese population was accompanied by an inevitable process of acculturation. Cultural vibrations ran through novels, poetry, films, music, and theater in the 1960s and 1970s. But adaptation in the fields of art and literature from characteristically Chinese to that of Chinese American was as slow and painful as on the social and religious fronts. In the late nineteenth and early twentieth centuries, Chinatown literature and art were pre-

TABLE 6

**Chinese Population in Major U.S.
Metropolitan Areas, 1960**

Name	Total	Percent of Total U.S. Chinese Population	Male	Female	Male/Female Ratio
San Francisco-Oakland	53,250	22.4%	29,928	23,322	128
Honolulu	38,875	15.5%	19,723	19,152	103
New York	36,503	15.4%	22,509	13,994	161
Los Angeles-Long Beach	19,402	8.2%	10,902	8,500	128
Sacramento	6,457	2.7%	3,540	2,917	121
Chicago	5,866	2.5%	3,552	2,314	154
Boston	5,564	2.3%	3,463	2,101	165
Seattle-Everett	4,611	1.9%	2,686	1,925	140
Washington D.C. & vicinity	3,925	1.7%	2,361	1,564	151
Philadelphia & vicinity	2,544	1.1%	1,527	1,017	150
Total	176,997	73.8%			
Total Chinese Population in U.S.A.	237,292	100.0%			

dominantly China-oriented, and artists looked to the old country for inspiration. Creative works before World War II, written almost exclusively in Chinese language, were rare and rather unsophisticated. Chinese-language newspapers and periodicals, such as the *Chung Sai Yat Po* (1900–1950) and the *Chinese Youth Magazine* (1917–1924), featured poetry, fiction, satire, humor, and writings in history and biography. In the 1880s and 1900s, Chinese literary societies in San Francisco, New York, and Chicago frequently sponsored verse contests and poetic couplet competitions. The tones and themes of these literary activities were as Chinese as their counterparts in China. Even as late as the 1940s a number of poets, such as Wenquan (Hot Springs), still tried to make direct connections between Chinatown literature and Chinese Maoist literature. But because of McCarthyism this self-styled "ethnic literary movement" died out in the 1950s.[47] However, two New York Chinese-language literary journals, the *Zhong-Mei zhoubao* (China-U.S. Weekly, 1942–1970) and the *Dahua xunkan* (Great China Trimonthly, 1942–1964), continued to attract readership. The former published 1,600 issues; the latter, 917.[48]

The rise of an acculturated generation ultimately entailed the development of art and literature in a Chinese-American context. Be-

TABLE 7

**Chinese Population in Major U.S.
Metropolitan Areas, 1970**

Name	Total	Percent of Total U.S. Chinese Population	Male	Female	Male/Female Ratio
San Francisco-Oakland	88,402	20.3%	45,393	43,009	106
New York	77,099	17.7%	41,486	35,613	116
Honolulu	48,897	11.2%	24,533	24,364	101
Los Angeles-Long Beach	41,500	9.5%	21,840	19,660	111
Boston	12,157	2.8%	6,585	5,572	118
Chicago	11,995	2.8%	6,449	5,546	116
Sacramento	10,457	2.4%	5,307	5,150	103
Washington & vicinity	7,858	1.8%	3,910	3,948	99
Seattle-Everett	7,701	1.8%	4,030	3,671	110
Philadelphia & vicinity	4,832	1.1%	2,586	2,246	115
Total	310,898	71.5%			
Total Chinese Population in U.S.A.	435,062	100.0%			

yond the world of chop suey and laundry, Chinese Americans were becoming more educated, more English-speaking, reading more books and seeking ethnic self-definition in art and literature. American-born Chinese writers began to adopt themes from American life, attacking discriminations in the immigration laws and the evils of racism, and speaking in terms of alienation and anguish in contemporary American life. Creative works became a vehicle by which Chinese Americans could characterize their sensibilities as members of a minority group and could develop their ethnic consciousness. Over and over, they expressed the pain of cultural estrangement and *alexia,* or the deprivation of a natural language of identity. Short-lived English journals like the *Chinese Mind* (1940s in New York) and the *Chinese Students Monthly* (1936-1937 in Chicago) reflected the Chinese quest for identity.

Modern precursors of the Chinese-American identity crisis provided a number of interesting works dealing with the image of the Chinese in America and telling quite different stories about their experiences in the United States. Pardee Lowe wrote *Father and Glorious Descendant* in 1937, and in 1945 Jade Snow Wong wrote *Fifth Chinese Daughter,* an autobiography. Both served to improve the image of the

Chinese, an image that had been severely damaged by Earnest Bramah Smith's series on Kai Lung, by Earl Derr Digger's Charlie Chan
books with their cinematic offshoots, and by Sax E. Rohmer's Fu
Manchu novels. In 1957, C. Y. Lee's *Flower Drum Song,* which was later
made into a movie, clearly demonstrated the conflict between the
Chinese and American cultures. Relations between parents and children, between sexes, and emotional and social breakdowns in the
novel underscored a definite sign of gradual acculturation in Chinese-
American society. Diana Chang's *Frontier of Love* (1956) and Louis
Chu's *Eat A Bowl of Tea* (1961) dealt with the values and relationships of
Chinese men who struggled in the womanless and childless American
society in the 1940s. These stories also showed how the old bachelor
sojourners, in their effort to preserve Chinese culture, fought a losing
battle against acculturation.

These books, though faintly familiar to nonethnic Chinese, enjoyed
only limited readership. Major publishers continued to be skeptical of
the marketability of Chinese-American writing until 1976 when Maxine Hong Kingston's semiautobiographical novel, *The Woman Warrior,*
became a best seller and was selected as the best nonfiction work of
the year by the National Book Critics Circle. Actually, two years before the appearance of *The Woman Warrior,* the ideas of Chinese Americans were voiced in *Aiiieeeee! An Anthology of Asian American Writers,*
composed of selected works by Frank Chin, Paul Chin, Lawson Fusao
Inada, and Shawn Hsu Wong. In 1983 Frank Chin and his colleagues
published yet another volume, titled *The Big Aiiieeeee!* and further displaying in forceful terms the struggle of the Chinese for a new identity in American society. They spoke arrestingly to a new generation,
who found that they were neither characteristically Chinese nor
white, that the central issues of their lives were cultural alienation and
estrangement. But most striking was these authors' relentless attacks
on the destructive stereotype of Asian Americans: "The white stereotype of the Asian. . . . is the only stereotype completely devoid of
manhood. Our nobility is that of an efficient housewife. At our worst
we are contemptible because we are womanly, effeminate, devoid of
all the traditionally masculine qualities of originality, daring, physical
courage, and creativity."[49]

Maxine Hong Kingston shared the cultural alienation and estrangement with Frank Chin and other American-born Chinese. In
her later work, *China Men,* Mrs. Kingston attempted to reconcile traditional Chinese culture with the white culture in America, to come to
terms with the tensions between Chinese-American perceptions of
Chinese heritage and American realities, hence, to minimize the conflicts between American-born Chinese, who were nourished in American soil, and their immigrant forefathers, who had strong and deep
roots in China. Designed as an interlocking story with *China Men, The*

Woman Warrior tells the experience of a Chinese American woman who had to overcome sexual, racial, and national barriers. It vividly unfolds the painful process of acculturation of a minority people while explaining what being a Chinese American means.[50] Non-Chinese readers generally considered Kingston as a fair representative of the Chinese-American minority group, but her Chinese critics repeatedly complained that Kingston did little research and that her writing was myths fused with dreams and imagination. They assailed her for inaccurate translations and for changing details of Chinese legends in her books and, worst of all, compared her books to fortune cookies and chop suey, foods made exclusively for American consumption as the Chinese do not eat them at home. Kingston's reply was that she cared little about accuracy, explaining, "I just want to write stories, stories that fly away."[51] Clearly, the Chinese identity crisis surfaced as a result of Kingston's works, but the future direction of Chinese-American art and literature remained in a stage of uncertainty.

Nowhere was the rising Chinese ethnic awareness more evident than in the founding in San Francisco of the Chinese Historical Society of America (1963) and the Chinese Culture Foundation (1967), both being dedicated to promotion of Chinese-American culture. In the Chinese communities of Honolulu, Los Angeles, and New York, similar societies were subsequently established, and under their auspices, various historical projects attempted to recover history from deceit and distortion by telling it from the Chinese point of view. It should be pointed out that there was always a difference between the way Chinese viewed themselves and the way they were viewed in a racist society. Two films dealing with the Chinatown of New York illustrated that difference. One was made by the American Playhouse Series and called "Nightsong"; the other, issued by the Third World Newsreel, was called "From Spikes to Spindles." While the former generally ridiculed and degraded the Chinese-American community and presented a lurid view of Chinatown's gang wars and sweatshops, the latter condemned the exploitation of garment workers and emphasized the complexities of Chinese-American society. More important, instead of characterizing the Chinese Americans as passive, assimilated Uncle Toms, the Chinese-made film portrayed Chinese Americans as an awakening urban minority, fed up with economic and social ills, fighting fiercely for a better tomorrow.[52]

7. Chinese Christian Faith

In addition to art and literature, the changing religious affiliation of Chinese Americans can also serve to gauge their degree of acculturation. After the 1920s native Chinese religions, such as Buddhism and Taoism, lost ground even among the older Chinese. Confucianism was still taught because of programs of the Chinese-language schools. However, old Chinatown Buddhist and Taoist temples no longer served as places of worship because the new generation had not been taught the religious practices of their forebears. On the contrary, more and more Chinese became Christians. Churches and missions established and undertaken by and for the Chinese were found in almost all the large Chinese communities in the United States. Sunday schools were opened by Chinese Christians in many cities and towns. By 1922 the number of missions undertaken by or in conjunction with Chinese Christians totaled 41, encompassing a variety of denominations (see Table 8).[53]

TABLE 8

Chinese Christian Churches and Missions, 1920s

Denomination	Number
Baptist	5
Congregational	7
Cumberland Presbyterian	2
Episcopal Protestant	2
Independent Baptist	2
Independent Missions	4
Interdenominational	3
Methodist Episcopal	10
Presbyterian	5
United Christian Missions	1
Total	41

But Chinese religious acculturation, when compared with language adaptation, went much slower and has been far less impressive. In spite of the fact that Chinese Christian population had probably tripled by the end of World War II, the vast majority of the new arrivals still affiliated with traditional Chinese religions. An alternative adaptation, nonaffiliation, also steadily increased, particularly among the student immigrants. Nevertheless, the American-born Chinese, many growing up in non-Chinese neighborhoods and attending American public schools, were more ready to embrace Christianity, as evidenced by the increasing number of Chinese churches and Christian population. According to a 1955 survey conducted by the National Council of Churches, the Chinese had established and administered 62 Protestant churches in the mainland United States and 4 in Hawaii. Of these 66 churches, 47 were denominational, 5 were interdenominational, and the rest were categorized as independent. The denominational Chinese churches were led by the Southern Baptist Convention, which had 11, followed by American Baptist and Presbyterian, each with 7; Methodist, Congregational, Episcopal, Nazarene, and Lutheran completed the list. By 1968, approximately 20 percent of Chinese in San Francisco had become members of the Christian churches.

In terms of regional distribution, the majority of the Chinese churches were found in California and the major American cities where the Chinese population was located. San Francisco had 8; Los Angeles, 5; Sacramento and Oakland, 4; Fresno, 2; and San Diego, Stockton, Locke, San Mateo, and Watsonville each had one Chinese church. North of California there were 2 in Portland, founded respectively in 1874 and 1885; Seattle had the only Chinese Presbyterian Church. In the Rocky Mountain region, three Protestant churches were run exclusively by the Chinese, while eight others existed in the Southern states. There were only five such religious establishments in the Midwest but New York had six, one of which, the Chinese Lutheran Church, had the largest membership of any Chinese Protestant church in America. Finally, seven Chinese churches were scattered in the cities of Boston, Philadelphia, and Washington. Of the four Hawaiian Chinese churches, three were Congregational Christian and one Protestant Episcopal.[54]

In addition to these Protestant churches, Chinese Americans also established Roman Catholic congregations. By the 1950s there was a substantial number of Chinese Catholics in San Francisco as well as in other U.S. metropolitan areas, such as Chicago, Philadelphia, and New York. While the Paulist Fathers supervised the San Francisco Chinese parishioners, the Maryknoll Fathers, the order that also conducted foreign-mission work of the Catholic Church in Hong Kong and Taiwan, carried on various types of programs for Chinese Catholics in the rest of the United States. Catholic workers carried the apostolate to the Chinese immigrants in urban slums, and also offered English classes for adult pupils as well as schoolchildren. They also provided transportation for church members to attend mass and to look for jobs. Like their Protestant counterparts, Chinese Catholics in America soon took over their own church administration. By 1955 there were at least seven Chinese priests who supervised respectively All Souls Church, St. Agnes, St. Monica, and St. Thomas Churches in San Francisco. On September 5, 1959, when the Chinese Catholics of America convened their eighth national meeting in New York they claimed to have a membership of more than 2,000 people.[55]

The size, program, membership, and budget of these Chinese churches varied greatly, ranging from store-front efforts with small congregations to well-organized churches and diversified programs. In the case of Hawaiian Chinese churches, they were all self-supporting, had an average membership of nearly 600 and an average budget of more than $10,000. On the other hand, Chinese Protestant churches in the South attracted very small audiences and had to rely heavily or entirely upon denominational boards for support. Several churches, such as the one near the University of Chicago and three located in New York City, were composed mostly of Chinese students. Attendance at these Chinese churches was naturally small; Chinese Christians, under the circumstances, usually met weekly to worship or find fellowship. These types of churches tended to be more mobile and unstable, maintained limited programs, and were generally isolated from other religious bodies. On the other hand, affluent churches not only provided parsonages and large sanctuaries but also had kitchens, playgrounds, libraries, nurseries, and air-conditioned modern facilities. The same situation applied to the Chinese Catholic churches. Chicago's St. Theresa Chinese Catholic Mission not only had a large membership but operated a St. Theresa School on 23rd Street for Chinese children. On the other hand, Chinese Catholic missions in Washington, D.C., and Philadelphia were poorly equipped and their sanctuaries much too small to provide adequately for their parishioners.

Chinese churches were dedicated mainly to serving Chinese, and their programs were accordingly run by a Chinese pastor or ordained priest, with occasional services provided by a visiting white minister or Caucasian father. The Chinese attended services on Sunday afternoon and sometimes held Wednesday night prayer meetings and occasional family night dinners. As with other American churches, their worship included the traditional Bible reading, sermon, prayer, singing, and similar Christian rituals. More often than not the Chinese churches also sponsored youth fellowship clubs, women's guilds, and education and English classes for new immigrants. Services were conducted often in the Taishan dialect or in Cantonese, but since 1965 Mandarin Chinese or English has been more common. However, in Sunday School classes, a survey conducted by Cayton and Lively reported that 267 out of 298 services held in 33 churches were conducted in English, as the great majority of the Chinese youngsters were native-born.[56]

In spite of the fact that an increasing number of Chinese have accepted Christianity, Chinese Christians remain a minority in the Chinese-American community. Deep-rooted Chinese cultural heritage and strong social organizations in the Chinatowns have resisted Christianity. New immigrants and those who were steeped in the Chinese cultural background have found the Chinese concept of syncretic religion incompatible with monotheistic Christianity. The majority of Chinese in America justify their religious preference by arguing that to be a moral person one does not need to be religious, and to be religious one does not need to be Christian. Indeed, a large percentage of the Chinese churchgoers still have not abandoned the harmonious and syncretic Chinese religious view. Some probably join churches for social and educational reasons.

This does not mean that Chinese heritage will always make Chinese Americans unresponsive to Christianity; that has been proven not to be the case. The past decade has witnessed a continued growth in church population. This growth is a part of Chinese acculturation. In the process of Americanization, church organizations serve similar social and political functions to those provided by the earlier Six Companies and clan/family associations. In the past few decades American values have inspired native-born Chinese Americans to strive for individual success and to supplant traditional Chinese responsibility to family and ancestors as the motivation for behavior. As Americans create caucuses to fight social ills and to eradicate racism in the churches, the caucuses have elevated several Chinese Americans to conspicuous leadership positions, among them Wilbur W. Y. Choy, who became the first Chinese bishop in the United Methodist Church in 1972.

8. Transition in Social and Economic Lives

Chinese religious organizations and churches were at once part of the Chinese community and also linked directly with the larger society. They functioned not only inside Chinatown but in and as part of the larger society that surrounded and permeated the Chinese community. Consequently, any change in Chinese social and economic lives must also be viewed in the context of the larger society. In 1943, when America was looking forward to victory in the biggest and most destructive war of all time, it was a nation of 132 million people, of which 78,000, or 0.05 percent, were Chinese. The majority of the Chinese (52 percent) were native-born American citizens. Although the once lopsided ratio between men and women had narrowed, from 15 to 1 in 1910 to 3 to 1 in 1950, a disproportionate number of Chinese men still lived without wives and families. Other significant changes had also taken place; in particular, the Chinese community by the 1960s was almost wholly urban. The transition period of the post–World War II era also witnessed an increasing number of Chinese going into business and a remarkable growth in the number of Chinese in professional occupations.

The Chinese learned to raise capital by pooling their savings, instead of going through normal bank financing. A group of men, say 12, formed a hui for a 12-months' duration. For example, each put $50 into the hui each month, and the person who bid the highest interest rate would have the use of the $600-minus-interest. As the 11 other men waited for their turns to bid on the remaining 11 monthly pools, they could plan ahead for continuing to earn the interest or for bidding on the money needed to set up a small shop. In this way many Chinese were able to change their status from laborers to merchants or entrepreneurs. Deeply motivated, frugal, hardworking, and noted for their sobriety, many Chinese soon became men of substance with families. Others gained merchant status by persuading established Chinese merchants to take them in as partners.

Among the Chinese businesses, hand laundry, which was considered the economic mainstay of Chinatowns, remained popular, particularly with the newly arrived immigrants in the 1940s, 1950s and 1960s. Chinese laundry workers, as a matter of economic necessity, put in long working hours for modest wages. They did all the washing, ironing, folding, and drying by hand. Often challenged by large, mechanized, non-Chinese commercial businesses, they had to provide free, or at minimal cost, "personal services," such as mending tears and sewing on buttons. However, modern technical developments played a significant role in the decline of that business, and it was edged out almost entirely by home washers and dryers. Figures from 1970 show that only 4,800 Chinese were employed as laundrymen and that, by 1983, only 1,000 Chinese laundries (as against about 4,000 in 1930) remained in the New York metropolitan area; five shirt presses shared their dwindling business. It appears likely that in the near future the Chinese hand laundry will disappear because of retirement of foreign-born laundrymen and cessation of the flow of illiterate immigrants. In the meantime, new forms of survival for veteran Chinese laundrymen have emerged. Some opened coin laundries. Others brought their ironing skills into Chinese garment factories as pressers.[57]

Many Chinese also engaged in retail businesses, such as vegetable growing, peddling, and market retailing. Before emergence of the giant supermarket industry, Chinese grocers, mostly small-scale family enterprises, could make modest profits. By effectively utilizing these modest profits, many provided their children with good educational opportunities. However, when the younger and better educated Chinese had access to the primary labor market, very few wanted to follow their father's footsteps. One survey indicated that when Chinese grocers were asked: "Would you want your children to go into this line of work after you?" 62 percent of the Chinese petty merchants said "No."[58] By the late 1960s most of the Chinese retail stores were found either in small Southern rural communities or in the ghettoes of urban communities, the so-called neighborhood markets which, to a certain degree, still fulfill the needs of those depressed areas.

In addition to the hand laundry and retail store businesses, Chinese continued to operate restaurants; as a matter of fact, in recent years restaurants have gained a slight increase in the percentage of Chinese work force. The 0.8 percent increase between 1960 and 1970 was due mainly to the influx of new immigrants from Hong Kong, who were unable to find employment commensurate with their education, experience, or qualifications. Chinese restaurants have survived also because of an increasing demand for delicate Chinese cuisines in large American cities. There has been a change, however, in the composition of the Chinese labor force in the restaurant business. More Chinese have become owners and managers of restaurants, while fewer have been employed as waiters and dishwashers. Moreover, Chinese restaurants since 1950 have offered more than chop suey and Cantonese cuisine, featuring a variety of renowned Chinese dishes, notably Sichuanese, Hunanese, Peking, Northern Chinese, Mongolian, and Formosan.

Collateral to urbanization of the Chinese population during the transition period was a remarkable growth of Chinese professionals and a simultaneous decrease in the number of Chinese manual laborers (see Appendix 5). The percentage of household workers, for example, declined from 6.2 percent in 1940 to only 0.8 percent in 1970. The proportion of farmers decreased similarly from 3.8 percent in 1940 to 0.6 percent in 1970, while less than 1 percent of the Chinese work force remained in retail industry by 1970.[59] The censuses of 1930 and 1940 reveal a paucity of Chinese professional men but, during the next three decades, the number of Chinese professionals rose from a mere 2.5 percent of the total male population to a 28.9 percent. The dramatic occupational change was evident not only for Chinese males but also for females; 19.4 percent of the Chinese women were employed as professionals in 1970. The almost tenfold increase among the Chinese professional/technical workers far exceeded that of the whites or of the nation as a whole. Moreover, by 1970, the percentage of Chinese employed in the professional/technical category had surpassed every other category, including service workers.[60] These phenomena reflect a conscious effort on the part of the Chinese to raise their status through industriousness and, above all, education.

The majority of native-born Chinese youths have chosen to study medicine, pharmacy, engineering and technology, business administration, and other professional fields emphasizing tactile or quantitative skills rather than requiring written or oral fluency in English. It has been suggested that technical professions that require dexterity, design, and quantitative skills attracted the Chinese in America because they offered occupational independence and prestige, and did not require expert use of English. This has resulted in a scarcity of Chinese in the legal profession, such as judges, legal clerks, lawyers, and paralegals. Once again, however, there are cultural as well as linguistic explanations for these patterns. While the legal profession enjoyed high status and good income in Western society, the best minds in traditional Chinese society studied Confucian classics and aspired to pass the civil-service examinations so that they could become degree holders and work for the Emperor. They thereby enjoyed the status of a scholar-official-landowner gentry. Because of this tradition, though it has been slightly modified in modern times, law is still used as little as possible in Chinese society. At the present time, there are about 5,500 lawyers among the 1 billion people in China and only about 120 lawyers in the highly commercialized city of Taibei; but the United States has 612,593 practicing lawyers for its 224 million citizens.[61] In major Chinese cities lawyers continue to play only a subsidiary role and do not enjoy the same status as their American counterparts. But with a disproportionately small number of lawyers in their population, the Chinese minority once again find themselves in an unfavorable situation in the complexity of contemporary American society.

VI

CONTEMPORARY CHINESE-AMERICAN SOCIETY

Within four seas all men are brothers.

—Confucius

That patience is a noble virtue of the
Chinese people no one who knows them
will gainsay. There is so much of this virtue
that it has almost become a vice with them.

—Lin Yutang

1. New Immigrants since 1965

The U.S. Census shows that there were 806,027 Chinese in the 50
states of the Union as of 1980 and that the Chinese had overtaken the
Japanese to become America's largest Asian population. Although
this figure represents an increase of 239.68 percent since the 1960 Census, which had recorded 237,292, a growing number of researchers
and civic leaders argued that the Chinese, along with other ethnic minority groups, were severely undercounted in the 1980 Census. Privately sponsored population projections in the San Franciso-Oakland
area and New York City estimated that the margins of error might
have ranged as high as 25 to 50 percent.[1] Problems in counting Chinese arose from the reluctance of respondents to report an ethnic
identification that still carried a social stigma, as well as the inability of
unlearned people to understand the complex census questionnaires.
Many Chinese were probably listed in the "others" category, which
was intended to include only persons of American Indian, Eskimo,
and Aleutian heritage. Others did not respond or could not respond
to census inquiries because they feared any contact with the federal
government. In the light of these census deficiencies, knowledgeable
insiders in the Chinese community believe that the total number of

151

Chinese in the United States, including students and illegal aliens, exceeded the one million mark in 1980.

The phenomenal increase of the Chinese population during the past two decades was due to a combination of two factors. First, from June 4, 1962, to the end of 1965, President John F. Kennedy, in response to a puzzling and massive exodus of Chinese refugees to Hong Kong in May, 1962, invoked the provisions of existing legislation and permitted 15,000 Chinese to enter the United States as "parolees." Second, this was followed by the abolition, on October 3, 1965, of the discriminatory and anti-Chinese immigration quota system. The Act of 1965 provided a ceiling of 170,000 annually for immigrants from the entire Eastern Hemisphere; each foreign state was subjected to a numerical limitation of 20,000 visas. Independent countries of the Western Hemisphere—formerly unrestricted by number — were now limited to a ceiling of 120,000. The 170,000 ceiling was divided into seven categories, with specific percentages allocated for each category: (1) unmarried sons and daughters of U.S. citizens, 20 percent or 34,000; (2) spouses, unmarried sons or daughters of permanent residents, 20 percent, or 34,000; (3) those with exceptional ability, professionals, scientists, artists, 10 percent, or 17,000; (4) married sons and daughters of U.S. citizens, 10 percent, or 17,000; (5) brothers and sisters of U.S. citizens, 24 percent, or 40,800; (6) skilled and unskilled labor, 10 percent, or 17,000; and (7) refugees, 6 percent, or 10,200. The Act of 1965 placed no numerical limit on immediate relatives, including spouses, minors, unmarried children and parents of adult citizens, who could come to the United States for visits or other lawful purposes.[2]

The Act of 1965 was twice amended in 1970; the impact of these amendments was good news for would-be Chinese immigrants from Taiwan, Hong Kong, and Southeast Asia. Indeed, the period between 1965 and 1974 can rightly be characterized as the "golden years" of Chinese immigration because, from October 3, 1965, to July 4, 1971, as many as 115,509 Chinese were admitted to the United States as immigrants, almost equally distributed between males and females. Moreover, during the same period, 42,392 Chinese already in America on a temporary basis were able to readjust their status to permanent residents with the intention of become American citizens by naturalization. The following table clearly reveals the startling results of what turned out to be the nation's most liberal immigration law toward the Chinese.[3]

In 1980 over half of all Chinese in the United States still lived in the Pacific states; however, an increasing number had settled in the East, notably New York, New Jersey, and Massachusetts, and in such Mid-

TABLE 9

Chinese New Immigrants, 1965–1974

	Subject to Numerical Limitations	Not Subject to Numerical Limitations	Total
1965	1,152	3,617	4,769
1966	12,900	4,708	17,608
1967	19,712	5,384	25,096
1968	12,386	4,048	16,434
1969	17,258	3,635	20,893
1970	14,699	3,257	17,956
1971	14,598	3,024	17,622
1972	18,447	3,283	21,730
1973	17,405	4,251	21,656
1974	18,367	4,318	22,685
	146,924	39,525	186,449

Source: Immigration and Naturalization Service Annual Report, 1965–1974

western states as Illinois, Michigan, and Ohio. The greatest percentage increase since 1970 was in the South, especially in Texas and Florida. Eleven percent of the Chinese population resided in the South in 1980 as compared with only 8 percent in 1970. Coincidental to these changes were slight decreases in percentages of Chinese living in Hawaii and California, in spite of the fact that California remained the state with the largest Chinese population, at a figure of 322,340, and Hawaii led all states, with the highest Chinese population percentage at 5.8 (see maps 4 and 5).

Chinese population was overwhelmingly urban in the 1980 census. The largest concentrations were in the New York-New Jersey metropolitan area and the San Francisco Bay Area, each of which listed more than 100,000 Chinese residents. Other urban and suburban counties also showed high rates of population gain for the Chinese. In Los Angeles, the Chinese population grew 129 percent between 1970 and 1980 while the county's growth was only 6 percent. San Diego showed a 139 percent gain for the Chinese as compared with an overall population gain of 37 percent. About 97 percent of American Chinese lived in urban areas: other cities showing marked gains included Houston, Chicago, Boston, Dallas, Seattle, San José, Detroit, Philadelphia, Phoenix, Washington, D.C., Honolulu, and Sacramento. Other cities that had concentrations of over 4,000 Chinese included Stockton, Anaheim-Santa Ana-Garden Grove, and Fresno in California; Portland, Oregon; Miami-Fort Lauderdale; and Baltimore. Chinese population grew only modestly in rural counties.

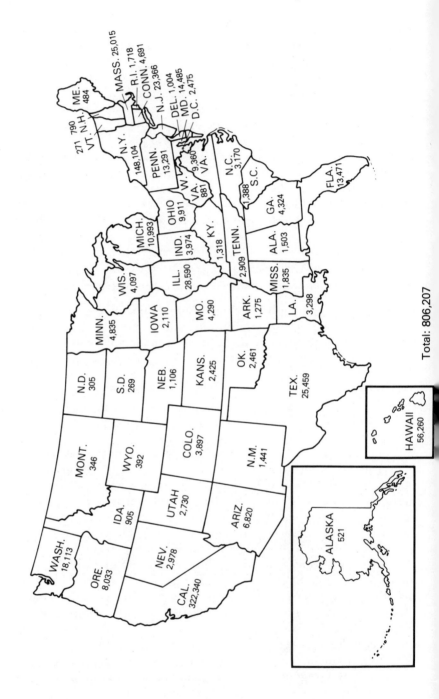

Map IV. Chinese Population by State, 1980

Total: 806,207

MASS. 25,015
R.I. 1,718
CONN. 4,691
N.J. 23,366
DEL. 1,004
MD. 14,485
D.C. 2,475

ME. 484
VT. 271
N.H. 790
N.Y. 148,104
PENN. 13,291
W. VA. 881
VA. 9,360
N.C. 3,170
S.C. 1,388

MICH. 10,993
OHIO 9,911
IND. 3,974
KY. 1,318
TENN. 2,909
GA. 4,324
ALA. 1,503
FLA. 13,471

WIS. 4,097
ILL. 28,590
MISS. 1,835
LA. 3,298

MINN. 4,835
IOWA 2,110
MO. 4,290
ARK. 1,275

N.D. 305
S.D. 269
NEB. 1,106
KANS. 2,425
OK. 2,461
TEX. 25,459

MONT. 346
WYO. 392
COLO. 3,897
N.M. 1,441

IDA. 905
UTAH 2,730
ARIZ. 6,820

WASH. 18,113
ORE. 8,033
NEV. 2,978
CAL. 322,340

HAWAII 56,260

ALASKA 521

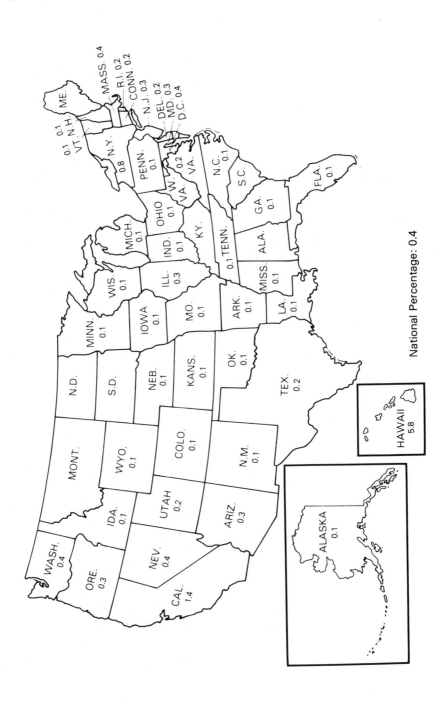

Map V. Percentage of Chinese in U.S. Population by State, 1980

National Percentage: 0.4

MASS. 0.4
R.I. 0.2
CONN. 0.2
N.J. 0.3
DEL. 0.2
MD. 0.3
D.C. 0.4
ME.
N.H. 0.1
VT. 0.1
N.Y. 0.8
PENN. 0.1
W. VA. 0.2
VA. 0.1
N.C. 0.1
S.C.
OHIO 0.1
MICH. 0.1
IND. 0.1
KY.
TENN. 0.1
GA. 0.1
ALA.
FLA. 0.1
WIS. 0.1
ILL. 0.3
MO. 0.1
ARK. 0.1
LA. 0.1
MISS. 0.1
MINN. 0.1
IOWA 0.1
N.D.
S.D.
NEB. 0.1
KANS. 0.1
OK. 0.1
TEX. 0.2
MONT.
WYO. 0.1
COLO. 0.1
N.M. 0.1
IDA. 0.1
UTAH 0.2
ARIZ. 0.3
WASH. 0.4
ORE. 0.3
NEV. 0.4
CAL. 1.4
HAWAII 5.8
ALASKA 0.1

TABLE 10

Chinese Population in Major U.S.
Metropolitan Areas, 1980

1. San Francisco-Oakland-Berkeley	169,016
2. New York, Newark, Jersey City	157,237
3. Los Angeles, Long Beach	94,521
4. Honolulu	52,301
5. Chicago & vicinity	25,489
6. San Jose	22,745
7. Boston & vicinity	22,467
8. Washington, D.C. & vicinity	18,250
9. Sacramento	15,440
10. Seattle-Tacoma	15,270
11. Anaheim-Santa Ana-Garden Grove	14,575
12. Houston	14,235
13. Philadelphia-Wilmington	12,210
14. San Diego	8,618
15. Detroit-Ann Arbor	8,143
16. Miami-Fort Lauderdale	6,826
17. Dallas-Fort Worth	5,663
18. Portland, Oregon	5,285
19. Stockton, CA	4,392
20. Baltimore	4,237
21. Phoenix	4,185
22. Cleveland-Akron-Lorain	4,034

Source: *1980 U.S. Census.*

Chinese in America were still treated, at least in government ethnic reckonings, as a singular minority group, even though they are as diversified and, to a certain extent, as individualistic as Americans of European origin. Like other Americans, the Chinese community included those who had been established in America for several generations, along with newly arrived immigrants, economically disadvantaged and non-English-speaking workers, wealthy businessmen, high-school dropouts, and Ivy-League trained Ph.D.s. Unlike the early "faceless and nameless" Chinese immigrants of the nineteenth century, contemporary Chinese Americans included such nationally recognized personalities as news reporter Connie Chung of NBC, Senator Hiram Fong, Republican activist Anne Chennault, world-renowned architect I. M. Pei, prominent California politician March Fong Eu, ice skating champion Tiffany Chin, astronaut Taylor Wang, and computer wizard Dr. An Wang. Unlike early Cantonese-speaking peasants from rural villages, many of the recent arrivals were well educated and spoke the standard Mandarin plus the distinct Taiwan or Shanghai dialect. Not only did these recent arrivals speak different Chinese dialects and organize associations completely independent of the Six Companies, they also preferred different cuisines and supported mutually hostile political groups. In short, the presence of sharp ethnic and class distinctions and a politically fragmented population were characteristics of the post-1965 Chinese-American community.

2. Chinese Women in a Changing American Society

The Immigration Act of 1965 helped to alter the historically lopsided ratio between Chinese males and females in America. In 1950, for every 162 Chinese males there was only 100 females, but two decades later the ratio was narrowed to 107 males for 100 females. This situation, coupled with a rapidly changing environment in the United States, was to affect the destiny of hundreds of thousands of Chinese-American women. The 1970s witnessed a record number of young Chinese women attending U.S. colleges and universities, and more than half of Chinese women in America worked outside their homes. Education and employment entailed a social and psychological new look. Chinese women gradually dissolved inhibitions imposed by their native traditions and obtained greater individual satisfaction. They were indeed quite different from the female characters of thirty or forty years earlier described by such writers as Jade Snow Wong and Maxine Kingston.[4]

In order to appreciate this dramatic change and to understand the double burden of being Chinese and female that contemporary Chinese-American women have to bear, one must remember women's roles as prescribed by Chinese traditions. In a traditional Chinese society, women were subordinate to men. Confucius ranted: "Women and inferior men are hard to get along with; they get out of hand when befriended and they resent it when kept at a distance." Chinese wives were often called "Nei Ren," or "inside person." To keep women in shackles, Confucian doctrine created what was known as the three obediences and the four virtues. The three obediences were "obedience to the father when yet unmarried, obedience to the husband when married, and obedience to the sons when widowed." Thus, traditionally, Chinese women were placed under control of the male sex from the cradle to the grave. From father to husband to son, the Chinese female was systematically subordinated by men. The four virtues were: (1) "woman's ethics," meaning a woman must know her place and act in every way in compliance with the old ethical code; (2) "woman's speech," meaning a woman must not talk too much, taking

care not to bore people; (3) "woman's appearance," meaning a woman
must pay attention to adorning herself with a view to pleasing the opposite sex; and (4) "woman's chore," meaning a woman must willingly
do all the chores in the home.

Clearly, Chinese traditions had placed primary emphasis on the
role of woman as wife and mother, dictating that her status, fulfill-
ment, and economic livelihood depended on men. However, since the
turn of the twentieth century, such rigid ideas were challenged, as
well-to-do girls flocked to modern schools and young widows were
permitted to marry for a second time. As soon as Chinese women emigrated to America, they discovered a society that seemed to them
more of a matriarchy than a patriarchy, as characterized by Lin Yutang and Philip Wylie in the 1940s. They were shocked that divorce
and remarrying were not besetting sins. Although Chinese women
rarely approved of smoking, drinking, and boisterous public behavior, they envied the freedom and property rights enjoyed by their
American counterparts. In particular, they liked the American concept of love and marriage. Acculturated Chinese women began to in-
sist on the right to fall in love and to be married without parental
arrangement. Others showed affection in public, a behavior considered by their grandmothers and mothers as licentious and immoral.
By the 1970s, many young, educated, middle-class Chinese American
women, undoubtedly inspired by the feminist movement of the larger
society, even tried to reverse the roles in which Chinese traditions
had cast them, roles that they believed demeaned their status and falsified their identity. They became more aggressive, assertive, and self-
confident, and dared to challenge masculine authority.

In 1981, Judy Yung of San Francisco received a grant from the U.S.
Department of Education and began the first national research study
on the history of Chinese-American women. She found important regional variations in the degree of acculturation. In a multiracial society such as Hawaii, where there was less discrimination, Chinese
women appeared to be more assertive, assimilated, and economically
more successful. In the rural South, such as Arkansas and Mississippi,
Chinese women remained more submissive and complacent, maintaining a middle status between whites and blacks. In metropolitan
areas, such as San Francisco and New York, Chinese women were
largely foreign-born. They spoke little or no English, lived in substandard conditions, and were less acculturated.[5]

The plight of urban Chinese women of lower-income families appears to contradict the "successful image" of the Chinese minority
often depicted by the media. Living in overcrowded ghettoes and
struggling for survival, most of these women worked as sewing-

machine operators for garment industries. Violations of minimum wage laws, failure to pay unemployment insurance or overtime, and the illegal use of child labor have been chronic injustices in the garment industry of America's Chinatowns. In 1981 an estimated 146 garment shops or sweatshops existed in San Francisco's twenty-block rectangular Chinatown; 99 were nonunion. These shops employed some 3,500 women and produced about 50 percent of San Francisco's apparel.[6] Most of the shops lacked adequate fire exits, toilet facilities, and ventilation. The apparel industry was seasonal and greatly influenced by fluctuations in fashion, and time restraints were often critical. Frequently owners, pressured by big garment cartels, overworked their laborers. Many Chinese women continued to work in their homes after the shops closed for the day. Since a substantial number of them were illegal aliens, they were paid in cash and received no social security benefits. Time cards were frequently falsified to circumvent minimum-wage laws. Some employers required their employees to work exclusively at home in order to speed up production.

Most of the Chinatown sewing shops, including those in New York City, were subcontractors who worked for major firms, such as Fritzi of California, which did all the cutting and designing. Consequently, Chinatown sewing shops made business connections, sometimes illicit, with manufacturers of their choosing, and set up whatever operations the manufacturers wanted. The margin of profit was generally slim, so contractors tried to avoid union labor. In July, 1981, the California legislature passed a bill requiring every garment manufacturer to register with the Division of Labor Standards Enforcement. Businesses were also required to submit detailed information, including the number of employees and the names of contractors. Nevertheless, some garment employers continued to break the laws and exploit non-English speaking Chinese workers.

According to a survey conducted by Chalsa Loo and Paul Ong, three-fourths of Chinese garment workers in San Francisco, aged 18 and over, frequently felt depressed and were not proud of their occupation. Only one-fourth of those who were married felt that they received respect and emotional support from their husbands. And yet only a few of them expressed the desire for a better husband. As they were foreign-born, their ethnic consciousness remained strong and Chinese values and norms persisted in their community life. Accordingly, they did not relate comfortably with persons outside their own ethnic subgroup. In fact, three-fourths of the women said they would not join in a rent strike to obtain better security if a robbery or an assault occurred in their housing project.[7] It was apparent that these women, in spite of their working and living conditions, were reluctant to publicize their problems or to attempt to solve them with outside assistance. Most of them seemed unaware of the social, political, and economic demands of the larger society.

In contrast to the garment workers in America's Chinatowns, however, thousands of Chinese-American women during the past two decades have made inroads into the high-paid labor market. Education, hard work, merit, and, for some, affirmative action were factors that contributed to their socio-economic successes. Chinese female doctors, professors, dentists, pharmacists, business managers, accountants, librarians, and laboratory researchers abound, and their numbers have been steadily increasing as hundreds continued to complete Ph.D., M.D., M.A., M.BA., and D.D. degrees from leading U.S. universities. Before 1960 only a few Chinese-American women had attained national prominence, such as Katherine Hsu, a doctor specializing in perfecting a drug to prevent child tuberculosis; Ah Quon McElrath, a labor organizer in Hawaii for over 40 years; and Helen Pon Onyett, an army colonel.[8] Subsequent Chinese-American society, on the contrary, produced a great many prominent and influential female personalities. Among them were Lorraine C. Wang, probably the richest Chinese woman in the United States; Anne Chennault, Republican Party activist, who had direct access to the White House; Connie Chung, NBC anchorwoman; March Fong Eu, California's secretary of state; and Lily Lee Chen, Mayor of Monterey Park, California. These women, and many others, are predisposed toward assertive political advocacy. They feel themselves to be capable, self-confident, and reliable.

Neither the garment workers in Chinatown ghettoes nor these extremely successful women represented the majority of Chinese American women. A profile of the average, contemporary Chinese-American woman would be somewhere between these two groups. In 1970, 58 percent of Chinese women in the 18–24 age group were enrolled in school, and 31 percent of Chinese women in the 25–34 age group were employed in professional and technical positions (as opposed to only 17 percent in 1960). However, positions and earnings were not always commensurate with educational attainment. Chinese women continued to be subject to discrimination as Chinese and as females. In spite of the fact that 23 percent of the Chinese women were college graduates in 1970, only 13.3 percent of them earned more than $10,000 a year, while 28 percent of the white women with college education and 34 percent of the black women earned these income levels.[9] Of Chinese women who did not have college degrees, most were employed as file clerks, office machine operators, typists, and in other low-paying jobs. Although 60 percent of Chinese families had two wage earners, as opposed to the national average of 51 percent, their median family income in 1970 was only $10,610; the U.S. average was $9,590.[10]

In addition to existing racial and sexual discrimination, the Chinese cultural heritage may have been equally important in dictating employment patterns of Chinese American women. In 1973 Derald Sue and Barbara Kirk made a study on the relationship between college-graduate Chinese women's personalities and their occupational preferences. Of the 236 women investigated, they found that a vast majority preferred more structured environments, where there was less uncertainty and ambiguity, and fewer unpredictable situations. Chinese-American women favored such occupations as housewife, teacher, stenographer-secretary, office clerk, dietician, occupational therapist, nurse, dentist, laboratory technician, and engineer.[11] The study suggested that contemporary Chinese-American women were still predominantly interested in domestic and domestic-related jobs. As the acceptance of education for Chinese girls became more general in the Chinese American community, many girls went to college because of parental pressure. However, many did not view their schooling as preparation for attaining well-paid jobs. College education was viewed rather as satisfying their parental expectations or as a means of finding better husbands. Pauline L. Fong's survey of several hundred Asian-American female students, ranging from seventh grade through post-baccalaureate levels, corroborated this pattern, i.e., Chinese-American women have higher educational aspirations and expectations than they do work aspirations. Chinese women have not been so competitive in the work world as other minorities.[12] In short, Chinese women still appeared unsure about combining professional employment with family life.

Given that traditional Chinese culture defined women as weak, subservient, and compliant, Chinese-American women have changed dramatically during the past three decades. It is not likely that the freedoms so recently won would easily be relinquished. Contemporary Chinese-American women are much more conscious of their individual rights; their fathers, brothers, and husbands have in the meantime shown greater sensitivity to their problems and needs. As acculturation progresses, it seems likely that Chinese American women will become socially less pliant and emotionally less docile, enjoying more freedom and rights than their grandmothers and mothers.[13]

3. Chinese Children and Youths in a Multiracial Society

In spite of the influence of the women's liberation movement, a great majority of Chinese American women continued to cling to their Chinese heritage and pride, believing that taking care of a home and educating the young were more important and rewarding than having a job or living independently. The persistence of traditional attitudes among Chinese-American women was perhaps best reflected in the upbringing of their children, whose remarkable achievements at every level of schooling in recent years have drawn the attention of not only the media, but also of many prominent behavioral and social scientists. Chinese-American children appeared better adjusted to school than other ethnic groups; generally they were less apt to fight with other children and are more compliant to the teacher's commands. How does one explain the fact that Chinese children consistently have high testing scores and lower delinquency rates? Are the Chinese-American children the embodiment of the best from the East and the West?

Responding to these and other related questions, social scientists have offered different answers, but all of them attribute Chinese high achievement and ability to home environment and the continuing influence of Chinese cultural values and familial structure. Chinese child-rearing imbued children with a stronger motivation to learn and with greater compliance to adult demands than were common in Western cultures. Chinese parents were more severe than white parents in weaning, toilet training, control of aggression, and sexual conduct, apparently contributing to less juvenile delinquency and lower rates of teenage pregnancy.[14] But Chinese upbringing also emphasized kinship dependence rather than independent initiative. While white parents insisted on privacy for all individuals, Chinese parents usually maintained a complete community of interests with their children. Inside white American houses, space and possessions were individualized, and a child's physical environment established strong lines of individual rights. Inside Chinese houses, children shared rooms with parents and had freedom to use their parents' possessions; likewise, parents had the freedom to use their children's belongings. While white parents refused to allow their youngsters to enter the real world of adults, Chinese parents invited their children to take part in their social activities. Children were welcomed to dinners, weddings, theaters, and other adult parties, rather than being turned over to a babysitter. Because they were included in family and social gatherings, Chinese children had opportunities to observe the behavior of adults and to interact with them. [15]

Reared in close-knit, integrated families, Chinese children were more likely to develop a mutual dependence upon their family rather than becoming self-centered. They were taught to give up pleasure or comfort in favor of someone else and to give in during a quarrel. Positive values of sharing, noncompetitiveness, and control of violent temper were stressed. This may explain why Chinese children appear less dominant than whites, generally showing humility and underestimating their worth. They are also more sensitive to group pressure than whites, and this accords with their well-known unwillingness to speak out or to contradict their professors in university seminars. As a Chinese child was continuously in contact with adult models of behavior after whom he patterned his own behavior, at an earlier stage, he established a more realistic view of people and things, whereas the white child understood little of the world of human reality which awaited him. Several studies suggested that Chinese high-school graduates tend to have a more balanced and realistic view of life, the world, and its inhabitants than do white American youths. For white students, school is the stage at which they become aware of the gap between the real and the ideal. Consequently, when confronted with frustrating situations, Chinese youths have already been taught to feel sad, but white youths often react with anger.[16]

Child rearing in a Chinese-American family, therefore, has been highlighted by strong parental role models. Whether the parent was an engineer, a doctor, or a professor who could provide an intellectually stimulating home environment, or a grocer, a restaurant worker, or a laundryman who worked long hours for small wages, he trained his child to bring honor to his family. The teachers of Chinese-American children discovered that, if a note was sent home about a child's infraction of the rules, almost invariably the father appeared the next day and apologized for his failure in the proper upbringing of the child. Often if a white or black child did poorly in school, his parents believed that the teacher or school had failed. Chinese parents, however, believed that the student was not trying hard enough. Parental pressures, diligence, and a favorable social environment pushed Chinese children to succeed academically. Since the 1920s the smaller, lighter, and physically less well-developed Chinese children have been the equal of, or higher than, whites on nonverbal intelligence tests. Recently, Philip Vernon reported that mean IQs on verbal group tests of Chinese children were 97, a little below the white average, but their mean IQs on nonverbal and spatial tests were 110, much above the average whites. Moreover, Chinese students were superior in arithmetic, history, geography, and, surprisingly, in spelling as well.[17]

In mathematics and science, Chinese students consistently scored the highest of any ethnic group on Scholastic Aptitude Tests, taken each year by a million high school students who plan to enter college. In 1982, in its 41st national competition for talented young American scientists between the ages of 13 and 17, the Westinghouse Company gave out 40 awards, and 5 of the recipients were ethnic Chinese. The next year, in a Science Talent Search conducted by the same company, a contest that attracted 1,000 entrants, Chinese youngsters swept 6 of the top 10 awards. In 1984 Chinese once again accounted for 9 of the 40 semifinalists and 3 of the top 10 winners. Jay Luo, a 12-year-old mathematical boy wonder, became the youngest college graduate in the world when he finished undergraduate courses at Boise State University in May, 1982. Luo immediately was enrolled at Stanford University's graduate program for studies in mathematics.[18]

Luo and the several dozen Westinghouse winners, who had mean IQs near 180, were exceptional cases, but reports from major U.S. universities confirmed a stunning increase in the numbers of Chinese students. At Ohio State University, Asian (mostly Chinese) enrollment jumped 122 percent from 1976 to 1981. In the 1981 academic year more than 20 percent of the students at Berkeley were Asian, while Cornell's freshmen class registered 9 percent Asian. During the 1983–84 academic year, Chinese students made up about 8 percent of Harvard's freshman class and 16 percent of all students at the Juilliard School.[19] Moreover, the Chinese dropout or transfer rates were generally much lower than for whites or blacks. The 1980 Census indicated that the Chinese were the best educated group in American society. If recent trends continue there will be a highly disproportionate number of Chinese-American doctors, engineers, artists, writers, scholars, pharmacists, scientists, advanced mathematicians, computer experts, and various kinds of technocrats by the year 2000.

While clearly contributing to their upward mobility, the strict home environment of Chinese youngsters also produced stress and high anxiety levels and apparently encouraged introverted behavior. Increased education will probably undermine the familial patterns that have set the Chinese apart. Until high-school age, Chinese youngsters remain relatively isolated from the wider, dominant culture. After they scatter to high schools and colleges in various parts of the country, they participate more in the mainstream of American culture. Within the framework of the more permissive American culture, many of the Chinese customs appear much too rigid to the younger generation. Some Chinese Americans have felt intense psychological stress as a result of these pressures. Irving S. K. Chin, representative of the Chinese community in New York, testifying in 1970 before the Sub-Committee on Education of the U.S. Senate Committee on Labor Public Affairs, cited the tragic example of a 21-year-old Chinese who was enrolled at New York University in the computer field, but due to social isolation and other personal problems, became a dropout and eventually took his own life.[20] Others rebelled against their strict upbringing. In order to prove themselves as American as possible, some rejected their Chinese heritage. They became devotees of rock music, dated non-Asians, and generally flouted the traditional morality of their parents.

While youth rebellion in the Chinese community could hardly be assigned to any single cause, it is clear that one factor that undermined parental authority was the continued language handicap of new arrivals. Immigrant parents with college degrees but English deficiencies often found themselves unable to utilize their education, and were forced to take jobs as skilled technicians or, in some instances, in such unskilled jobs as dishwashers or janitors. The language handicap further lessened their chance of getting into the labor market, particularly in the construction and building trades. Because available employment for the non-English-speaking adult was low-paying and the cost of urban living high, most immigrant families lived in subsistence housing, and many suffered chronically from malnutrition. The immigrant father earned little, so the mother frequently was forced to work as well, leaving the children unattended. The close-knit family structure suffered. These lower-income youngsters, like their American counterparts, became restless recruits for leather-jacketed teenage gangs. The 1960s and 1970s saw a gradual rise of juvenile delinquency, previously unknown in Chinatowns. Many immigrant parents who had transplanted their families to provide a better education for their children were bitterly disappointed when their children failed in school. At the same time, the menial job held by the father was seen by some immigrant children as an equally debasing sign of failure on the father's part.

Alienation and bitterness developing in such circumstances were illustrated at Galileo High School in San Francisco in 1969. During that academic year the 2,802 student body of Galileo High School was made up of 1,535 Chinese (64.8 percent), but its teaching and administrative staffs were over 95 percent white and about 3 percent Chinese. Foreign-born Chinese children were generally given only 20 to 45 minutes of daily English instruction and then placed in the regular classroom. Some of the white teachers, who had difficulties with Chinese pronunciation, called the children by numbers instead of their names. The foreign-born teenagers, frustrated by cultural and language problems and alienated from the other students, were involved in frequent and violent incidents, on and off campus. During 1969–1970 Galileo had more suspensions than any other high school in California. It also ranked among the highest in the number of disciplinary transfers. San Francisco police figures on arrests and citations of juveniles indicated that the Chinese delinquency problem increased by 600 percent during the period 1964–1969.[21]

The most notorious of the Chinese teenage gang leaders was Joe

Fong, a figure in the mold of Little Pete in the nineteenth-century tong war era. Son of a grocery store owner, Joe Fong went to Galileo High School, and together with several alienated immigrant students, formed the Wah Ching (or Chinese Youth) gang. The club soon grew into a violent and criminal organization. Since Joe Fong was native-born, he was later excluded from the gang after a bitter internal strife. To counteract the Wah Ching power, Joe Fong thereafter re-cruited native-born Chinese teenagers, who called themselves the Joe Boys. Throughout the 1970s the two gangs attacked each other and terrorized the San Francisco Chinatown in a binge of vandalism, ex-tortion, and murder. Their gang war drew media attention when the Joe Boys, on September 5, 1977, entered the Gold Dragon Restaurant and sprayed gunfire throughout the main dining lounge. The bullets were intended for Michael Louis, leader of the Wah Ching gang, and his followers. They killed seven innocent bystanders instead. The San Francisco Chinatown community was stunned, but residents gener-ally adopted a "code of silence," partly because they feared the ven-geance of the gangsters. The late Mayor George Moscone offered a $25,000 reward for information leading to the arrest and conviction of the criminals. After nearly four and a half years, the Golden Dragon murderers were finally tried and convicted. The desperate social conditions which created the gangs were more difficult to rem-edy. Similar tragedies were later repeated in New York Chinatown and in Seattle's "International Quarters," where 13 older Chinese were killed by two young immigrants from Hong Kong, on the night of February 18, 1983.

Gang violence and lawlessness in Chinatowns have often been mag-nified out of proportion by journalists. As a result the tourist business was adversely affected, provoking Chinatown merchants to become hostile toward young Chinese immigrants. Serious rifts developed within the Chinatown societies. This discontent encouraged the be-ginning of job-training programs and youth counselling throughout Chinatowns. For instance, the San Francisco Summer Youth Pro-gram sponsored a series called "Chinatown Open Forum" for discus-sing the unique problems of the Chinese community. The Economic and Youth Opportunities Agency sponsored a number of educational and service programs, such as college counselling, advice about draft status, Mandarin and English classes, youth employment service, and classes for prospective citizens. In Los Angeles the Chinese commu-nity set up a Teen Post, which had an office, library, ping-pong table, and meeting places. The club regularly sponsored social and recre-ational events.[22] Of course, such social services relieved only the symptoms of the deeper economic disorders in America's China-towns.

4. Red Guards versus Old Guards

As non-English-speaking Chinese desperately clung to low-paying jobs, they often lived precariously. Because the poor resided in unhealthy conditions, worked long and strenuous hours, lacked proper exercise facilities, and frequently suffered from malnutrition, health problems abounded in Chinatowns. Tuberculosis was especially prevalent. A recently published report by the City and County of San Francisco Department of Public Health indicated that the Chinese had a TB rate more than double that of the general population. A comprehensive report published November 9, 1970, by Action for Boston Community Development (ABCD) revealed that health conditions among Boston's Chinese were worse than those of any other minority group. Infant mortality among Chinese in 1966 was 66.7 per thousand, two and one-half times greater than in Boston as a whole. New tuberculosis cases were 192 percent greater than in the rest of the city, and the death rate 129 percent greater.[23] In September, 1970, Boston's Tufts Medical Center screened a total of 510 Chinese: about half of them suffered from one or more of the following conditions—tuberculosis, chronic bronchitis, emphysema, hypertension, arrhythmia, diabetes, kidney disease, or vision defect.[24] Moreover, because of their physical isolation and the psychological pressures resulting from economic and social problems, mental illness, and suicide were serious problems.

An increasing feeling of entrapment and powerlessness among some poorer Chinese Americans in California was translated into action when a small handful of young men in 1968 formed the Chinatown Red Guards to protest a long-smoldering list of social grievances. Riding the wave of anti-Vietnam War sentiment and taking their cue from the Black Panther Party, which had just formed across the Bay in Oakland, the Red Guards in San Francisco attacked the blatant discrimination and racist attitudes of the dominant society. They addressed the issues of social ills of Chinatowns, the neglect of the Chinese elderly, and the unsanitary conditions in their community. The movement also had an important branch in New York. In February, 1970, a bilingual paper, *Getting Together,* was founded by I Wor Kuen in New York City. The paper challenged the authority of the older establishment in Chinatowns and criticized its inability to deal effectively with whites and willingness to accept a role inferior to the white society. It alleged a propensity of older Chinese merchants to exploit their own economically disadvantaged Chinese brethren. In Philadelphia a group of young Chinese Americans founded the Yellow Seeds, in 1971, to provide educational, recreational, and referral services. It published irregularly a bilingual newspaper of the same name, calling for a new leadership to solve the new problems of Chinese Americans.[25] Because of a lack of funds and their radicalism, neither the *Getting Together* nor the *Yellow Seeds* could generate broad community support. The radicals had soon joined with American liberals and civil-rights activists who also wanted to abolish legal and political barriers for America's minority groups in general, making common cause with other protesters.

The traditional old guards of Chinatowns, generally wealthy and influential citizens, viewed such political activism as alien, disreputable, and a threat to the social tranquility of the Chinese community. Most residents of Chinatowns, frightened by the association of the young militants with violence, drugs, hippies, and the permissiveness of the counterculture, also reacted conservatively. Particularly, the emotional issue of busing pushed these Chinese into a conservative stance. Beginning in 1967 a group of antibusing white mothers came to San Francisco Chinatown seeking a united front against busing children to black ghetto schools. Chinatown PTA leaders and several Chinese-language newspapers, such as the *Young China* and the *Chinese Times,* agreed and became leaders in the anti-busing crusade. With moral support form white organizations, in August, 1971, the Chinese filed petitions for an injunction against the court busing order. Justice William O. Douglas denied their petitions, and the Chinese resorted to boycott. When schools opened on September 13, 1971, the Chinese absentee rate was higher than 90 percent. In the meantime, Chinese mothers organized three "Freedom Schools" which claimed to have an attendance of about 1,450 pupils and more than 1,000 on a waiting list. Dozens of volunteers taught in these schools.[26]

But the Freedom Schools, due primarily to a lack of money and to conflicts of interest, immediately ran into trouble. The schools had left fund raising to community elders who belonged to the Chinese Six Companies, the Chinatown Chamber of Commerce, and the Chinese-American Citizens Alliance. These three conservative organizations linked busing to anti-Communist propaganda. When several volunteer teachers and members of the Chinese Parents Association refused to participate in a demonstration against the admitting the People's Republic into the United Nations, their conservative elders charged that they were un-Chinese and Communist dupes. When the conservative elders subsequently withdrew their support, the Freedom Schools could not maintain a full staff of qualified teachers or purchase standard texts. By mid-November, 4,226 Chinese elementary pupils had returned to the public schools, which was about two-thirds of the enrollment of 6,263 at the end of the previous school year. By the end of December, several hundred more Chinese children returned, and the boycott collapsed.[27]

The antibusing crusade was as dramatic as it was paradoxical. It was the first issue in decades that had brought the "silent majority" of the Chinese community together in social protest. While the upheavals of the 1960s had done much to increase the group identity of Blacks, Chicanos, and Indians, the angry antibusing protest had helped to stimulate a new Chinese-American group awareness. However, it exposed a basic weakness of the Chinese community; Chinese Americans were a politically fragmented minority group with an unbridgeable gap not only between the old generation and the young generation but also between different ideological groups. It also revealed, for the first time, that many Chinese parents bore deep prejudices against blacks and perhaps against other ethnic groups as well. The majority of Chinese in America by the 1970s were characterized by some as "bananas," having yellow skins but acting like whites.

However, the New Left ideology of the 1960s, which rejected white America's traditional middle-class values and preached a need for violence, did stir a great number of young Chinese to protest. Chinese students, traditionally silent on the campuses, now spoke out and engaged in political debate. The first sign of such activity occurred when they took part in demonstrations, sit-ins, marches, burnings, riots, and other violent protests. As the counter-culture protest flourished, Chinese students worked closely with other "Third World" radical elements to promote their common causes. They particularly supported demands by students for courses teaching the true history and culture of Third World people. Student radicals charged that students in American history were taught only about Chinese building of railroads, the Japanese bombing of Pearl Harbor, and the Filipinos' being called "little brown monkeys."

On November 6, 1968, a general student strike was called by the San Francisco Third World Liberation Front, which consisted of blacks, Latin Americans, Chinese, and Filipinos. Student mobilization for the strike included also the Students for a Democratic Society, the most active of the student organizations in the 1960s. The strike turned violent on November 26 when the president of San Francisco State resigned and S. I. Hayakawa was appointed president of the college. Although picket lines and marches were broken by thousands of club-swinging policemen, the San Francisco strike captured the attention of other students all over the nation. Across the bay, the University of California at Berkeley had a similar strike on January 21, 1969, calling for betterment of conditions of Third World students. Other campuses, such as at U.C.L.A. and the University of Washington, followed a less violent form, but the demands were similar: "some kind of programs should be established to determine a need, gather data through research, perceive goals and directions and solve problems through action."[28] Out of these protests came a variety of Asian-American Studies programs that were offered at the major universities of California, Hawaii, New York, and Washington, where Chinese made up a significant portion of the student body.

The leaders of student radicalism were mostly American-born Chinese youths. They soon discovered that their revolutionary speeches and programs gained little support from the majority of foreign-born Chinese students and that their own inability to read and speak Chinese was a major hindrance to effective college organizing. According to a report published by the Institute of International Education, during the academic year of 1970–71 a total of 21,355 Chinese from foreign countries were studying in American universities and colleges. Of this figure, 9,210 came from Taiwan, 9,040 from Hong Kong and 3,105 from Southeast Asia. During the decade of the 1970s the number of foreign-born Chinese students matched the rising tide of Chinese immigrations to America and eventually outnumbered that of the American-born Chinese. When the same institute reported its annual statistics on foreign students for the academic year of 1980–81, Chinese students from Taiwan ranked second in number (behind Iranians) with a total of 19,460, and Chinese from Hong Kong ranked eighth with a figure of 9,660. But two years later, Taiwan became the leading foreign country to send students to American universities and colleges (21,960), surpassing the former pacesetter, Iran (20,360).[29] In addition, several thousand ethnic Chinese came to study in the United States from Malaysia, Indonesia, Thailand, Singapore, the Philippines, Brazil, Uruguay, Peru, Bolivia, Jamaica, and Colombia.

The overwhelming majority of foreign-born Chinese students pursued graduate degrees. More than 70 percent of them chose agriculture, education, engineering, public and business administration, science, and technology. The general academic record achieved by foreign-born Chinese students was very high. This was especially true of those doing graduate work. They gained a reputation with American professors of being excellent students and men and women of high ability, which was understandable because they represented a select group of Chinese youths. When they arrived in the United States, most aspired to return and become responsible and leading citizens of their own society. Their lofty ideals, however, were gradually diluted by practical realities. As they gained personal maturity and confidence through experiences in America, their thinking and philosophy of life often underwent unexpected changes. Being exposed to American society and its economic opportunities at a very impressionable time of their lives, hundreds of thousands of them, upon completing their study, opted to stay in the United States and become permanent residents or citizens.

As students these foreign-born Chinese often found it difficult to identify with their American-born fellow Chinese. Aside from the language barrier, American-born Chinese had cultural and political backgrounds different from foreign-born Chinese students. The foreign-born thought of themselves as Chinese, and were so viewed by their professors and fellow students. The American-born Chinese, on the other hand, might look and eat like Chinese but talked and behaved like Americans. American-born Chinese students loved football games and rock-and-roll music, joined fraternities and sororities, held bridal showers, and exchanged Valentine cards. Foreign-born Chinese students considered such customs strange and un-Chinese. American-born Chinese coeds smiled at strangers; foreign-born Chinese coeds would never do so. An American-born Chinese student might challenge the authority of university administration and confront a professor in the classroom; a foreign-born Chinese student displayed Confucian piety toward his teachers. American-born Chinese students often complained that Asians did not appreciate the historical struggle of Chinese immigrants against such racist policies as the exclusion acts and the hardships suffered by the early Cantonese laborers. The foreign-born Chinese, on the other hand, complained that the ABC (American-born Chinese) youths were too narrow and clannish and that they lacked knowledge of Chinese culture. In the light of these differences, it was no wonder that foreign-born Chinese students generally stood on the sidelines when their ABC classmates battled against the college administrators and picketed classes in the late 1960s and early 1970s. It is also understandable that while American-born Chinese students were unhappy with persistent racism in America and often involved in Chinatown politics, foreign-born Chinese were mainly concerned with the future of China and Taiwan and faced the difficult decision of whether to remain loyal to the Nationalist government on Taiwan or switch allegiance to the People's Republic of China.

5. Protecting Diaoyutai Movement

In the early 1970s, a so-called "Unification Movement," led by foreign-born Chinese students, sponsored demonstrations not against American social injustices or the Vietnam War but against the Kuomintang's ineffectiveness in foreign affairs. Peking's leadership reacted ineptly toward the movement and failed to improve its relationship with the overseas Chinese in the United States. Since signing an agreement in 1955 with the Indonesian government, Peking's policy toward overseas Chinese was to encourage naturalization on a vol-

untary basis. But, once naturalized, a Chinese immigrant lost his
Chinese citizenship. The Nationalist government on Taiwan, on the
other hand, retained a policy of dual citizenship so that a naturalized
Chinese, no matter where he lived, was permitted to carry a Chinese
passport and was accorded the rights of a citizen of the Republic of
China. Under this arrangement a number of overseas Chinese actually held offices in the Nationalist government. For those who chose
to remain Chinese, both Peking and Taiwan urged them to abide by
local law and to respect local customs and habits. Both governments
pledged to continue to protect the emigrant's legitimate rights and interests. But while the Taiwan government maintained that those who
became citizens of another country were still "overseas Chinese," Peking referred to them as "naturalized Chinese" or "people of Chinese
origin." While the Peking regime welcomed both overseas Chinese
and naturalized Chinese to visit their homeland and their relatives,
the government on Taiwan actively made contact with the Chinese
living abroad, naturalized or otherwise, sponsored a variety of programs to woo their support, and briefed them about Taiwan's economic development and cultural achievements. In short, Taiwan's
policy toward the overseas Chinese in general and the Chinese in
America in particular was one of courtship, while Peking's attitude
was one of indifference.

   In spite of these differences a sizable segment of Chinese-American
community came to favor the mainland Chinese government. The
People's Republic emerged from the Korean War as a new world
power. In spite of the fact that it was not accorded membership in the
United Nations, Peking's representatives played an important role in
the Geneva Conference on Indo-China in 1954 and at the Conference
of Asian-African states, held at Bandung, Indonesia, in 1955. Within a
decade of these meetings, the People's Republic bolstered its international standing by detonating its first and second atomic bombs on
October 16, 1964 and May 14, 1965, at Lop Nor in China's northwest
Xinjiang province. The fact that Peking had become the fifth nuclear
power in the world generated a frenzy of pride in the Chinese-
American community, where expressions of approval for the People's
Republic hitherto had been very rare. A handful of Chinese intellectuals and those who opposed Kuomintang politics began to talk about
a peaceful unification program.

   This idea found new support when a territorial dispute between
Taiwan and Japan over a potential oil deposit in the Okinawa archipelago developed into a diplomatically embarrassing issue for the
Kuomintang regime. On August 29, 1969, Japanese geologists reported the discovery of huge oil deposits in the Diaoyutai Islands (Japanese called them the Sengaku Islands) area in the East China Sea.

The islands, then administered by the United States as part of the Ryukyu Islands Chain, were about 100 miles northeast of Taiwan, 50 miles from the China mainland, and 240 miles from Okinawa. In 1893, the Empress Dowager of the Qing government awarded the islands to Sheng Xuanxuai as his property for the purpose of collecting medicinal herbs. Accordingly, both Peking and Taiwan claim that the Diaoyutai Islands were historically and politically part of the territory of Taiwan.[30] But the United States government, based on the Nixon-Sato communiqué of November 21, 1969, pledged to return Okinawa and other U.S.-held Ryukyu Islands to Japan in 1972. When Dr. Hiroshi Niino of Tokai University speculated that the underwater oil field could be one of the ten largest in the world, the Japanese government immediately announced that $280,000 would be allocated for exploration and development of the oil fields.

As this crisis unfolded, Chinese students across the United States voiced opposition to the Japanese action and began the Protecting Diaoyutai Movement. It started in September, 1971, when several hundred Chinese students and scholars met at Ann Arbor, Michigan, to discuss "urgent national issues." The meeting denounced the manner in which the Kuomintang government had handled the Diaoyutai issue and appealed to Taiwanese authorities to stand firm in negotiations with Japan. The students wanted dignity and justice restored in China's diplomacy, which they believed had been marred by a series of concessions and defeats. But the Kuomintang government, lacking real muscle and confidence in its diplomacy and fearful of an unmanageable outcome, interpreted the protest movement as pro-Communist and subversive. Recent Congressional testimony has alleged that the Kuomintang maintained a web of agents in major U.S. colleges and universities to engage in surveillance of Chinese students and professors.[31] However, the tactics of the Kuomintang did not discourage the movement. Many Chinese began reexamining their relations with the Nationalist government and showed a willingness, for the first time, to openly criticize the Kuomintang leadership.

At the outset, the centers of the Protecting Diaoyutai Movement were the University of Michigan, the University of California at Berkeley, the University of Chicago, and the State University of New York at Stony Brook. Chinese students from other major campuses also participated in a series of demonstrations, carrying banners and shouting such slogans as "Fight, Fight, for Diaoyutai!" and "We Want Justice, When? Now!" as they marched through the streets of New York, Washington, D.C., Chicago, and many college towns. They demanded the return of Chinese territories and attacked the Kuomintang's weak foreign policy and Japanese new imperialism. In early March of 1971, 523 Chinese professors in American universities and colleges signed a petition addressed to President Chiang Kai-shek, demanding that he concede not one inch of territory to the Japanese.[32] Across the United States, Chinese intellectuals held a series of seminars, conferences, and workshops to discuss Chinese "urgent national issues." In December, 1971, more than 200 Chinese scholars attended a "Chinese Unification Seminar" sponsored by the Chinese students of Columbia University. In January, 1973, a similar conference was held in Philadelphia where the "Taiwan Problem" was the discussion topic. The following spring a similar conference was held at Berkeley.[33]

In the early 1970s, major U.S. campuses were enlivened by a flowering of Chinese student organizations of various political shades. Publications discussing the future of Taiwan and the future of China poured from mimeograph and photocopy machines. Notable examples included: Buffalo's *The Buffalo*, Pittsburgh's *Unification Correspondence*, Chicago's *Diaoyutai Dispatches*, Berkeley's *Berkeley Dispatches* and *Berkeley Green Seedlings*, Michigan's *Brief News on National Affairs*, and Honolulu's *Friends of China*. In addition, *Spring and Autumn from the U.S. Capital* appeared in Washington, Stony Brook Chinese published the *Brook's Correspondence*, The Chinese in New Jersey and Illinois printed, respectively, the *New Jersey Correspondence* and the *Brief Reports on Current Issues,* and the Houston Chinese students wrote the *America South Correspondence.*[34] The majority of these publications were handwritten in Chinese before being mimeographed, and their circulations were generally limited to 2,000 copies. The articles were mostly polemical rather than analytical, emotionally charged, and propagandistic in tone. Among the popular topics were the new socialist motherland, Taiwan society, the Kuomintang policies, how to deal with new imperialism, and similar subjects.

Chinese students involved in the Diaoyutai dispute regarded themselves as spokesmen for the Chinese people because their brethren in Taiwan and in mainland China were not free to express ideas contrary to the policy of their respective governments. In this sense, the intellectual dissenters of the Diaoyutai movement reflected a self-image much in the pattern of Confucian tradition, which has always assigned to its intellectual elite an important role as critics of the political order. Often this responsibility had been discharged only at the level of symbolic remonstrance, but on occasion criticism of government policy had been more forcefully expressed, as in the case of protests against the Versailles Peace Treaty in 1919 and against the Japanese aggression of 1937. But the student protest of the Diaoyutai period was far different in scope and intent. The tone of its challenge to Kuomintang authority was less reminiscent of the traditional style of Confucian remonstrance and more suggestive of the kind of intellectual dissent that was so familiar to American colleges and universities during the 1960s anti-Vietnam War era and the civil-rights campaign. In short, it was the Americanization of foreign-born Chinese students that inspired them to take to the streets to proclaim their lack of confidence in the Kuomintang policies.

6. Chinese Americans and the Unification of China

Politically, the Protecting Diaoyutai movement and the ensuing Unification campaign had limited effect. They did succeed in embarrassing the Kuomintang government, and opened channels for dialogue between the Chinese in America and the Communist leadership in Peking. But the movement had no impact on the Diaoyutai dispute; the Kuomintang regime remained in power and Chinese students' overtures to socialist China were not altogether appreciated. These movements also failed to generate popular support among the heterogeneous Chinese groups in America. Following the deaths of Chairman Mao Zedong, Premier Zhou Enlai, and Marshal Zhu De in 1976, the image of the People's Republic suffered a sharp decline. Crimes allegedly committed by the "Gang of Four" were gradually revealed, and the misery of the Chinese people under Communist rule began to become clearer. The Chinese in America learned that hundreds of thousands of Chinese intellectuals had been sent to labor camps and that millions of Chinese people had been executed, imprisoned, or starved to death. Instead of seeing the happy, smiling, prosperous utopian society described by American visitors to China in the early 1970s, after the beginning of Ping Pong Diplomacy, the overseas Chinese who visited China were appalled that living standards were still terribly low, that party leaders had become privileged elites with private food stores, chauffeured limousines, and servants, and that corruption had become a way of life again.

Chinese living in America once more had to reassess support for unification under Communist rule or the Kuomintang system. Many were disillusioned and felt that they had been naively misled by Communist propaganda. Many of the Protecting Diaoyutai Movement's leaders learned a bitter political lesson and renounced all unification activities. The Protecting Diaoyutai movement and the Unification campaign withered away by the beginning of 1978. In the meantime, the Kuomintang government refurbished its policy toward the Chinese intellectuals in America, devising a series of programs to attract and hold their allegiance. For example, it subsidized such pro-Taiwan professional groups as the Chinese American Association for Science and Technology, the New England Association for Chinese Professionals, and the Chinese American Librarian Association. It stepped up goodwill activities by sending youth missions, opera troupes, and Chinese films to major U.S. campuses and Chinatowns. Its officials held receptions for Chinese participants at annual conferences of the Association for Asian Studies. It invited prominent Chinese American scientists and scholars, community leaders, youth representatives and athletes to visit Taiwan to attend seminars, Double-Tenth national day celebrations, overseas Chinese conferences, and national reconstruction conferences. Chinese visitors from the United States were given preferential treatment on the government-owned China Airlines. In general, the Kuomintang government did a much better job in courting the Chinese in America than did the People's Republic.

After the downfall of the "Gang of Four" and the emergence of Deng Xiaoping, the Peking regime took a number of steps to stir overseas Chinese patriotism and to encourage unification of the Chinese nation. On New Year's Day, 1979, the Chinese Communist Party called for establishing of three links and four exchanges between the People's Republic and the Nationalist government as first steps toward a peaceful reunification. The three links referred to mails, trade and air, and shipping services. The four exchanges called for the exchange of relatives and tourists, academic groups, cultural groups, and athletes. These overtures were immediately rejected by Taiwan. The Chinese in America were divided on the Communist proposals because, on the same day that the three links and four exchanges were proposed, the United States established diplomatic ties with the People's Republic, ending the nearly 30-year lapse in relations and, in the eyes of many, deserting Nationalist China. Left-wing Chinese in America were elated; die-hard Kuomintang supporters were enraged; the majority of Chinese Americans remained undecided.

At this unsettled juncture in the formation of Chinese-American opinion, the highest official delegation in Chinese history visited the United States. At the invitation of President and Mrs. Jimmy Carter, Vice-Premier Deng Xiaoping made an official visit to the United States from January 29 to February 4, 1979. During his three-day stay in Washington, D.C., Deng held talks with Carter, including discussions on the future of Taiwan. On the evening of January 30, Deng attended a reception given by the U.S.-China Peoples' Friendship Association and the National Association of Chinese Americans and Overseas Chinese in the United States, while hundreds of Chinese demonstrators shouted anti-Communist slogans outside the hall. In his speech Deng announced that Chinese Americans were welcome to visit China, to tour the country, to locate relatives and friends there, to offer suggestions, and to give assistance to China in its drive for modernization. On the question of Taiwan, Deng declared: "After the normalization of relations between China and the United States, the chances of bringing Taiwan back to the embrace of the motherland and reunifying the country in a peaceful way have increased."[35] Many disagreed with Deng's optimism, but his visit put renewed pressure on the Kuomintang leadership.

In September, 1981, Deng's comrade-in-arms, Marshal Ye Jianying, made a nine-point peace talk proposal on behalf of the Chinese Communist government, calling on the Kuomintang of Taiwan to talk with the Chinese Communist Party as equals. Ye announced that the Chinese Communists would allow Taiwan to maintain its military, economic, and social autonomy. Peking's new peace-talk proposals once again attracted the attention of the international as well as the Chinese-American community. But Taiwan continued to dismiss these proposals as gimmicks designed to deceive the people of the world. The Nationalists pointed out that all such proposals had two accompanying preconditions: first, the Taiwan government was to be considered a "provincial government" under jurisdiction of the Peking regime; second, the invasion of Taiwan by force was not ruled out if peace talks failed. In other words, as the Kuomintang government pointed out, the long-standing tactic of the Chinese Communists was to use negotiation as a prelude to military action.[36] The Kuomintang newspapers and its friendly organizations in America, such as the Six Companies, the Anti-Communist League, the Taiwan Benevolent Association of America, and the American University of Chinese Students Association, sponsored a series of forums and seminars and placed advertisements to discredit Peking's peace overtures.

The propaganda warfare continued into the presidency of Ronald Reagan, who had spent much of his political career castigating the Chinese Communists and supporting the Nationalist Chinese government on Taiwan. Peking, evidently annoyed by the Reagan administration's slower pace toward full normalization, reactivated the Taiwan issue by publicizing a U.S. arms sales agreement with Taiwan. The Reagan administration quietly negotiated with Peking, seeking a formula that would neutralize the tricky Taiwan issue. The result was a second U.S.—China communiqué, issued August 17, 1982, which called for limiting and eventually ending American arms sales to the Kuomintang government. But the United States had done little to actually curtail arms sales to Taiwan when Reagan made his historical five-day visit to the People's Republic in the spring of 1984. Reagan claimed to have laid the groundwork for a new partnership that could serve both nations well, yet he was determiend not to do anything which could be interpreted as a sellout of Taiwan. During his stay in China, both sides tried to avoid any public disagreement over Taiwan

that would affect the harmony of the visit. Official statements suggested that the Chinese leaders did not press Reagan about the speed
with which Americans should carry out the agreement of the communiqué. However, Taiwan remained the most troublesome issue in the
building of Sino-American relations.

While Peking was unable to force Washington to cut all ties with
Taiwan, it did make a deal with Great Britain on Hong Kong's future
after 1997, providing for Hong Kong's economic self-rule under Peking's political authority. Since early 1984, Communist Chinese leaders have suggested that the Hong Kong model could be used to unify
the mainland and Taiwan. They believed that the continued modernization of the mainland, coupled with continued efforts to diplomatically isolate Taiwan, could be the carrot and stick that would
eventually compel the Kuomintang to begin bargaining for peaceful
unification. To accelerate this process, Peking designated Deng Ying-
cao, widow of the late premier Zhou Enlai, to direct a new united
front campaign, with winning support of the Chinese in America as its
immediate goal. Consequently, 1984 witnessed an increasing number
of contacts between the Communist officials and their Chinese compatriots in the United States. In the summer of 1984, for example, Peking sent a Triad team (secret societies organized before 1949),
headed by an 84-year-old man, to visit the Chinese Freemasons in San
Francisco, New York, Boston, Washington, D.C., and other major
U.S. cities. Almost simultaneously, it dispatched the deputy governor
of Guangdong province and several officials from southern China to
induce Cantonese immigrants to visit the mainland by promising to
return their confiscated properties and to allow their relatives to join
them abroad.[37] And following the politically motivated assassination
in October, 1984, of Henry Liu, a Chinese-American journalist and
the author of a biography critical of Taiwan's president, Jiang
Jingguo (Chiang Ching-kuo), Peking stepped up its anti-Kuomintang
propaganda in America and began to make contact with several
Chinese-American groups that previously favored the Nationalist
government.

To strengthen the bond between mainland China and the Chinese
in America, Peking appointed a Mr. Lin, vice president of the Taiwan
Benevolent Association of America, as deputy chief of China's Olympic team, whose extraordinary performance in Los Angeles had
aroused the spirit of the Chinese Americans. In dealing with Chinese
scholars and scientists, Peking employed tactics formerly used by the
Kuomintang by holding study tours, summer camps, and seminars.
Notable among such activities was the 1984 summer camp held in the
port city of Daren, which was attended by more than 140 Chinese
from America.[38] Peking asked several American experts on China to

help publicize the inauguration of the North America edition of the first Chinese-language newsweekly, the *Liaowang* (Outlook), from the People's Republic. Those who gave their endorsement included A. Doak Barnett of Johns Hopkins University, Arthur H. Rosen, President of National Committee on U.S.-China Relations, John Service of the University of California at Berkeley, Harrison E. Salisbury of *The New York Times,* and Thomas P. Bernstein of Columbia University.[39]

How did the Chinese in America react to the new overtures from Peking? In general, the older Chinese immigrants, some of whom had suffered under communist rule, tended to be more cautious and remained either neutral or loyal to the Kuomintang. But many young Chinese, who played down the importance of Marxist ideology but took pride in China's achievements, have shown some enthusiasm toward the mainland. In the final analysis, however, the unification issue continued to divide the Chinese-American community and to provide a battleground on which different political groups claimed their trophies and exaggerated the casualties they inflicted upon their enemies.

7. The Taiwanese Independent Movement in America

Complicating the complex political entanglement between the pro-Peking and pro-Kuomintang forces were the aspirations of Taiwanese Americans, whose number by 1985 had swollen to an estimated 100,000. Among them, more than 6,000 were holders of Ph.D. degrees from American universities. An estimated 50,000 of these Taiwanese have participated in activities sponsored by the Taiwan Provincials' Association, an organization once pronounced seditious by the Kuomintang government. How then does this new element fit into the multidimensional relationships among the pro-Kuomintang, the American-born Chinese, and the pro-Peking Unification groups? And how did the Taiwanese Independent Movement in America influence the already complicated U.S.-China relations?

Both the Communist and the Kuomintang governments regard Taiwan as an integral part of China, a view acknowledged by the United States and confirmed in the Shanghai Communiqué signed by the late Premier Zhou Enlai and former President Richard Nixon. Yet the wishes of the native Taiwanese people—that is, people of Chinese stock who had settled earlier on the island and who constitute approximately 85 percent of the island's population—have been ignored. The Taiwan problem is more than a piece of unfinished business left over from the Chinese civil war. Actually, with the exception of the years 1945–1949, the island has not been part of mainland China since 1895, in spite of the fact that the native Taiwanese are ethnically Han Chinese and culturally Sinic. Because of long political separation from mainland China, Taiwan's history, economy, and customs have diverged from those of China proper. Moreover, before approximately 2 million Chinese civilian refugees fled to Taiwan in 1949, the seeds of discord between the majority Taiwanese and the minority mainland Chinese had already been sown by Chiang Kai-shek's soldiers, who took control of Taiwan's garrison following the Japanese surrender in the fall of 1945.

The Chinese military rulers, at the outset, treated the Taiwanese as a conquered people. The Taiwan islanders, in spite of the fact that many had served in the Japanese military during World War II, deeply resented the treatment. A general uprising broke out February 28, 1947, resulting in the slaughter of several thousand Taiwanese, among them doctors, lawyers, teachers and college students, and other leaders. Some were probably Communist sympathizers, trying to pave the way for an easy Communist takeover. According to George Kerr, an American official in Taiwan, the uprising was caused by the "foreignness," rudeness, and arrogance of the Chinese forces of occupation.[40] Even though the revolt was ruthlessly crushed, the 2.28 incident has since become a rallying point for a fledgling Taiwanese nationalism. Taking cues from neighboring states, such as Korea, Vietnam, the Philippines, and Indonesia, the Taiwanese nationalists have used the martyrdom and blood of the 2.28 incident to rally other dissident Taiwanese behind their independence movement. Because they were constantly under surveillance and the island provided no sanctuary for antigovernment activities, leaders of the movement slipped out of the country, first to Japan in the 1950s, then to the United States and Canada in the 1960s and 1970s. Thus, in the past two decades, the Taiwanese Independent Movement's major battleground against the Kuomintang regime was in America instead of Taiwan.

The movement slowly increased its activities as more and more Taiwanese students came to study, many eventually settling in the United States. During the period 1950–1983, a total of 74,000 college graduates from Taiwan were enrolled in American colleges and universities; of this number only 10,033, or less than 13 percent, returned to Taiwan.[41] Of the more than 87 percent student-immigrant Taiwanese, many joined and ultimately became stalwarts in the Taiwanese Independent Movement. However, the road to becoming a revolutionary convert was often tortuous and hazardous. Prior to their American experience, nearly all of the Taiwanese students had gone through a carefully designed program of indoctrination, by which the Kuomintang regime hoped to produce model citizens in accordance with its ideology, that is, one who adhered to Chinese culture and to the teachings of Confucius, Dr. Sun Yat-sen, and Chiang Kai-shek.

However, after exposure to the more liberal American education and after learning more about Western traditions and of modern China, many of the young Taiwanese underwent a painful process of what psychologists call "marginalization," both intellectually and emotionally. No longer mere provincial youths, their minds were liberated and, not infrequently, they were torn between the values of the two cultures. Exposed to liberal professors who more often than not criticized the Kuomintang record on the mainland and attributed the debacle of 1949 to the corruption and ineffectual leadership of the Kuomintang, many became converts to the independence movement.

In addition, liberal American news media, with their blunt and even relentless remonstrations against U.S. officials, exerted enormous influence on the political views of the Taiwanese student-immigrants. They were forced to compare the American democratic and open society with the political system of their native land. In spite of economic development and educational accomplishments by the Nationalists, people in Taiwan were deprived of basic rights to freely elect their own government (although elections were held at local levels). Since 1949, real power has remained in the hands of about two dozen older Chinese and a handful of Taiwanese "collaborators." For 37 years Taiwan has been under martial law, the longest period in modern world history. Although the martial law was mild and the Kuomintang government rarely used force, strikes were not allowed, free speech was curtailed, the right of assembly was restricted, and censorship of publications was often practiced.[42] Such restraints distressed the Taiwanese in America. Their anguish was increased by the fact that Kuomintang diplomacy had been on the defensive in its battle against the Communists since the late 1960s. Neither did the changing U.S. policy toward Taiwan help their grievances. In short, the majority of Taiwanese in America, groping in political confusion and cultural transition, added to their intellectual and emotional baggage many new and foreign concepts and values. In such a process of marginalization, they became culturally more Occidental and politically more American, while maintaining many elements of Taiwanese identification. These were people most likely to become infatuated with the Taiwanese Independent Movement.

The Taiwanese Independent Movement first drew the attention of the American public in April, 1970, when two young Taiwanese nationalists, one an architect and the other a Ph.D. candidate in journalism, attempted to assassinate Jiang Jingguo, older son of Chiang Kai-shek and Chiang's successor and President of the Kuomintang government on Taiwan. The attempt took place near the entrance of the New York Plaza Hotel on April 24, 1970. The abortive assassination immediately piqued the interest of the American news media in Taiwanese grievances and Taiwanese activities in the United States. Following the incident, the Kuomintang allegedly stepped up its security measures and established a network of spies in American colleges and universities. According to a report published by *Newsweek*, there were in the 1970s as many as five agencies of the Kuomintang government (including the equivalents of the U.S. National Security Agency, FBI, and Defense Department) gathering intelligence in the United States. They were loosely controlled through Taiwan's Embassy, which since 1979 was called Taiwan's Coordination Council for North American Affairs (CCNAA). On several occasions *Newsweek* reported that Kuomintang officials in Taiwan kept tabs on which American universities needed more informants and which students and professors needed to be watched. When the Kuomintang got a negative report about a student or a professor, it usually issued a warning to the student. Further transgressions would prompt a visit by a security agent to the student's family in Taiwan. Revoking passports, blacklisting, subtle threatening, and even imprisonment were used to deal with dissident Taiwanese in the United States.[43]

The Kuomintang government denied that it subsidized the ubiquitous informers on American campuses or that it sponsored any spying scheme in the United States. Such denials, however, were contradicted by, among other cases, the arrest of Rita Yeh and the violent deaths of Henry Liu and Dr. Chen Wencheng. Yeh was the daughter of a veteran Chinese officer and a former University of Minnesota student who allegedly attended a Communist Chinese movie while studying in the United States. Not long after her return to Taiwan she was sentenced to a 14-year prison term in January, 1981, by the martial law court. Chen was a professor of computer science at the Carnegie-Mellon University in Pittsburgh. He allegedly raised funds for the dissident magazine *Formosa Weekly*. In the summer of 1981 Chen went to Taiwan for a family visit and was brought to the Taiwan Garrison Headquarters and interrogated for 13 hours. Later, his battered body was found on the pavement beneath the fire escape of the National Taiwan University Research Library. Many Taiwanese around the world were outraged at the violent death of the 31-year-old professor. But his death also aroused the concern of the United States Congress, whose House Foreign Affairs Sub-Committee scheduled a series of hearings between July and October, 1981. Afterward, Congressman Jim Leach, Republican of Iowa, said: "Without question, agents of the Taiwan government have engaged in harassment, intimidation, and monitoring of Taiwanese Americans."[44] Leach called on the United States government to investigate Professor Chen's death and to determine whether Nationalist spies were violating the Foreign Agents Registration Act.

Congressman Leach's concern was shared by a number of liberal lawmakers, notably Senator Edward Kennedy (Democrat of Massachusetts), Senator Claiborne Pell (Democrat of Rhode Island), and Congressman Stephen Solarz (Democrat of New York). They brought pressure on the State Department to take action, including a cutback on the number of Kuomintang government personnel allowed in the United States. They urged that arms sales to Taiwan be made contingent on a certification by the President that the Kuomintang had ended surveillance activities in America. It appeared that the Congressional sources were convinced of the seriousness of the problem.

Other examples of suppression surfaced in Taiwan. For example, a Harvard-trained woman lawyer, Lu Xiulian, who once spoke at a human-rights rally in the city of Gaoxiong, was arrested December 10, 1979. Miss Lu and seven Taiwanese activists were later charged with trying to subvert the Kuomintang government. They were court-martialled and received harsh sentences; one to life imprisonment and the rest to prison terms of 14 and 12 years. Many Taiwanese charged that torture was used to extract false confessions during detention of the so-called Gaoxiong 8 and 33 other dissidents who were being tried in civil court. While the United States government remained silent on the Gaoxiong incident, the Taiwanese in America took to the streets to protest. Between August, 1979, and July, 1980, angry Taiwanese attacked Kuomintang buildings and personnel in the United States. The more publicized incidents included breaking the windows of the CCNAA in Washington, D.C., ransacking the Kuomintang-subsidized newspaper headquarters in New York, bombing the China Airlines offices in Los Angeles and Chicago, and harassing CCNAA personnel throughout the United States.[45] These acts were later declared terrorist acts by local officials, such as the attorney general of California, and denounced by a number of conservative lawmakers, including Senator Jeremiah Denton (Republican of Alabama), Senator Barry Goldwater (Republican of Arizona), and Congressman Henry Hyde (Republican of Illinois). When the Reagan administration took office, violent acts against the Kuomintang stopped abruptly in the United States but they continued on the island of Taiwan, where three bombs were set off in the offices of Kuomintang-controlled newspapers April 26, 1983.[46]

While taking radical action against the Kuomintang, the Taiwanese nationalists also realized the importance of public relations and began to utilize the congressional lobby to advance their cause. In February, 1982, they organized the Formosan Association for Public Affairs

(FAPA) in Short Hills, New Jersey, dedicated to promoting the interests and welfare of the Taiwanese people. The North America Taiwanese Professors' Association, which had a memberhsip of over 300, also became politically more active. The Formosan Association of Human Rights, which was headquartered in New York and had local chapters throughout the nation, stepped up its activities. Through meetings, publications, and public speeches on behalf of Taiwan's political prisoners, these groups helped to develop public concern about the human rights situation on Taiwan and to enlist assistance from other international organizations on human rights. They also waged a national letter campaign, inundating the White House and the Congress with post cards, letters, and telegrams. One immediate result was overwhelming approval of a Senate Foreign Relations Committee resolution, passed November 15, 1983, stating in essence that the future of Taiwan should be settled peacefully, free of coercion, and in a manner acceptable to the people of Taiwan.[47] Even though the resolution had no legal force, it was nevertheless a source of concern for both Peking and the Kuomintang, on grounds that the Taiwanese plea for self-determination had the support of a substantial number of U.S. Senators.

In order to generate maximum support of the Taiwanese in America, the independent movement leaders resorted to propaganda techniques that had been effectively utilized by other revolutionary movements in modern times. Publishing of the *Formosa Weekly*, which led to the arrest of the Gaoxiong 8 in the first place, was resumed in Southern California. The organ of the Taiwan Independence League, the *Independent Taiwan*, after publishing its last issue (no. 112) on June 28, 1981, began the biweekly *Taiwan Tribune* to meet the demand of an increasing readership. The *Asian Journal*, published in 1981 as a moderate, business-oriented paper, also assumed an anti-Kuomintang stance. The Gaoxiong Incident became the impetus for encouraging hundreds of thousands of Taiwanese, in the months that followed, to march through the streets of New York, Washington, D.C., Los Angeles, Houston, Boston and other U.S. cities to publicize their quest for an independent Taiwan.

But the support for Taiwan independence among the Taiwanese in America was not uniform, despite their common belief that the Kuomintang government was repressive, corrupt, and undemocratic. Within the movement, there were several factions, each with its own program and unique leadership. For example, the Taiwan Independence League, which was the oldest and also the largest political group, emphasized "freedom, democracy and human rights" and favored a plebiscite supervised by the United Nations to allow the inhabitants of Taiwan to decide their own future. Members of this league were mostly well educated and successful professionals and were generally fervent nationalists. They consistently rejected both the Nationalist and the Communist claim to Taiwan. The second group, known as the Self-Rule Taiwanese Clique, consisted of many Taiwanese exiles who at one time or another served in Taiwan's local governments. Some members of this group, the Kuomintang believed, had made contact with Peking, seeking an autonomous status for Taiwan. Taiwanese Presbyterians, whose leadership had a history of altercations with the Kuomintang, formed a third group. They demanded that martial law be lifted, political prisoners be released, Kuomintang political commissars be removed from the Taiwan army, and that popular elections be held for all officials, including the president, the governor, the two metropolitan mayors and all parliament representatives. Finally, there was a younger group of Taiwanese socialists, who admired the Scandinavian type of social democracy; they called for equitable distribution of land and capital and efficient welfare programs for the needy and the poor, along with other reforms.

It was clear that mutual dissent masked a rich diversity in the Taiwanese nationalist movement in America and that the faction-ridden leadership had failed to persuade the United States government to openly support its cause. For its part, the United States appeared to be committed to a policy of realism, as former President Nixon once said, "There is no more important guarantee to Taiwan security than a strong China-U.S. relationship." Nevertheless, the Taiwanese nationalist movement in America helped to speed up the Taiwanization of the Kuomintang; more and more Taiwanese have filled in the rank and file of the Kuomintang party, and nearly all the current military recruits are native-born Taiwanese. Moreover, equal education and an increasing rate of intermarriage between the Taiwanese and mainland Chinese have helped to erase old ethnic differences. Also, political realities and mutual interests have forced the two groups to hang together. Out of the gradual and inevitable Taiwanization of the Kuomintang, a new society, a new economy, and a new political entity have emerged on what the Portuguese once called "Ila Formosa—the Beautiful Island." This may be the most important contribution of the Taiwanese Independent Movement in America. It is an exaggeration to say that Taiwan is the 51st state of the United States, but what has transpired in Taiwan suggests that the Taiwanese in America and the United States government will certainly play a very significant role in the future of Taiwan.

The Taiwanese in America are a second wave of student-immigrants whose sojourner outlook toward their residence in America is similar to that of the nineteenth-century Chinese laborers. But while motivation for the earlier Chinese immigration was basically economic, political considerations were equally important for the massive student immigration of the post–1960 era. Some came to America to wage war against the Kuomintang, but many left Taiwan fearing an imminent invasion and eventual occupation of the island by the Communist Chinese. Like the first wave of the Chinese student-immigrants of the 1940s, these people have a working knowledge of English, a professional education in an American university, and financial resources that put them economically in the middle class. At least one out of every three Taiwanese American families has a child taking music lessons in either piano, violin, or cello. Over 90 percent of their college-aged children are attending college, and a vast majority of the families are reported to have their own homes with an average equity of over $50,000, plus savings accounts and liquid assets. Although they are involved, one way or the other, in the future development of Taiwan, they participate only tangentially in the main American society. In general, they are occupationally integrated, but they socialize primarily with their immediate ethnic group, or in Milton Gordon's term, their "ethclass".[48] Accordingly, there is a big gap between the Cantonese-speaking population of America's Chinatowns and the Taiwanese-speaking population in the suburbs of American metropolitan cities. Contemporary Taiwanese student-immigrants adhere to values, sentiments, attitudes, and beliefs entirely different from those of the Cantonese bachelor sojourners but reminiscent of the Chinese students stranded by World War II. Certainly, their extrinsic cultural trait has added one more new ingredient to the already pluralized American culture, and their struggle for success and recognition has helped to vivify the highly diversified American nation.

EPILOGUE

The history of the Chinese in America has been marked by cultural conflicts, political alienation, and a stream of economic and social injustices. In the midst of this, American views of the Chinese have changed from highly unfavorable in the nineteenth century, to more realistic in the 1930s and 40s, to highly favorable in recent years. This study divides Chinese Americans into sojourners, American-born citizens, and student-immigrants, recounting the unique historical experience of each group.

The bitter experience of the laboring sojourners resulted primarily from their own resistance to acculturation, as shown in their close-knit Chinatown enclaves, the hierarchical system of self-governance, and the Chinese consul generals' strong influence over their associational life. Their problems were further compounded by the prejudiced and stereotyped white perception of them. The common characterizations of the Chinese—heathen, evil, filthy, treacherous, and labor scabs—were false, but the American community at large regarded the Chinese as unassimilable and unworthy of the rights of citizenship. Consequently, the Chinese were excluded from the political life of the nation and became a benighted minority. Geographical concentration of the Chinese in a few pockets on the West Coast was both a manifestation of and a factor in contributing to their segregation and separatism.

But the Chinese could not escape the influence of a new and energetic culture. As they became involved in the transformation of America, they themselves were concomitantly transformed. By the time a generation of American-born Chinese came along, the unsavory image of the Chinese had begun to change and so had the attitudes of the Chinese younger generation. By World War II the Chinese had improved their status educationally and economically and had successfully dispelled many of the stereotypes about them. They increasingly interacted with white Americans, adopted Anglo-American names, and attended Christian churches. Yet, despite this acculturation and their relatively improved social and economic conditions, the ABC often found themselves culturally perplexed and psychologically troubled; consequently they suffered in varying degrees from an identity crisis.

Later a group of student-immigrants, who came mostly from

187

middle- and upper-class Chinese society, not only helped to heighten Chinese pride but also drastically changed American perception of the Chinese. In the 1960s and '70s the adjectives commonly used to characterize the Chinese were smart, quick, industrious, reliable, efficient, and fun-loving. Student-immigrants understood the pluralistic and legalistic nature of American society. They believed that they represented the best of the East, and in making contributions to this powerful and vibrant country, they wanted to make full use of their Chinese inheritance. Indeed, the massive student immigration since 1960 has significantly improved the collective worth of the Chinese, both quantitatively and qualitatively.

It is evident that the Chinese in America can no longer be studied as a homogeneous group as they usually were prior to the 1960s. In one way they were a unique minority people, having common ancestry and embracing the same ideal. In many ways they were several subgroups among one people as the Chinese population became far more heterogeneous. By the 1970s the Chinese-American population included males and females of different ages, professionals and students who spoke diverse dialects, and merchants and laborers from various parts of Asia. Furthermore, the course of American history affected each of these groups in discrete and unique ways.

The diversified and increasingly individualistic population has made it difficult to generalize about the quality of Chinese-American life. For hundreds of thousands, the Chinese success story has ended with careers as scientists, engineers, pharmacists, and entrepreneurs. The success story also included the fact that one out of every three Chinese in America was a college graduate, while only 17 percent of the white population attained that level. By 1980 the median family income of Chinese Americans had equalled that of white families. On the other hand, a substantial number of Chinese remained unassimilated; the "Chinaman's chance" was still probably less than that of the white majority. The main hindrance to assimilation remained the language barrier. In the 1970s between 20,000 and 30,000 Chinese in the San Francisco-Oakland area and about 75 percent of the Chinese population in Boston spoke little English or none at all.[1] Those Chinese who did not speak English, whether Cantonese or non-Cantonese, skilled or unskilled, found themselves locked into low-paying, menial work in and around Chinatowns.

Increasing numbers of non-English-speaking immigrants caused a population explosion in the already congested Chinese urban quarters. As a result, the ability of the Chinese to provide instant employment for new arrivals became increasingly strained and contributed to a collage of economic and social problems. The Chinese restaurant business became saturated, hand laundries were replaced by automatic facilities, and the old garment factories declined. There had always been underemployment, but the inundation of new immigrants caused even more unemployment, and by the mid-1960s the capacity of Chinatowns to exist as isolated economic islands had vanished. Job problems compounded Chinatown's poor housing, deficient education, and substandard health facilities. Since the 1960s America's Chinatowns have been plagued by crimes and gang violence, sometimes perpetrated by organized rings.

These recent social and economic problems have caused a breakdown in the traditional Chinese community structure in America. The once-powerful Chinese Consolidated Benevolent Association and its umbrella subsidiary associations have proven increasingly anachronistic in the new and large population. Traditional values provided by the old leadership have been challenged. The old elite, often inward-looking and wealthy entrepreneurs, has been replaced by a new elite of better educated, white-collar professionals. As contacts with the non-Chinese community widened, the hitherto impenetrable Chinatown boundary, which tended to isolate its members from the dominant society, has been broken. Moreover, prejudice and discrimination against the Chinese has declined, and more and more affluent Chinese live outside Chinatown, breaking the traditionally voluntary segregation. Consequently, the main functions of America's Chinatowns have shifted from defensive necessities to business purposes. One may, therefore, conclude that as young Chinese continue to move out of Chinatown, eventually Chinatown will exist primarily as a commercial district instead of a residential area.[2]

As the center of gravity of the Chinese community has shifted away from Chinatown and as the traditional leadership has gradually been replaced by a new elite, Chinese social relationships have become more complex and more Americanized. Traditional situation-centered social ties, such as kinship, clanship, and huiguan networks, which were based exclusively on personal relationships among the Chinese themselves, began to be replaced by individual-centered social relationships between the Chinese and other ethnic groups and among the different social and cultural Chinese groups as well. Professional colleagues, business partners, friends, and neighbors were more important relationships than distant cousins, huiguan brothers, or someone from the same ancestral home or with the same surname. As these new social ties worked to lessen the Chinese desire to maintain their ethnic and cultural purity, more interracial marriages and more interactions between the Chinese and other ethnic groups took place. Another powerful means of facilitating Chinese assimilation was America's educational system. The Chinese have taken full advantage of it. In part, education is indoctrination, and the young Chinese who learned American history and values became as American as their classmates. Like most other educated Americans, modern Chinese professionals found job opportunities throughout the nation, further breaking out of their cultural isolation. This in turn accelerated Chinese integration into the economic, social, and political fabric of America's mainstream.[3] For it is the contact with people of different cultures and different races that takes away some of their nativistic attitudes and makes them more like other members of the big melting pot. By the 1980s it appeared that the Chinese were well on their way to following the Japanese, the Italians, the Jews, and other minorities who, through travail and joy, hope and frustration, had participated in the great American melting pot experience.

In spite of such sanguine prospects, the Chinese continued to remain behind whites economically. Chinese males still earn less than their white counterparts with the same educational experience. While the proportion of Chinese males in professional and managerial occupations is higher than that of any other population group, income levels of Chinese men are generally lower. In fact, while Chinese may have higher family median incomes, as indicated in both the 1970 and 1980 censuses, Chinese males earn only 75 percent as much as white males. There is a feeling in the Chinese community that subtle discrimination in employment will continue. For instance, Chinese Americans in civil service alleged that they had been continually passed over for promotion to supervisory positions in favor of whites who scored lower on written examinations. Many Chinese were convinced that a similar pattern of discrimination existed in the private sector. A study of AT&T Laboratories between 1972 and 1976 showed that whites took a median of nine years to reach supervisory jobs but Chinese took twelve years.[4] A report published in 1978 indicated that Chinese college professors published more professional articles than white colleagues, but were paid less.[5] Government agencies and private businesses frequently omitted Chinese Americans when forming minority programs, though Chinese Americans were always included when minority employment was calculated.[6]

In sheer economic terms, the Chinese in America have undoubtedly made significant headway since World War II, but social scientists use different criteria to judge success in culture. In the nineteenth century, one was successful if he could save enough money from his menial or manual labor to return to China a wealthy man. Now the Chinese complain that, even though statistically they are above average in income, more than 65 percent of the Chinese families have more than one wage earner. Thus, their economic progress remains questionable. In the past, Chinese culture emphasized restraint of strong feelings, obedience, harmony in human relations, and formality in interpersonal relations. Present-day Chinese Americans have learned spontaneity, assertiveness, competitiveness, and informality from American whites. Their struggle to get into America's middle class has resulted, for many, in severe psychological disorders, such as excessive conformity, alienation, lack of confidence, and low self-esteem.[7]

In 1983, when the published letters of Harry S Truman to his wife revealed that Truman as a young man despised the Chinese and the Japanese, many Chinese Americans quickly proclaimed that the age-old stereotype of the Chinese, and discrimination against them, remained much more pervasive than Chinese optimists had believed. They cautioned their fellow countrymen to take little comfort from the fact that the present target of American racial prejudice was the Vietnamese and the Japanese.[8] Cynics declared that Chinese were not and would never be equal to whites in terms of educational benefits, employment, parity in job compensation, and political opportunities.

On the other hand, much change had been accomplished. Who could have predicted in the days of early anti-Chinese furor that Hawaiians would elect a Chinese to the U.S. Senate in 1959 and that California voters would overwhelmingly choose, in 1978, a Chinese woman to be their Secretary of State? Who could have predicted, in the anti-coolie era, that in 1980, 85 percent of the Chinese families in eastern Arkansas would have a son or son-in-law who was a doctor? In November, 1984, when Dr. S. B. Woo, a China-born physics professor, was elected lieutenant governor of Delaware, even the pessimists agreed that the Chinese might one day find their place in the American sun.

In political terms, however, being a minority remained discriminatory. In addition, Chinese political life in America was exacerbated by the problems of China and Taiwan. The development of so many political subgroups within the Chinese-American community encouraged division rather than unity; differences between the Chinatown Chinese and non-Chinatown Chinese impeded the election of Chinese candidates on the county and state levels. Internal feuding, caused by the old country's political problems, was fratricidal and self-defeating. The one million Chinese, constituting a bare 0.4 percent of the total U.S. population and torn by perennial internal rivalry, seemed destined to continue a subordinate role in American political life.

In order to attain equality with other ethnic groups, the Chinese in America need to shift their loyalties, expectations, and political activities from self-entrenched and China-oriented or Taiwan-oriented isolation. One way to overcome being "a sheet of loose sand" and to forge a true unity would be the establishing of a national Chinese

American Foundation, similar to the National Italian American Foundation or the Anti-Defamation League of B'nai B'rith. Such an organization would transcend political, economic, and linguistic groups and aim at promoting Chinese American interests and fighting against injustice and stereotyping. Chinese Americans should realize that, whether they are pro-Peking or pro-Taiwan, whether they speak Mandarin, Cantonese, Taiwanese, or Shanghainese, whether they think of themselves as Taoist, Buddhist, atheist, or Christian, they are basically Chinese Americans.

Such a plea does not mean that in this diversified and pluralistic American society the Chinese need to give up their respective cultures and distinguishing characteristics. It does mean, however, that the Chinese should readily participate in what Akira Iriye and others have called America's neoplatonic experiment, that is, "men of diverse backgrounds may live in peace and harmony with one another, since they are all potential equals and share common destinies."[9] Indeed, it is in America that the Confucian ideal of cosmopolitanism and brotherhood of man has met head-to-head the Greek tradition of the unity of mankind. For all the disciples of Confucius in the United States, it is high time that they examine their experience in the spirit of Plato: "The intention of our law, which does not aim at making any one class in the State happy above the rest; it seeks rather to spread happiness over the whole State, and to hold the citizens together by persuasion and necessity, making each share with others any benefit which he can confer upon the State; and the law aims at producing such citizens, not that they may be left to please themselves, but that they may serve in binding the State together."[10]

APPENDIX 1
Total Population of California County
vs. Number of Chinese, 1870

County	Total Population	Chinese Population	Percentage of Chinese Population
Amador	9,582	1,629	17.00
Butte	11,403	2,082	18.25
Calaveras	8,895	1,432	16.10
El Dorado	10,309	1,559	15.12
Fresno	6,336	427	6.73
Inyo	1,956	29	1.48
Kern	2,925	43	1.47
Lake	2,969	119	4.00
Los Angeles	15,309	234	1.52
Nevada	19,134	2,629	13.74
Placer	11,357	2,409	21.21
Plumas	4,489	911	20.29
Santa Clara	26,246	1,520	5.79
Shasta	4,173	574	13.76
Sierra	5,619	809	14.40
Trinity	3,213	1,095	34.08
Tulare	4,521	99	2.19
Tuolumne	8,150	1,523	18.69
Yuba	10,851	2,333	21.50

Source: U.S. Congress, *Executive Documents, 10,* 42nd Cong., 1st sess. (Washington, D.C., 1871), Serial 1470.

APPENDIX 2
Chinese Population in Hawaii,
1853–1980

Year	Chinese	Total Population	Percentage of Chinese Population
1853	364	73,138	0.5
1866	1,206	62,959	1.9
1872	1,938	56,897	3.4
1878	5,916	57,985	10.2
1884	18,254	80,578	22.3
1890	15,301	89,990	17.0
1900	25,767	154,001	16.7
1910	21,674	191,909	11.3
1920	23,507	255,912	9.2
1930	27,179	368,336	7.4
1940	28,774	422,770	6.8
1950	32,376	499,794	6.5
1960	38,197	632,772	6.0
1970	52,039	769,913	6.8
1980	56,260	965,000	5.8

Source: *Hawaiian Annual,* 1853–1890, and U.S. Bureau of Census, 1900–1980.

193

APPENDIX 3
Chinese Arrivals in, and Departures from United States, 1882–1892

Year Ending June 30	Chinese Arrivals in U.S.A.			Chinese Departures from U.S.A.	Net gain or loss
	Imm.	*Non-Imm.*	*Tot.*	*All classes*	*All classes*
1882	39,579	——	39,579	10,366	+29,213
1883	8,031	2,151	10,182	12,159	−1,977
1884	279	3,194	3,473	14,145	−10,672
1885	22	5,330	5,352	19,655	−14,303
1886	40	4,809	4,849	17,591	−12,742
1887	10	3,754	3,764	12,155	−8,391
1888	26	2,751	2,777	12,893	−10,116
1889	118	1,945	2,063	10,226	−8,163
1890	1,716	154	1,870	8,056	−6,186
1891	2,836	171	3,007	8,924	−5,917
1892	2,728	462	3,190	6,696	−3,506

Source: U.S. Bureau of Census, *Historial Statistics of the United States, 1789–1945* (Washington, D.C., 1949).

APPENDIX 4
World War II Chinese Draftees and Casualties in the U.S. Army

State	Total Number drafted	Total casualties
Alabama	21	
Arizona	187	7
Arkansas	45	
California	5,048	92
Colorado	38	
Connecticut	52	
Delaware	15	
Dist. of Columbia	122	2
Florida	17	
Georgia	25	
Idaho	48	
Illinois	390	13
Indiana	44	
Iowa	17	
Kansas	17	
Kentucky	15	
Louisiana	51	2
Maine	18	
Maryland	39	
Massachusetts	436	15
Michigan	181	4
Minnesota	56	1
Mississippi	91	2

Missouri	34	
Montana	36	
Nebraska	10	
New Jersey	202	5
New Mexico	14	
New York	2,680	40
North Carolina	13	
North Dakota	9	
Ohio	167	6
Oklahoma	26	
Oregon	214	5
Pennsylvania	169	4
Rhode Island	54	
South Carolina	4	
South Dakota	5	
Tennessee	11	
Texas	137	2
Utah	51	1
Vermont	2	
Virginia	51	
Washington	271	7
West Virginia	11	
Wisconsin	51	6
Wyoming	19	
Alaska	2	
Hawaii	820	
Other Territories	5	
Total	12,041	214

Source: Historical Center of the Defense Department and *World War II Honor List of Dead and Missing.*

APPENDIX 5
**Major Occupational Groups of the Chinese
in the U.S., By Decade and Percent
1940–1970**

Major Occupational Groups	1940	1950	1960	1970
Total Employed	36,454	48,409	98,784	181,190
Professional/Technical	2.8%	7.1%	17.9%	26.5%
Managers	20.6%	19.8%	12.7%	8.9%
Sales Workers	11.4%	15.9%	6.6%	4.3%
Clerical Workers	11.4%	15.9%	13.8%	16.8%
Craftsmen	1.2%	2.9%	5.2%	5.4%
Operators	22.6%	17.1%	15.0%	14.8%
Laborers, except farmers	0.7%	1.7%	1.3%	2.3%
Farmers	3.8%	2.6%	1.0%	0.6%
Service Workers	30.4%	28.8%	18.8%	19.6%
Private Household Workers	6.2%	2.6%	1.0%	0.8%
Not Reported	0.3%	1.5%	6.5%	——

Source: U.S. Census Bureau, Decennial Censuses (1940, 1950, 1960, 1970).

NOTES

I. The Nineteenth-Century Chinese Immigration

1. *Liang shi* (History of the Liang Dynasty), LIV, biography 48 on "Eastern Barbarian Fusang."

2. Levi Hollingworth, a Philadelphia merchant, later helped the three Chinese to petition Congress for assistance and sent them to their ancestral land in China.

3. Hubert Howe Bancroft, *History of California 1860–1890* (San Francisco, 1890), p. 336.

4. *DaQing huidian shili* (Precedents and Edicts Pertaining to the Collected Statutes of the Qing Dynasty) (1220 juan, Shanghai, 1899). The 1963 Taiwan reprint with continuous pagination in 19 volumes is cited here, see juan 775, pp. 1–2.

5. Ping-ti Ho, *Studies on the Population of China, 1368–1953* (Cambridge, Mass., 1959), Appendix I.

6. Wen-chang Chu, "The Background of the Chinese Immigration into the United States," M.A. thesis, University of Washington, 1949, pp. 58–60.

7. Ho, *Population of China*, p. 283.

8. Liang Renzai, *Guangdong jingji dili* (Economic Geography of Guangdong) (Peking, 1956), p. 21; also see Ho, *Population of China*, pp. 203 and 283. Though overall, the percentage of cultivated land in Guangdong was only 16 percent, in the Pearl River Delta it was above 50 percent.

9. *Xinning Xianzhi* (Gazetteer of the Xinning District) (Taiwan reprint, 1965), XIV, p. 24a.

10. Hunter Miller, ed., *Treaties and Other International Acts of the United States* (Washington, D.C., 1931), IV, p. 567.

11. Hosea Ballou Morse, *The International Relations of the Chinese Empire* (3 vols., London, 1918), II, p. 166; also see Gao Degun, *Pilu Huaqiao shihua* (The Story of Overseas Chinese in Peru) (Taibei, 1956) and Stewart Watt, *Chinese Bondage in Peru* (Durham, North Carolina, 1951).

12. Lee Tom-yin, *The Chinese in Jamaica* (Kingston, Jamaica, 1957), pp. 10–12; also "Coolie Trade," in U.S. Congress, *House Report 443*, 36th Cong., 1st sess. (1860), Serial 1069, p. 28.

13. Harley F. MacNair, *The Chinese Abroad* (Shanghai, 1924), p. 211.

14. H. N. Palmer to William L. Marcy, November 9, 1885, U.S. Congress, *House Executive Documents 105*, 34th Cong., 1st sess. (1856), Serial 859, p. 71.

15. Peter Parker to Daniel Webster, May 21, 1852, ibid., pp. 94–96.

16. *Encyclopedia Britannica* (Cambridge Universtiy Press, 1910), 11th edition, VII, p. 77.

17. Russell H. Conwell, *Why and How: Why the Chinese Emigrate, and the Means They Adopt for the Purpose of Reaching America* (Boston, 1871), p. 87.

18. Parker to Secretary of State Marcy, February 12, 1856, *House Executive Documents 105*, Serial 859, p. 73.

19. Attorney General Jeremiah S. Black to Secretary of State Case, March 11, 1859, *House Report 443*, Serial 1069, p. 28.

20. T. H. Hyatt to Secretary of State Marcy, May 1, 1855, *House Executive Documents 105,* Serial 859, p. 67.

21. "An Act to Prohibit the Coolie Trade by American Citizen in American Vessels," in *U.S. Statutes, 1859–62,* 37th Cong., 2nd sess. (1862), Vol. XII, pp. 340–41.

22. Charles I. Bevans, ed., *Treaties and Other International Agreements of the United States of America, 1776–1949* (Washington, D.C., 1971), Vol. VI, p. 682. More on the controversy of the Burlingame Treaty, see Shih-shan H. Tsai, *China and the Overseas Chinese in the United States, 1868–1911* (Fayetteville, Arkansas, 1983), chapter 2.

23. Bowring to Lord Malmesbury, January 5, 1853, in *The British Blue Books* (London, 1953), under "Emigration," p. 83.

24. Pao-yun and Li to the U.S. Commissioners, October 7, 1880, *Papers Relating to the Foreign Relations of the United States* (China, 1881) (Washington, D.C., 1881), Enclosure 2 in No. 6, p. 173. This series of documents will hereafter be cited as *USFR.*

25. *San Francisco Examiner,* August 23, 1888. Also see Gunther P. Barth, *Bitter Strength: A History of Chinese in the United States, 1850–1870* (Cambridge, Mass., 1964) pp. 61–62.

26. Zhu Shijia, *Meiguo pohai huagong shiliao* (Historical Materials Concerning America's Persecution of Chinese Laborers) (Peking, 1958), pp. 71–72.

27. For more, see Shih-shan H. Tsai, "The Chinese in Arkansas," *Amerasia Journal,* VIII (Spring/Summer, 1981), pp. 1–18.

28. S. Wells Williams to George Seward. June 30, 1876, *USFR* (China, 1876), p. 61.

29. U.S. Bureau of the Census, *Ninth Census, the Statistics of the Population of the United States* (Washington, D.C., 1872), Vol. I, pp. 692–762.

30. Henry Degroot, "Mining on the Pacific Coast," *Overland Monthly,* VII (August, 1871), pp. 151–58.

31. George S. Boutwell and Rossiter Raymond to James G. Blaine, March 16, 1871, "Mining Statistics West of the Rocky Mountains," U.S. Congress, *Executive Documents 10,* 42nd Cong., 1st sess. (Washington, D.C., 1871), Serial 1470, p. 89.

32. Ibid., pp. 33–54.

33. Ibid., pp. 176–77.

34. Berne Bright, "Blue Mountain Eldorados: Auburn, 1861," *Oregon Historical Quarterly,* LXII (September, 1961), p. 236.

35. Robert E. Wynne, "Reaction to the Chinese in the Pacific Northwest and British Columbia, 1850–1910," Ph.D. dissertation, University of Washington, 1964, pp. 49–50.

36. Boutwell and Raymond, "Mining Statistics West of the Rocky Mountains," p. 7, 28, 145.

37. Chen Lanpin, *ShiMei jilue* (A Brief Account of My Mission to America), in Wang Xiji, ed., *Xiao fanghu zhai yudi congchao* (Collections of Essays on Chinese and Western Geography, Politics and Others) (26 vols., Taibei, 1962), Vol. XII, p. 61.

38. Boutwell and Raymond, "Mining Statistics West of the Rocky Mountains," p. 187.

39. A. K. McClure, *Three Thousand Miles through the Rocky Mountains* (Philadelphia, 1869), p. 372.

40. Liu Boji *Meiguo huaqiao shi* (History of the Overseas Chinese in the United States) (2 vols., Taibei, 1976), Vol. I, p. 87.

41. *Oregon State Constitution 1859,* Article II, Sec. 6; Article XV, Sec. 8; also *Statutes of Oregon 1862,* "An Act to provide for taxing Negroes, Chinamen," Sec. 1.

42. *Statutes of Washington Territory 1863–1864,* "An Act to Protect Free White Labor against Competition with Chinese Coolie Labor and to Discourage the Immigration of the Chinese in the Territory," January 23, 1864, Sec. 1, 8.

43. Daniel Cleveland to Minister Browne, July 27, 1868, in *USFR* (China, 1868), p. 533.

44. Boutwell and Raymond, "Mining Statistics West of the Rocky Mountains," pp. 4–6.

45. "Testimony of Leland Stanford, U.S. Pacific Railway Commission," U.S. Congress, *Senate Executive Documents 51,* 50th Cong., 1st sess. (Washington, D.C., 1887), Serial 2507, p. 2523.

46. Edwin L. Sabin, *Building the Pacific Railway* (Philadelphia, 1919), p. 125. For more details, also see Tze-kuei Yen, "Chinese Workers and the First Transcontinental Railroad of the United States," Ph.D. dissertation, St. John's University, 1977.

47. A letter from E. B. Crocker to Congressman Cornelius Cole, dated April 12, 1865, in Catherine C. Phillips, *Cornelius Cole, California Pioneer and United States Senator* (San Francisco, 1929), p. 138.

48. "Testimony of J. H. Strobridge, U. S. Pacific Railway Commission," *Senate Executive Documents, 51,* Serial 2507, pp. 3139–40.

49. *Alta California,* November 9, 1868.

50. For more, see George Krause, "The Chinese Laborers and the Central Pacific," *Utah Historical Quarterly,* Vol. XXXVII (Winter, 1969), pp. 40–57.

51. *Sacramento Reporter,* June 30, 1870.

52. *Alta California,* November 9, 1868.

53. Erle Heath, "Trail to Rail," *Southern Pacific Bulletin,* XV (1927), chapter 15, p. 12.

54. Alexander P. Saxton, "The Army of Canton in the High Sierra," *Pacific Historical Review,* XXXV (May, 1966), p. 141.

55. Wynne, "Reaction to the Chinese," pp. 84–85.

56. Ibid.; cf. *New Northwest* (Portland, Oregon), December, 1881.

57. Edward J. M. Rhoads, "The Chinese in Texas," *Southwestern Historical Quarterly,* LXXXI (July, 1977) pp. 3–6; also Sylvia Krebs, "The Chinese Labor Question: A Note on the Attitudes of Two Alabama Republicans," *Alabama Historical Quarterly,* XXXVIII (Fall, 1976), pp. 214–16.

58. For more, see Laurence Fong, *The Chinese Experience in Arizona and Northern Mexico,* (Tucson, 1979) and Nancy Farrar, *The Chinese in El Paso,* Southwestern Studies Monograph No. XXXIII (El Paso, 1972).

59. "Testimony of Colonel William W. Hollister," in "Report of the Joint Special Committee to Investigate Chinese Immigration," U.S. Congress, *Senate Report 689,* 44th Cong., 2nd sess. (Washington, D.C., 1877), Serial 1734, pp. 768–78. This document will be hereafter cited as "Report of Joint Special Committee."

60. David Horace, "Wheat in California," *Overland Monthly,* 1 (November, 1868), p. 452.

61. For more on Chinese agricultural labor, see George F. Seward, *Chinese Immigration in Its Social and Economic Aspects* (New York, 1881), pp. 69–79.

62. "Testimony of George D. Roberts," in "Report of Joint Special Committee," pp. 436–37.

63. "Report of the Immigration Commission," in U.S. Congress, *Senate Doc-*

ument, 633, 61st Cong., 2nd sess. (Washington, D.C., 1911), Serial 5684, pp. 325–329 and 432. Also see George Chu, "Chinatowns in the Delta: The Chinese in the Sacramento-San Joaquin Delta, 1870–1960," *California Historical Society Quarterly*, XLIX (March, 1970), pp. 22–26.

64. Ira B. Cross, *History of the Labor Movement in California* (Berkeley, 1933), pp. 57–58. For a detailed analysis of the Chinese manufacturing labor in California and its relationship with the white labor, see an excellent study by Ping Chiu, *Chinese Labor in California, 1850–1880: An Economic Study* (Madison, Wisconsin, 1967), chapters 6 and 7.

65. Otis Gibson, *The Chinese in America* (Cincinnati, 1877), p. 59. Also a letter from A. F. Adams to Frederick Bee, June 12, 1879, *National Archives Microfilms*, M 98, Roll 1.

66. *Alta California*, October 7, 1888.

67. Robert J. Schwendinger, "Chinese Sailors: America's Invisible Merchant Marine, 1876–1905," *California History*, LVII (Spring, 1978), pp. 62–63.

68. Navy Muster Rolls, *USS Olympia*, June, 1898, Record Group 24, Washington National Records Center, National Archives and Record Service. Also see William F. Strobridge's interesting account, "Chinese in the Spanish American War and Beyond," a paper read in the Second Chinese-American Studies Conference, San Francisco, October, 1980.

69. For more, see Thomas Chinn et al., *A History of the Chinese in California: A Syllabus* (San Francisco, 1969), pp. 36–41; also George B. Goode, *The Fisheries and Fishing Industries of the U.S.* (2 vols., Washington, D.C., 1887), Vol. I, p.748, and Vol. II, pp. 623–24.

70. Gordon B. Dodds, *The Salmon King of Oregon* (Chapel Hill, North Carolina, 1959), pp. 6 and 26; also Chinn, *A History of the Chinese in California*, pp. 41–42.

71. Robert A. Nash, "Chinese in the California Fisheries," *East-West*, January 22, 1969.

72. Robert W. Shugg, *Origins of Class Struggle in Louisiana* (Baton Rouge, 1939), pp. 254–55.

73. For more, see Etta B. Peabody, "Effort of the South to Import Chinese Coolies, 1865–1870," M.A. thesis, Baylor University, 1967.

74. Powell Clayton, *The Aftermath of the Civil War in Arkansas* (New York, 1915), p. 213.

75. Rhoads, "The Chinese in Texas," p. 6.

76. Katharine Coman, "The History of Contract Labor in the Hawaiian Islands," *Publications of the American Economic Association* (New York, 1903), 3rd series, Vol. IV, No. 3, pp. 11–12.

77. Ibid., p. 65. Also see Hawaiian Sugar Planters' Association (ed.), *The Story of Sugar in Hawaii* (Honolulu, 1926).

78. "Report of the Commissioner of Labor on Hawaii, 1901," in U.S. Congress, *Senate Documents 169*, 57th Cong., 1st sess. (Washington, D.C., 1902), Serial 4231, p. 34.

79. U.S. Public Health, *Public Health Report*, XV (February 9, 1900), p. 305.

80. Coman, "Contract Labor in Hawaiian Islands," p. 36.

81. Doris M. Lorden, "The Chinese-Hawaiian Family," *The American Journal of Sociology*, XL (January, 1935) p. 454.

82. Ibid., p. 460.

83. Donald Rowland, "The United States and the Contract Labor Question in Hawaii, 1862–1900," *Pacific Historical Review*, II (September, 1933), p. 259.

84. Figures for 1853–1890 come from the Hawaiian census as published in

the *Hawaiian Annual* while figures from 1900 onward come from the U.S. Bureau of Census.

85. Louis J. Beck, *New York's Chinatown* (New York, 1899), pp. 11–12.

86. Liang Qichao, *Xindalu youji* (Travels in the New Continent) (Shanghai, 1936), pp. 105–6.

II. The Development of the Early Chinese Community

1. Francis L. K. Hsu, *Americans and Chinese: Two Ways of Life* (New York, 1970).

2. Arthur Waley, tr., *The Way and Its Power* (Boston, 1935), pp. 241–42.

3. Arthur Waley, tr., *The Analects of Confucius* (London, 1938), pp. 105–6.

4. Professor Sucheng Chan of the University of California at Santa Cruz disputes this charge. Examining the ten California counties with the most numerous Chinese between 1860 and 1910, Chan claims that the Chinese population was not completely segregated into an ethnic economic enclave and that the Chinese did own property and did pay their share of taxes. For more, see her paper, "The Occupational Structure of Rural Chinese Immigrant Communities in Nineteenth-Century California," read at the 96th annual meeting of the American Historical Association, Los Angeles, December 28–30, 1981.

5. A. W. Loomis, "What our Chinamen Read," *Overland Monthly*, I (December, 1868), p. 530.

6. The *Chinese Digest*, May 15, 1936.

7. Wang Hungyi, "Wei Zhonghua wenhua zengguang de Dean Lung" (Dean Lung's Effort to Promote Chinese Culture), in *Zhonghua wenhua yuekan* (Monthly Journal of Chinese Culture), VIII (Taibei, 1975), No. 2.

8. Joan B. Trauner, "The Chinese as Medical Scapegoats in San Francisco, 1870–1905," *California History*, LVII (Spring, 1978), p. 73.

9. Ibid., pp. 70–86.

10. Yung Wing to Secretary of State Evarts, March 9, 1888, National Archives Microfilms, M 98, Roll 1.

11. California Legislature, "Senate Special Committee on Chinese Immigration," published in *Western America: Frontier History of the Trans-Mississippi West, 1550–1900* (New Haven, Conn., 1975), Reel 88, No. 908, pp. 110–11, 116.

12. Otis Gibson, *The Chinese in America* (Cincinnati, 1877), p. 264. For more on the Opium War, see Hsin-pao Chang, *Commissioner Lin and the Opium War* (New York, 1964).

13. Liu Boji, *Meiguo huaqiao shi* (History of the Overseas Chinese in the United States) (Taibei, 1976), Vol. I, p. 120.

14. Zhang Yinhuan, *Sanzhou riji* (Diary of the Three Continents) (8 juan, Kyoto, 1896), VII, Guangxu 14/11/4 [December 6, 1888]. A Chinese silver dollar was worth approximately $1.75 U.S. dollars in gold at that time.

15. The figures are calculated from the U.S. Census of 1860–1900; the Hawaiian Chinese figures come from Romanzo C. Adams, *The People of Hawaii* (Honolulu, 1925), p. 8.

16. *Report of the Joint Special Committee to Investigate Chinese Immigration*, U.S. Congress, *Senate Report 689*, 44th Cong., 2nd sess., 1877, Serial 1734, p. 145.

17. Otis Gibson, *Chinese in America*, p. 156.

18. Li Gui, *Huanyou diqui xinlu* (New Journal Around the Earth) (4 juan, Nanjing, 1877), juan 3. For more, see also Lucie Cheng Hirata, "Chinese Im-

migrant Women in Nineteenth Century California," in *Women of America, A History*, eds., Carol R. Berkin and Mary B. Norton (Boston, 1979), pp. 224–36.

19. *Report of Joint Special Committee*, pp. vi and 28.

20. Otis Gibson, *Chinese in America*, p. 157.

21. For more on Confucian creed, see Herrlee G. Creel, *Confucius and the Chinese Way* (New York, 1960).

22. For more on Taoism, see Laurence G. Thompson, *The Chinese Way in Religion* (Encino, Calif., 1973), pp. 46–76.

23. For more on Buddhism, see ibid., pp. 77–129.

24. Horace R. Cayton and Anne O. Lively, *The Chinese in the United States and the Chinese Christian Churches* (New York, 1955), chapter III, no page numbers.

25. Ibid.

26. Gibson, *Chinese in America*, pp. 341–42.

27. Stanford Lyman, *Chinese Americans* (New York, 1974), p. 122.

28. There is an interesting personal account on the Hakkas by Han Suyin, whose mother was Flemish and whose father was a Hakka from the province of Sichuan. See *The Crippled Tree* (New York, 1965).

29. William Hoy, *Chinese Six Companies* (San Francisco, 1942), p. 2; also H. Mark Lai and Philip P. Choy, eds., *LuMei sanyi zong huiguan jianshi* (A Brief History of the Whole San-yi Association in the United States) (San Francisco, 1975), pp. 57 and 75. H. Mark Lai claims that William Hoy's account on the early history of the Six Companies is erroneous. According to Lai's date, the first huiguan were set up by San-yi and Si-yi in 1851. Then came Yanghe in 1852; Ningyang split off from Si-yi in 1854, then Hehe split from Si-yi in 1862, with the remainder changed to Gangzhou in 1867.

30. Hoy, *Six Companies*, pp. 10–16; also William Speer, *The Oldest and the Newest Empire: China and the United States* (Hartford, Conn., 1870), pp. 556–65.

31. Liu Boji, *Overseas Chinese*, Vol. I, pp. 150–153.

32. A. W. Loomis, "The Six Chinese Companies," *Overland Monthly*, I (September, 1868), pp. 225–26.

33. Ibid., p. 221.

34. William Speer, "Democracy of the Chinese," *Harper's New Monthly Magazine*, XXXVII (November, 1868), p. 845.

35. Loomis, "Six Companies," p. 224.

36. Li Gui, *New Journal Around the Earth*, juan 3.

37. Chen Lanpin, *ShiMei jilue* (A Brief Account of My Mission to America), in Wang Xiji, ed., *Xiao fangfu zhai yudi congchao* (Collections of Essays on Chinese and Western Geography, Politics and Others) (26 vols., Taibei, 1962), Vol. XII, pp. 59–60.

38. For more, see Hoy, *Six Companies*, pp. 6–10.

39. Stanford M. Lyman, "Conflict and the Web of Group Affiliation in San Francisco's Chinatown, 1850–1910," in *The Asian American: The Historical Experience*, ed., Norris Hundley, Jr. (Santa Barbara, 1976), p. 33.

40. Liang Qichao, *Xindalu youji* (Travels in the New Continent) (Shanghai, 1936), pp. 111–19.

41. L. F. Comber, *Chinese Secret Societies in Malaya*, Monographs of the Association for Asian Studies, VI (New York, 1959), p. 1; pp. 20–21. Also see Jean Chesneaux, *Secret Societies in China* (Ann Arbor, 1971).

42. For more on the Hong League nationalism, see Liu Lianke, *Zhongguo banghui sanbainian geming shi* (History of the Three Hundred Years' Revolution of the Chinese Secret Societies) (Taibei, 1975).

43. A. D. C. Newbold and C. B. Wilson, "The Chinese Secret Societies of the Tien Tihuih," *Journal of Royal Asiatic Society* (Northern Ireland and England, 1841–42), pp. 120–30.

44. Liang Qichao, *Travels in New Continent*, p. 118.

45. Ling Shanqing, ed., *Taiping yeshi* (Unofficial History of the Taipings) (Shanghai, 1929), XIV, p. 6.

46. Liu Boji, *Overseas Chinese*, Vol. I, p. 428.

47. Stewart Culin, "Chinese Secret Societies in the United States," *Journal of American Folk-Lore*, III (January-March, 1890), pp. 39–41.

48. Ji Ying to Sir John F. Davis, September 23, 1846, and February 8, 1847, in *Chinese Repository* (Canton, 1847), pp. 428, 480.

49. C. N. Reynolds, "The Chinese Tongs," *The American Journal of Sociology*, XL (March, 1935), pp. 617–19.

50. *San Francisco Evening Bulletin*, May 6 and May 8, 1869.

51. Zhang Yinhuan, *Diary of the Three Continents*, I, pp. 70–80.

52. San Francisco Six Companies to Chinese Foreign Ministry, Guangxu 28/1/27 [March 6, 1902] in *Qing Cables* in the Academia Sinica Archives of Taiwan.

53. Reynolds, "Chinese Tongs," p. 622.

54. Clifford Geertz, *The Interpretation of Cultures* (New York, 1973), p. 44.

III. American Exclusion against the Chinese

1. See Gunther Barth, *Bitter Strength: A History of Chinese in the United States 1850–1870* (Cambridge, 1964); Mary R. Coolidge, *Chinese Immigration* (New York, 1909); Francis L. K. Hsu, *The Challenge of the American Dream: The Chinese in the United States* (Belmont, Calif., 1971); Stuart C. Miller, *The Unwelcome Immigrant: The American Image of the Chinese 1785–1882* (Berkeley and Los Angeles, 1969); Elmer C. Sandmeyer, *The Anti-Chinese Movement in California* (Urbana, Ill., 1939); and Alexander P. Saxton, *The Indispensable Enemy: Labor and the Anti-Chinese Movement in California* (Berkeley and Los Angeles, 1971).

2. Sandmeyer, *Anti-Chinese Movement*, pp. 71–72. For more on America's racial prejudice against the Chinese, see Cheng-Tsu Wu, *"Chink!"* (New York, 1972).

3. An excellent monograph on Chinese legal status in America is Milton R. Konvitz's *The Alien and the Asiatic in American Law* (Ithaca, 1946).

4. "Report of the Joint Special Committee to Investigate Chinese Immigration," U.S. Congress, *Senate Report 689*, 44th Cong., 2nd sess., 1877, Serial 1734, pp. 768–69, 778, 787–89.

5. Ibid., pp. 767, 1201–2.

6. Ibid., pp. 1138.

7. Ibid., p. viii.

8. U.S. Congress, *House Reports 62*, 45th Cong. 3rd sess. (Washington, D.C., 1880), Serial 1866, p. 1.

9. James G. Blaine, Republican of Maine, made these remarks. See Frederick W. Williams, *Life and Letters of S. Wells Williams* (New York, 1889), p. 430.

10. Memorandum, Chinese Legation, February 18, 1879, National Archives Microfilms (hereafter cited as *NAM*), M 98, Roll 1.

11. Williams, *Life and Letters of Williams*, pp. 430–31. For the entire veto message, see James D. Richardson, *A Compilation of the Messages and Papers of the Presidents, 1789–1897* (Washington, D.C., 1900), Vol. VIII, pp. 514–20.

12. Hayes twice recorded the Chinese problem in his diary, respectively on February 20 and February 23, 1879. For more, see T. Harry Williams, ed., *Hayes: The Diary of a President, 1875–1881* (New York, 1964), pp. 187–90.

13. James B. Angell, *Reminiscences of James Burrill Angell* (New York, 1912), p. 131.

14. Li Zongtong, *Li Hongzao xiansheng nianpu* (A Continuation of the Chronological Biography of Mr. Li Hongzao) (Taibei, 1969), pp. 270–354.

15. Shirley W. Smith, *James Burrill Angell: An American Influence* (Ann Arbor, 1954), pp. 122–24. Also James B. Angell, "The Crisis in China," *Atlantic Monthly,* LXXXVI (October, 1900), pp. 436–37.

16. Smith, *James Burrill Angell,* pp. 136–37.

17. *San Francisco Evening Bulletin,* January 10, 1881.

18. Ping Chiu, *Chinese Labor in California, 1850–1880* (Madison, Wis., 1963), pp. 127–38.

19. The subtitle of Miller's *Unwelcome Immigrant* is "The American Image of the Chinese, 1785–1882," and his thesis is that America's negative image of China and the Chinese originated from the Eastern Coast and that the Exclusion Act of 1882 was only an inevitable culmination of such perception.

20. *U.S. Congressional Record,* 47th Cong., 1st sess. Vol. XIII, 1882, pp. 1480–81.

21. Ibid., pp. 1515–23, 1586–91, 1634–46, 1702–6.

22. Ibid., p. 1753.

23. Ibid., p. 2227.

24. Bao-yun and Li Hongzao to U.S. Commission, October 7, 1880, *Papers Relating to the Foreign Relations of the United States* (China, 1881) (Washington, D.C., 1881), p. 174. This series of documents will hereafter be cited as *USFR.*

25. Wu Rulun, ed., *Li Wenzhong gong quanji* (Complete Works of Li Hongzhang) (Taibei, 1962), translated message to Zongli Yamen, VIII, pp. 207–9.

26. James B. Angell, "Diplomatic Relations Between the United States and China," *Journal of Social Science,* XVII (October, 1882), p. 35.

27. Memorandum, Chinese Legation, April 1, 1882, *NAM,* M 98, Roll 1.

28. For the entire veto message, see Richardson, *Messages of the Presidents,* Vol. VIII, pp. 112–18.

29. *United States Statutes 1881–83* (Washington, D.C., 1883), Vol. XXII, pp. 58–61.

30. Xu Shoupeng, charge d'affaires, to Secretary Frelinghuysen, May 20, 1882, *NAM,* M 98, Roll 1.

31. U.S. Bureau of Census, *Historical Statistics of the United States, 1789–1945* (Washington, D.C., 1949), pp. 33–35.

32. Frelinghuysen to Minister Zheng, January 6, 1883, and February 2, 1883, *USFR* (China, 1882), pp. 212–14.

33. *United States Statutes 1883–85* (Washington, D.C., 1885), Vol. XXIII, p. 115.

34. Ibid., pp. 116–18.

35. U.S. Bureau of Census, *Historical Statistics of U.S.,* p. 35.

36. William Mason, "The Chinese in Los Angeles," *Los Angeles County Museum of Natural History Quarterly,* VI (Fall, 1967), No. 2, p 16.

37. Gerald E. Rudolph, "The Chinese in Colorado, 1869–1911," M.A. thesis, University of Denver, 1964, pp. 107–21; also Roy T. Wortman, "Denver's Anti-Chinese Riot, 1880," *The Colorado Magazine,* XLII (Fall, 1965), pp. 275–291.

38. Bee to Chen Lanpin, December 1, 1880, and Chen to Secretary Evarts, January 21, 1881, *NAM,* M 98, Roll 1.

39. Blaine to Chen, March 25, 1881, *USFR* (China, 1881), pp. 335–37.

40. U.S. Congress, *House Report* (1885–1886), 49th Cong., 1st sess., No. 2044, Serial 2441, p. 27.

41. Ibid. See also Paul Crane and Alfred Larson, "The Chinese Massacre," *Annals of Wyoming*, XII (January, 1940), pp. 47–55 and 153–61.

42. *U.S. Congressional Record*, 49th Cong., 1st sess., 1886, Vol. XVII, pp. 4229, 5110–12, and 5184.

43. B.P. Wilcox, "Anti-Chinese Riot in Washington," *Washington Historical Quarterly*, XX (July, 1929), p. 205.

44. Jules Alexander Karlin, "The Anti-Chinese Outbreak in Tacoma, 1885," *Pacific Historical Review*, XXIII (August, 1954), pp. 271–83; also Karlin, "Anti-Chinese Outbreaks in Seattle, 1885–1886," *Pacific Northwest Quarterly*, XXXIX (April, 1948), pp. 103–30.

45. Karlin, "Anti-Chinese Outbreaks in Seattle," p. 129.

46. Ibid., p. 124; also see Secretary Bayard to Minister Zheng, November 7, 1885, *USFR* (China, 1885), pp. 197–98.

47. There is a correspondence dated August 14, 1959, between Miss Bess Glenn, Archivist in Charge, Justice and Executive Branch of the U.S. National Archives, and Mr. Gwen T. Coffin, Editor and Publisher of *Wallowa County Chieftain*, Enterprise, Oregon. Information concerning the trial was obtained from the Wallowa County Circuit Court Records in "Case of the State of Oregon versus Hiram Maynard, Hezekiah Hughes, and Frank Vaughn."

48. Memorandum, Chinese Legation, January 15, February 25, and March 18, 1887, *NAM*, M 98, Roll 2.

49. Wang Yanwei, ed., *Qingji waijiao shiliao* (Historical Materials Concerning Foreign Relations in the Late Qing Period, 1875–1911) (218 juan, Peking, 1932–1939), LXXVI, p. 1. Hereafter cited as *WJSL*.

50. *U.S. Congressional Record*, 50th Cong., 1st sess., 1888, Vol. XIX, p. 8226.

51. Memorandum, Chinese Legation, September 8, 1888, *NAM*, M 98, Roll 2.

52. For the entire opinion, see William L. Tung, *The Chinese in America, 1820–1973* (Dobbs Ferry, New York, 1974), Document 19, pp. 98–101.

53. Ira M. Condit, *The Chinaman as We See Him and Fifty Years of Work for Him* (New York, 1900), pp. 86–87.

54. The *San Francisco Chinese World*, January 22, 1910.

55. "Chinese Immigration," *House Report 4048*, 51st Cong., 2nd sess. (Washington, D.C., 1891), Serial 2890, pp. 1–594.

56. George E. Paulsen, "The Gresham-Yang Treaty," *Pacific Historical Review*, XXXVII (August, 1968), pp. 281–97.

57. Ibid., pp. 284–85.

58. *WJSL*, LXXXIX, pp. 30–34.

59. Ibid., XCIV, pp. 22.

60. For more about the Immigration Bureau, see Darrell H. Smith and Guy Herring, *The Bureau of Immigration: Its History, Activities, and Organization* (Baltimore, 1924).

61. Delber McKee, *Chinese Exclusion Versus the Open Door Policy 1900–1906: Clashes over China Policy in the Roosevelt Era* (Detroit, 1977), pp. 67, 216–17.

62. See John W. Foster, "The Chinese Boycott," *Atlantic Monthly*, XCVII (January, 1906), pp. 118–27; Chester Holcombe, "Chinese Exclusion and the Boycott," *Outlook*, LXXXI (December, 1905), pp. 1066–72; Margaret Field "The Chinese Boycott of 1905," in Harvard East Asian Research Center, ed., *Papers on China* (Cambridge, Mass., 1957); C. F. Remer, *A Study of Chinese Boycott* (Baltimore, 1933); and Shih-shan H. Tsai, "Reaction to Exclusion: The

Boycott of 1905 and Chinese National Awakening," *The Historian,* XXXIX (November, 1976), pp. 95–110.

63. Chen Jiyan of Hawaii, who was also the editor of a Chinese newspaper, the *Xin Zhongguo ribao* (New China Daily), for example, was believed to be the first one to suggest a boycott against the American goods.

64. Foster, "Chinese Boycott," pp. 112–23.

65. U.S. Department of State, *Consular Despatches* (hereafter cited as *CD*), Canton, October 27, 1905, *NAM,* M 101, Roll 19.

66. Foster, "Chinese Boycott," p. 125.

67. Zeng Shaojing's speeches are collected in A Ying, ed., *FanMei huakong jinyue wenxue ji* (An Anti-American Literary Collection on the Exclusion of Chinese Laborers) (Shanghai, 1960), pp. 666–70.

68. For more on anti-American boycott activities, see Tsai, "Reaction to Exclusion," pp. 98–99.

69. U.S. Department of State, *CD,* Canton, December 4, 1905, *NAM,* M 101, Roll 19.

70. Diary of John M. Hay, June 19, 1905, *John Milton Hay Papers,* Container 1, Library of Congress Manuscript Division.

71. Theodore Roosevelt to Francis B. Loomis and to Victor H. Metcalf, June 24, 1905, *Roosevelt Papers,* series 2, Letter Books, Library of Congress, Vol. 156, pp. 194 and 230.

IV. Living in the Shadow of Exclusion

1. The first Boxer Indemnity refund was paid in 1909 and at first each installment amounted to $1,600,000. For more, see Lo Xianglin, *Liang Cheng di chushi Meiguo* (Liang Cheng's Mission to America) (Hong Kong, 1977), pp. 19–40.

2. For more on the struggle between the reform and the revolution in America, see Eve L. Armentrout, "Competition between Chinese Reformers and Revolutionaries in the Americas, 1895–1911," Ph.D. dissertation, University of California, Davis, 1977.

3. Liang Qichao, *Xindalu youji* (Travels in the New Continent) (Shanghai, 1936), pp. 98–102.

4. "An Open Letter to Fellow Provincials," in Tang Zengchu, ed., *Guofu shuxin xuanji* (Selected Collection of Sun Yat-sen's Letters) (Taibei, 1954), pp. 22–25.

5. Wu Xianzi, *Zhongguo minzhu xianzhengdang dangshi* (Political Party History of China's Constitutional Democracy) (San Francisco, 1952), pp. 85–91.

6. Shih-shan H. Tsai, "The Emergence of Early Chinese Nationalist Organizations in America," *The Amerasia Journal,* VIII (Fall/Winter, 1981), p. 132.

7. Wong Sam Ark, *Hongmen geming shi* (The Revolutionary History of the Hong League) (Los Angeles, 1936) pp. 3–7; also Feng Ziyou, *Geming yishi* (Unofficial History of the Revolution) (Taibei, 1965), Vol. II, pp. 115–19.

8. For the entire text of the Triad constitution, see *Min Bao* (People's Journal), November 26, 1905, pp. 130–43.

9. Lo Jialun *et al., Guofu nianpu* (Chronological Biography of Sun Yat-sen) (Taibei, 1965), Vol. I, pp. 161–62.

10. Feng Ziyou, *Unofficial History,* Vol. IV, p. 140.

11. Liu Boji, *Meiguo huaqiao shi* (History of the Overseas Chinese in the United States) (Taibei, 1976), Vol. 1, p. 439.

12. Lo Jialun, *Biography of Sun,* p. 316.

13. The *Honolulu Chee Yow Sun Bo,* February 16, 1910, and Li Ling Ai, *Life Is for a Long Time* (New York, 1972), pp. 302–3.

14. I. Hsuan Julia Chen, "The Chinese Community in New York, 1920–1940," Ph.D. dissertation, American University, 1941, pp. 98–99.

15. *U.S. Congressional Record,* 78th Cong., 1st sess., 1943, Vol. LXXXIX, p. 8583.

16. Liu Boji, *Overseas Chinese,* Vol. II, p. 253; cf. Y. C. Hong, *A Brief History of The Chinese American Citizens Alliance* (no date, no publisher).

17. A two-year research project sponsored by the Chinese Culture Foundation with funding provided by the Office of Women's Educational Equity Act of Program, when completed, should yield more information and materials on the history of Chinese women in America.

18. "Reports of the Industrial Commission on Immigration," U.S. House of Representatives, 57th Cong., 1st sess., Document *184* (Washington, D.C., 1901), Serial 4345, p. 165.

19. *New York Herald,* November 28, 1896.

20. Luther C. Steward, Acting Commissioner, San Francisco, to Commissioner General, December 19, 1910, Record Set 85, National Archives.

21. *Chinese World,* February 26, 1911, and March 1, 1916.

22. Ibid., March 27, 1925; also *Young China Morning Paper,* July 1, 1925.

23. For the entire collection of written and carved poems, see Him M. Lai *et al., Island: Poetry and History of Chinese Immigrants on Angel Island 1910–1940* (San Francisco, 1980).

24. H. M. Lai, "Island of Immortals," *California History,* LVII (Spring, 1978), pp. 98–99.

25. This story is reported by Frances D'Emilio in "The Secret Hell of Angel Island," *American West,* XXI (May/June, 1984), p. 48.

26. William Tung, *Chinese in America 1820–1973* (Dobbs Ferry, New York, 1974), p. 21, 28. Also see Yon Chang Hong, "Chinese Immigration," J.D. thesis, University of Southern California, 1925, pp. 56–74.

27. Lai, *Island,* pp. 98–99.

28. *Chinese World,* December 15, 1910; also *Young China Morning Paper,* December 18, 1910. For more on hookworm disease, see John Ettling, *The Germ of Laziness* (Cambridge, Mass., 1981), pp. 1–6, 187–91.

29. *Young China Morning Paper,* October 20, 1927 & November 19, 1927; also *Chinese World,* January 30, 1922.

30. For more on the significance of the 1924 exclusion law, see Yamato Ichihashi, *Japanese in the United States* (Stanford, Calif., 1932), pp. 298–318.

31. Rose Hum Lee, "The Decline of Chinatowns in the United States," *The American Journal of Sociology,* LIV (March, 1949), p. 426.

32. *The 1920 U.S. Census.*

33. Lawrence Fuchs, *Hawaii Pono, A Social History* (New York, 1961), p. 98; cf. Clarence Glick, "Residential Dispersion of Urban Chinese," *Social Process in Hawaii,* II (1936).

34. Rhoads Murphey, "Boston's Chinatown," *Economic Geography,* XXVIII (July, 1952), No. 3, pp. 248–49.

35. William Mason, "Chinese in Los Angeles," *Los Angeles County Museum of Natural History Quarterly,* VI (Fall, 1967), No. 2, pp. 16–17.

36. Stuart H. Cattell, *Health, Welfare and Social Organization in Chinatown, New York City* (New York, 1962), p. 1.

37. Pardee Lowe, "Chinatown's Last Stand," *Survey Graphic,* XXV (February, 1936), pp. 89–90.

38. Rose Hum Lee, "Decline of Chinatowns," p. 423.

39. I. Hsuan Julia Chen, "Chinese Community in New York," p. 61.

40. Ibid.

41. *U.S. Congressional Record,* 78th Cong., 1st sess., 1943, Vol. LXXXIX, p. 8583.

42. H. M. Lai, "In Unity There is Strength: Chinese Workers' Fight For a Better Life," in *East-West,* May 1, 1974.

43. Ibid.

44. *Chinese Digest,* July, 1937; March, 1938; and July, 1938.

45. Jennie Matyas, *Jennie Matyas and the ILGWU,* University of California Institute of Industrial Relations (Berkeley, 1957), pp. 192–93.

46. H. M. Lai, "Chinese Workers," *East-West,* May 1, 1974.

47. Tsai Tingkai, *Haiwai yingxiangji* (Overseas Travel Impressions) (Hong Kong, 1935), August 26, to September 13, 1934.

48. Ibid., September 14 to September 19, 1934.

49. Ibid., November 3 to November 5, 1934.

50. Kum Pui Lai, "Attitudes of the Chinese in Hawaii Toward Their Language Schools," *Sociology and Social Research,* XX (November, 1935), No. 2, pp. 140–44.

51. Liu Boji, *Overseas Chinese,* Vol. II, pp. 569–76.

52. An old Chinese lady living in rural Arkansas still holds onto her over $1,000 worth of war bonds. She once asked the author to help her redeem her bonds but the Chinese authorities in Taiwan could only promise that once the Chinese mainland is recovered from Communism, all the World War II bonds would be processed.

53. Liu Boji, *Overseas Chinese,* Vol. II, pp. 581–83.

54. See articles and editorials of *San Francisco Examiner,* March 29, 1943; *New York Times,* March 1 and March 2, 1943; and *Los Angeles Times,* March 31, 1943.

55. Wu Xiangxiang, *Yen Yangchu juan* (Biography of Dr. James Y. C. Yen) (Taibei, 1981), pp. 492–93.

56. "Repeal the Chinese Exclusion Laws—the Minority Report," *House Report 732,* 78th Cong., 1st sess. (Washington, D.C., 1943), Serial 10763, p. 1.

57. "Message from the President of the United States Favoring Repeal of the Chinese Exclusion Laws," *House Document 333,* 78th Cong., 1st sess. (Washington, D.C., 1943), Serial 10793, pp. 1–2.

58. Ibid., p. 2.

59. *U.S. Congressional Record,* 78th Cong., 1st sess., 1943, Vol. LXXXIX, p. 8595.

60. Milton Konvitz, *The Alien and the Asiatic in American Law* (Ithaca, 1946), pp. 181–85, 231.

61. *U.S. Congressional Record,* 1943, *op. cit.,* p. 8583. There were an estimated 37,000 native-born Chinese when the bill passed Congress.

62. For a detailed account of the repeal legislation and America's relaxation of immigration restriction against the Chinese, see Fred W. Riggs, *Pressures on Congress: A Study of the Repeal of Chinese Exclusion* (New York, 1950).

63. Figures in this table are based on data from the historical center of the Defense Department and *World War II Honor List of Dead and Missing.*

64. Philip E. Vernon, *The Abilities and Achievements of Orientals in North America* (New York, 1982), p. 275.

65. Ibid., p. 16.

V. The Chinese-American Community in Transition:
The Post–World War II Era

1. For a detailed and careful study of America's entanglement in China, see Tang Tsou, *America's Failure in China* (2 vols., Chicago, 1963).

2. Rose Hum Lee, "The Stranded Chinese in the United States," *Phylon,* XIX (Summer, 1958), No. 2, pp. 180–81.

3. China Institute in America, *A Survey of Chinese Students in American Universities and Colleges in the Past One Hundred Years* (New York, 1954), pp. 17–19.

4. Wilma Fairbank, *America's Cultural Experiment in China, 1942–1949* (Washington, D.C., 1976), pp. 115–16.

5. Ibid., p. 139.

6. China Institute in America, *A Survey of Chinese Students,* p. 18.

7. Rose Hum Lee, "Stranded Chinese," p. 186.

8. Fairbank, *Cultural Experiment,* p. 141.

9. Liu Boji, *Meiguo huaqiao shi* (History of the Overseas Chinese in the United States) (Taibei, 1981), Vol. II, p. 417.

10. William L. Tung, *The Chinese in America, 1820–1973* (Dobbs Ferry, New York, 1974), p. 36.

11. *Chinese Communist Who's Who,* published by Institute of International Relations, Republic of China (Taibei, 1970), Vol. I, p. 152.

12. The figure cited here also includes the Chinese in Hawaii. The mainland U.S. total of 1950 shows only 117,629.

13. Lui Boji, *Overseas Chinese,* Vol. II, pp. 334–40.

14. Ibid., pp. 325–34.

15. Ibid., pp. 349–54.

16. Kum Pui Lai, "Attitudes of the Chinese in Hawaii," *Sociology and Social Research,* XX (November, 1935), No. 2, pp. 140-42.

17. According to a survey conducted by Dr. Peter Sih, by 1955 only 16 cities in the United States had Chinatowns, a decrease of 12 in 15 years. Cf. William Tung, *Chinese in America,* p. 37.

18. Shih-shan H. Tsai, "Chinese in Arkansas," *Amerasia Journal,* VIII (Spring/Summer, 1981), p. 14.

19. Milton Konvitz, *The Alien and the Asiatic in American Law* (Ithaca, New York, 1946), pp. 228–29.

20. Cf. Ling-chi Wang, "The Chinese-American Students in San Francisco," in *Chinese-Americans: Schools and Community Problems,* edited by Integrated Education Associates (Chicago, 1972), p. 54.

21. Each Chinese newspaper was required to send two copies of its daily issue to the United States State Department for file.

22. For a detailed history of the Chinese newspapers in the United States, see Karl Lo and H. M. Lai, *Chinese Newspapers of North America, 1854–1975* (Washington, D.C., 1977).

23. In the early 1970s, the *Union Daily* of Taiwan published its first issue in North America under the same name, the *Chinese World.* Relationship between the defunct *Chinese World* and the current one is yet revealed.

24. The *Chung Sai Yat Po* is available in microfilm beginning with the issue of January 30, 1906. Issues prior to that date are preserved in the Bancroft Library of the University of California at Berkeley.

25. The Chairman of the Board of the *Young China,* Chen Yuqing, was formerly Director of the Kuomintang Overseas Chinese Affairs Commission of Taiwan.

26. See *Young China,* May 5, 1952; *Chinese Journal,* March 12, 1952.

27. *China Daily News,* April 28, 1952.

28. Charges had been made that the *China Daily News* received subsidies from Peking. Whether or not these charges were true, the paper had by the early 1970s become the best propaganda vehicle for the People's Republic in North America.

29. For more on Chinese Hand Laundry Alliance, see Peter Kwong, *China-town, New York Labor and Politics, 1930–1950* (New York, 1979), pp. 61–81, 138, and 141.

30. H. Mark Lai, "A Historical Survey of the Chinese Left in America," *Counterpoint: Perspectives on Asian America* (UCLA, 1976), p. 73.

31. Liu Boji, *Overseas Chinese,* Vol. II, p. 532. Him Mark Lai, who was then the president of Min Qing, disputed Liu Boji's account.

32. James E. Sheridan, *Chinese Warlord, the Career of Feng Yu-hsiang* (Stanford, 1966), pp. 279–80.

33. "Statement by the Anti-Communist Committee for Free China," issued from its office at 16 Mott Street, New York, June 10, 1951.

34. Liu Boji, *Overseas Chinese,* Vol. II, pp. 541–42.

35. Victor Nee and Brett de Bary, "Chiang Still Runs the Show," *San Francisco Bay Guardian,* March 28, 1972.

36. *Chinese World,* April 13 and 14, 1956.

37. H. Mark Lai, Joe Huang and Don Wong, *The Chinese of America, 1785–1980, An Illustrated History and Catalog of the Exhibition* (San Francisco, 1980), p. 73.

38. Nee and de Bary, "Chiang Still Runs the Show," *op cit.,* March 28, 1972.

39. Warren Breed, "Six Companies dominate, but for how long?" *San Francisco Bay Guardian,* March 28, 1972.

40. *San Francisco Examiner,* August 14, 15, and 18, 1967.

41. Ibid., August 16 and 17.

42. The press conference was held at 843 Stockton Street, San Francisco, the office of the Six Companies on October 2, 1967. A press release was passed out to the persons attending this conference.

43. Lum's mimeographed statement was written at the request of the Chinese Six Companies and issued in early September, 1967.

44. This story was reported by Terry Drinkwater of CBS on March 3, 1982.

45. Sources of these figures come from U.S. Census data of 1940 and 1960.

46. *U.S. Census, 1960, Nonwhite Population by Race,* p. 217.

47. Marlon K. Hom, "Chinatown Literature during the Last Ten Years (1939–1949) by Wenquan," *Amerasia Journal,* Vol. IX (Spring/Summer, 1982), pp. 77–78.

48. Liu Boji, *Overseas Chinese,* Vol. II, p. 401.

49. Frank Chin et al., *Aiiieeeee! An Anthology of Asian American Writers* (Washington, D.C., 1974), p. 14.

50. Elaine H. Kim, "Visions and Fierce Dreams: A Commentary on the Works of Maxine Hong Kingston," *Amerasia Journal,* Vol. VIII (Fall/Winter, 1981), pp. 148–59.

51. *East-West,* May 13, 1981.

52. Christine Choy, "Recording Our Struggles," *Third World Caucus Bulletin* (December, 1983), pp. 9–10.

53. J. S. Tow, *The Real Chinese in America* (New York, 1923), p. 112.

54. For more details, see Horace R. Cayton and Anne O. Lively, *The Chinese in the United States and the Chinese Christian Churches* (New York, 1955), chapter

V, no page numbers.

55. Liu Boji, *Overseas Chinese,* Vol. II, pp. 450–52.

56. Cayton and Lively, *Chinese Christian Churches, op cit.*

57. D. Y. Yuan, "Division of Labor Between Native-Born and Foreign-Born Chinese in the United States: A Study of Their Traditional Employments," *Phylon* (Spring, 1969), p. 168. See also, New York Chinatown History Project, "Washing and Ironing: Chinese Laundry Workers in the U.S.," *Third World Caucus Bulletin* (December, 1983), pp. 5–6.

58. Charles Choy Wong, "Black and Chinese Grocery Stores in Los Angeles' Black Ghetto," *Urban Life,* Vol. V, No. 4 (January, 1977), pp. 459–61.

59. Betty L. Sung, *Chinese American Manpower and Employment* (Report to Manpower Administration, U.S. Department of Labor, 1975), p. 111.

60. Mely Giok-Lan Tan, "Social Mobility and Assimilation: The Chinese in the United States," Ph.D. dissertation, University of California, Berkeley, 1968, p. 84.

61. *Newsweek,* September 20, 1982, p. 33.

VI. Contemporary Chinese-American Society

1. *Asian Week,* April 29, 1982.

2. Louise Boggers, *Journey to Citizenship* (U.S. Funk & Wagnalls, New York, 1967), p. 27.

3. As a result of the Immigration Act of 1965, the flow of immigration has shifted from European to Asian countries. In 1965, the top four countries in the Eastern Hemisphere sending immigrants to the United States were the United Kingdom (27,528), Germany (24,045), Italy (10,821), and Poland (8,465). In 1975, the top four countries were the Philippines (31,751); Korea (28,362); China, including Taiwan and Hong Kong (18,136); and India (15,773). Figures come from U.S. Immigration and Naturalization Service Annual Report, 1975.

4. See Jade Snow Wong's autobiography, *Fifth Chinese Daughter* (New York, 1945) and Maxine Hong Kingston's semiautobiographical novel, *The Woman Warrior* (New York, 1976).

5. Judy Yung, "Researching Chinese American Women History," *Bulletin, Chinese Historical Society of America,* Vol. XVIII (September, 1983), p. 4.

6. "New Law As Garment Industry Abuses," *Asian Week,* April 30, 1981.

7. Chalsa Loo and Paul Ong, "Slaying Demons with a Sewing Needle: Feminist Issues for Chinatown's Women," *Berkeley Journal of Sociology,* Vol. XXVII (1982), pp. 77–88.

8. Judy Yung, "Chinese American Women," p. 3.

9. Pauline L. Fong, "The Current Social and Economic Status of Chinese American Women," *Bulletin, Chinese Historical Society of America,* Vol. XIX (April, 1984), p. 4; also see George Wilber, *Orientals in the American Labor Market, Minorities in the Labor Market* (Social Welfare Research Institute, University of Kentucky, 1975), pp. 140–41.

10. Philip E. Vernon, *The Abilities and Achievements of Orientals in North America* (New York, 1982), p. 11.

11. Derald Sue and Barbara Kirk, "Differential Characteristics of Japanese-American and Chinese-American College Students," *Journal of Counseling Psychology,* Vol. XX (March, 1973), pp. 142–48.

12. See Pauline L. Fong, "Education, Work, Family Aspirations of Contem-

porary Chinese American Girls and Women," *Bulletin, Chinese Historical Society of America,* Vol. XIX (September-October, 1984), pp. 2–18.

13. For more on the new role of Chinese American women, see Stacey Guat-Hong Yap, "Gather Your Strength, Sisters: The Emerging Role of Chinese Women Community Workers," Ph.D. dissertation, Boston University, 1983.

14. Vernon, *Abilities and Achievements,* pp. 29, 250.

15. For more, see Hennie H. Y. Yee, "Parenting Attitudes, Acculturation and Social Competence in the Chinese-American Child," Ph.D dissertation, Boston University, 1983.

16. Richard T. Sollenberger, "Chinese-American Child-Rearing Practices and Juvenile Delinquency," *The Journal of Social Psychology,* Vol. LXXIV (February, 1968), pp. 12–23; also Vernon, *Abilities and Achievements,* p. 260, and Francis L. K. Hsu, *Chinese and Americans* (New York, 1970), pp. 76–112.

17. Vernon, *Abilities and Achievements* p. 28.

18. The *Overseas Torchlight Weekly* (Taibei, Taiwan), February 19 and September 3, 1982; also *U. S. News & World Report,* April 2, 1984, p. 41.

19. *Newsweek,* November 8, 1982, p. 107; *U. S. News & World Report,* April 2, 1984, p. 42.

20. Irving S. K. Chin, "The Chinese in New York," *Chinese-Americans: Schools and Community Problems,* edited by Integrated Education Associates (Chicago, 1972), p. 21.

21. Ling-chi Wang, "Chinese Students in San Francisco," ibid., p. 55.

22. Chinese Chamber of Commerce of Los Angeles, *Los Angeles Chinatown* (Los Angeles, 1972), p. 33.

23. Betty Murphy, "Boston's Chinese: They Have Their Problems, Too!" in *Chinese-Americans,* pp. 29–30.

24. Ibid., p. 34.

25. *Yellow Seeds,* Vol. 1, No. 4, February, 1973; no. 6, September, 1973; & vol. 2, no. 2, May, 1974.

26. Min S. Yee, "Busing Comes to Chinatown," reprinted from *Race Relations Reporter* (January, 1972), pp. 70–71.

27. Ibid., p. 70.

28. *Asian/Pacific Newsmagazine,* a UCLA student publication (May/June, 1982), p. 12.

29. Institute of International Education, *Annual Report,* 1970–71; 1980–81; 1983–84.

30. "Proceedings and Debates", November 9, 1971, *U.S. Congressional Record,* 92nd Cong., 1st sess. (1972), p. 27.

31. *Time,* August 10, 1981, p. 19.

32. *Zhongyang ribao* (The Central Daily, Taibei), March 16, 1971.

33. *The Seventies* (A Chinese-language publication from Hong Kong), no. 147, April, 1982, p. 62.

34. Yeen-mei Wu Chang, *Tiao Yu T'ai Movement: Table of Contents* (Far Eastern Library, University of Washington, Seattle, 1972).

35. *Peking Review,* February 9, 1979, p. 11.

36. *Zhongyang ribao* (The Central Daily, Taibei), June 12, 1982.

37. *Overseas Torchlight Weekly* (Taibei, Taiwan), September 14, 1984.

38. *Liaowang* (The Outlook Weekly, Peking), No. 3 (September, 1984), pp. 15–17.

39. Ibid., Appendix.

40. For more on the 2.28 Incident and the conflict between the Taiwanese

and the mainland Chinese, see George H. Kerr, *Formosa Betrayed* (Boston, 1965).

41. Figures and percentage come from columnist Jack Anderson and a report in *Business Week*, May 17, 1982, p. 24B.

42. *Taiwan Tribune*, August 4, 1981.

43. See for example *Newsweek*, May 17, 1982, p. 73.

44. *Time*, August 10, 1981, p. 19.

45. *Independent Taiwan*, No. 107, January 1981, pp. 35–38.

46. *Overseas Torchlight Weekly*, September 7, 1984.

47. Tsung-kuang Lin & Wen-yen Chen, "An Analysis of the Senate Resolution 74 Survey Results," *Bulletin, North America Taiwanese Professors' Association*, Vol. IV (June, 1984), p. 18.

48. For more, see Milton M. Gordon, *Assimilation in American Life* (New York, 1964).

Epilogue

1. The number of the San Francisco-Oakland non-English speaking Chinese was estimated by Ling-chi Wang, "The Chinese Community in San Francisco," and the Boston figure comes from Betty Murphy, "Boston's Chinese: They Have Their Problems, Too!" both collected in *Chinese-Americans: Schools and Community Problems*, edited by Integrated Education Associates (Chicago, 1972), p. 15, 32.

2. This view is shared by such sociologists as D. Y. Yuan. For more, see Yuan's articles, "Chinatown and Beyond: The Chinese Population in Metropolitan New York," *Phylon*, XXVII, No. 4 (Winter, 1966), pp. 320–31; and "Voluntary Segregation: A Study of New Chinatown," *Phylon*, XXIV, No. 3 (Fall, 1963), pp. 255–65.

3. For more on the changing Chinese American community, see Bernard Wong, "Elites and Ethnic Boundary Maintenance: A Study of the Roles of Elites in Chinatown, New York City," *Urban Anthropology*, VI, No. 1 (1977), pp. 18–19.

4. *U.S News & World Report*, April 2, 1984, p. 43.

5. Philip E. Vernon, *The Abilities and Achievements of Orientals in North America* (New York, 1982), p. 10.

6. Wing-cheung Ng, "An Evaluation of the Labor Market Status of Chinese Americans," *The Amerasia Journal*, IV, No. 2 (1977), pp. 101–20; also see Betty Lee Sung, *Chinese American Manpower and Employment* (Report to Manpower Administration, U.S. Department of Labor, 1975) and Samuel Bowles and Herbert Gintis, *Schooling in Capitalist America: Educational Reform and the Contradictions of Economic Life* (New York, 1976).

7. For more, see Stanley Sue and Derald W. Sue, "The Reflection of Culture Conflict in the Psychological Problems of Chinese Americans," a paper presented at the First National Conference on Asian American Studies, Los Angeles, April, 1971.

8. One of those Chinese Americans who believes that there is still racial discrimination, though much less overt, is Albert H. Yee, a retired academic Dean at the University of Montana. See his impassioned speech, "The Best of the East and West—Their Future," given before the Chinese Historical Society of America at its 21st anniversary dinner. The speech was later printed in the *Bulletin, Chinese Historical Society of America*, XIX (May, 1984), pp. 2–8.

9. Akira Iriye, "Introduction," *The Asian American: The Historical Experience,* edited by Norris Hundley, Jr., (Santa Barbara, 1976), p. vii.

10. Plato, "Republic," in *The Western World,* ed., Wallace E. Adams *et al.,* Vol. I (New York, 1971), pp. 89–90.

BIBLIOGRAPHY

I. United States Government Documents

House Executive Document 105, 34th Cong., 1st sess. (1856), Serial 859.
House Report 443, 36th Cong., 1st sess. (1860), Serial 1069.
Executive Document 10, 42nd Cong., 1st sess. (1871), Serial 1470.
Senate Report 689, 44th Cong., 2nd sess. (1877), Serial 1734.
House Reports 62, 45th Cong., 3rd sess. (1880), Serial 1866.
House Report 2044, 49th Cong., 1st sess. (1885–86), Serial 2441.
Senate Executive Document 51, 50th Cong., 1st sess. (1887), Serial 2507.
Senate Document 169, 57th Cong., 1st sess. (1902), Serial 4231.
Senate Document 633, 61st Cong., 2nd sess. (1911), Serial 5684.
House Report 732, 78th Cong., 1st sess. (1943), Serial 10763.
House Document 333, 78th Cong., 1st sess. (1943), Serial 10793.
Hearings by the House Committee on Un-American Activities, 83rd Cong., 1st sess. (1954), Serial 11207.
Papers Relating to the Foreign Relations of the United States, China, 1868, 1876, 1881, 1883, 1885.
U.S. Bureau of Census, *Historical Statistics of the United States, 1789–1945* (1949).
U.S. Censuses, 1870–1980.
U.S. Congressional Record, 1882, Vol. XIII; 1886, Vol. XVII; 1888, Vol. XIX; and 1943, Vol. LXXXIX.
U.S. National Archives Microfilms: M 98, Roll 1; M 98, Roll 2; M 101, Roll 19, & Navy Muster Rolls, *USS Olympia,* June, 1898, Record Group 24.
Western America: Frontier History of the Trans-Mississippi West, 1550–1900 (Nev Haven, Conn., 1975), Roll 88, No. 908.

II. Chinese Language Materials

A Ying, ed. *FanMei huakong jinyue wenxue ji* (An Anti-American Literary Collection on the Exclusion of Chinese Laborers). Shanghai, 1960.
Chen Lanpin. *ShiMei jilue* (A Brief Account of My Mission to America). Taiwan reprint, 1962.
Guangdong local gazetteers: Districts of Guangzhou, Kaiping, Nanhai, Panyu, Xiangshan (Zhongshan), and Xinning.
Lai, H. Mark, and Choy, Philip, *LuMei sanyi zong huiguan jianshi* (A Brief History of the Whole San-yi Association in the United States). San Francisco, 1975.
Liang Qichao. *Xindalu youji* (Travels in the New Continent). Shanghai, 1936.
Liu Boji. *Meiguo huaqiao shi* (History of the Overseas Chinese in the United States). 2 vols. Taibei, 1976 and 1981.
Lo Xianglin. *Liang Cheng di chushi Meiguo* (Liang Cheng's Mission to America). Hong Kong, 1977.
Qing Cables, 1905–1911. Academia Sinica Archives of Taiwan.
Tsai Tingkai. *Haiwai yinxiangji* (Overseas Travel Impressions). Hong Kong, 1935.

Wang Yanwei, ed. *Qingji waijiao shiliao* (Historical Materials Concerning Foreign Relations in the Late Qing Period, 1875–1911). Peking, 1932–1939.
Wong Sam Ark. *Hongmen geming shi* (The Revolutionary History of the Hong League). Los Angeles, 1936.
Wu Rulun, ed. *Li Wenzhong gong quanji* (Complete Works of Li Hongzhang). Taibei, 1962.
Wu Shangying. *Meiguo huaqiao bainian jishi* (Records of Overseas Chinese in the United States for the Past One Hundred Years). Hong Kong, 1954.
Zhang Yinhuan. *Sanzhou riji* (Diary of the Three Continents). Kyoto, 1896.
Zhu Shijia. *Meiguo pohai huagong shiliao* (Historical Materials Concerning America's Persecution of Chinese Laborers). Peking, 1958.

III. Dissertations and Theses

Armentrout, Eve L. "Competition between Chinese Reformers and Revolutionaries in the Americas, 1895–1911." University of California at Davis, 1977.
Chen, Eugenia V. "Survey of Chinese Youth and Student Clubs in New York City—1945." University of Michigan, 1945.
Chen, I. Hsuan Julia. "The Chinese Community in New York, 1920–1940." American University, 1941.
Chen, Peter Wei-teh. "Chinese-Americans View Their Mental Health." University of Southern California, 1976.
Chu, Wen-chang. "The Background of the Chinese Immigration Into the United States." University of Washington, 1949.
Courtney, William J. "San Francisco's Anti-Chinese Ordinances. 1850–1900," University of San Francisco, 1959.
Daily, Carl Livingston. "The Chinese as Sojourners: A Study in the Sociology of Migration." City University of New York, 1978.
Han, Hsiao-min. "Roots and Buds: The Literature of Chinese Americans." Brigham Young University, 1980.
Hong, Yon Chang. "Chinese Immigration." University of Southern California, 1925.
Hsu, Susan Pien. "The Development of a Model Adult Education Center for the Chinese Community in New York." New York University, 1976.
Huang, Jerry Shao-shiong. "Mass Media Use and the Image of the People's Republic of China among Chinese Students in the Twin Cities Area." University of Minnesota, 1976.
Ng, Pearl. "Writings on the Chinese in California." University of California, Berkeley, 1939.
Peabody, Etta B. "Effort of the South to Import Chinese Coolies, 1865–1870." Baylor University, 1967.
Riddle, Ronald William. "Chinatown's Music: A History and Ethnography of Music and Music-Drama in San Francisco's Chinese Community." University of Illinois, 1976.
Rudolph, Gerald E. "The Chinese in Colorado, 1869–1911." University of Denver, 1964.
Tan, Mely Giok-Lan. "Social Mobility and Assimilation: The Chinese in the United States." University of California, Berkeley, 1968.
Wakeman, Frederic Evans, Jr. "Strangers at the Gate: Social Disorder in South China." University of California, Berkeley, 1965.
Wells, Marian K. "Chinese Temple in California." University of California,

Berkeley, 1962.
Woo, Deborah Anne. "Social Support and the Imputation of Mental Illness: Chinese Americans and European Americans." University of California, Berkeley, 1983.
Wynne, Robert E. "Reaction to the Chinese in the Pacific Northwest and British Columbia, 1850–1910." University of Washington, 1964.
Yap, Stacey Guat-Hong. "Gather Your Strength, Sisters: The Emerging Role of Chinese Women Community Workers." Boston University, 1983.
Yee, Jennie H. Y. "Parenting Attitudes, Acculturation and Social Competence in the Chinese-American Child." Boston University, 1983.
Yen, Tze-kuei. "Chinese Workers and the First Transcontinental Railroad of the United States." St. John's University, 1977.

IV. Newspapers and Magazines

Alta California, November 9, 1868; October 7, 1888.
Annals of the Chinese Historical Society of the Pacific Northwest, 1983.
Asian Week, April 30, 1981; April 29, 1982.
Bulletin, Chinese Historical Society of America, September, 1983; January, April, September, 1984.
Chinese Digest, May, 1936; July, 1937; March, 1938; July, 1938.
Chinese World, January 22, 1910; February 26, 1911; March 1, 1916; March 27, 1925; January 30, 1922; April 13 and 14, 1956.
Chung Sai Yat Po (China-West Daily), January 30, 1906.
East-West, January 22, 1969; May 1, 1974; May 13, 1981.
Huaqiao ribao (China Daily News), April 28, 1952.
Independent Taiwan, January, 1975; January, 1981.
Los Angeles Times, March 31, 1943.
New York Herald, November 28, 1896.
Newsweek, May 17 and September 20, 1982.
New York Times, March 1 and 2, 1943.
Overland Monthly, September, November, and December of 1868; August, 1871; May, 1894.
Peking Review, February 9, 1979.
San Francisco Bulletin, May 6 and May 8, 1869; January 10, 1881.
San Francisco Examiner, August 23, 1888; March 29, 1943; August 14, 15, 16, 17, 18, 1967.
Taiwan Tribune, August 4, 1981.
Time, August 10, 1981.
Tung-ngai san-luk (Oriental News), 1854.
U.S. News and World Report, December 26, 1966; April 2 and May 7, 1984.
Young China Morning Paper, December 18, 1910; July 1, 1925; October 20, 1927; May 5, 1952.
Zhongyang ribao (Central Daily), March 16, 1971; June 12, 1982.

V. General Works

A Survey of Chinese Students in American Universities and Colleges in the Past One Hundred Years. New York: China Institute in America, 1954.
Ai, Chung Kun. *My Seventy Years in Hawaii.* Hong Kong: *The Cosmorama Pictorial,* Publisher, 1960.

Ai, Li Ling. *Life is for a Long Time.* New York: Hastings House, 1972.
Barth, Gunther. *Bitter Strength: A History of Chinese in the United States, 1850–1870.* Cambridge, Mass.: Harvard University Press, 1964.
Char, Tim Yuke. *The Bamboo Path: Life and Writings of a Chinese in Hawaii.* Honolulu: Hawaii Chinese History Center, 1977.
Chen, Jack. *The Chinese of America.* San Francisco: Harper and Row, 1980.
Chin, Frank, *et al. AIIIEEEEE! An Anthology of Asian-American Writers.* Washington, D.C.: Howard University Press, 1974.
Chou, Cynthia L. *My Life in the United States.* North Quincy, Mass: The Christopher Publishing House, 1970.
Coolidge, Mary R. *Chinese Immigration* (1909). New York: Arno Press, 1969 (reprint).
Fessler, Loren W., ed. *Chinese in America: Stereotyped Past, Changing Present.* New York: Vintage Press, Inc., 1983.
Genthe, Arnold and Will, Irwin. *Pictures of Old Chinatown.* New York: Moffat, Yard & Co., 1908.
Getting Together. *Chinese-American Workers; Past and Present.* San Francisco: Getting Together, 1970.
Glick, Clarence E. *Sojourners and Settlers: Chinese Migrants in Hawaii.* Honolulu: Chinese History Center & the University Press of Hawaii, 1980.
Goo, Thomas York-Tong. *Before the Gods.* New York: Helios Book Publishing Co., 1976.
Hoexter, Corinne K. *From Canton to California: The Epic of Chinese Immigration* (including the biography of Dr. Ng Poon Chew). New York: Four Winds Press, 1976.
Hsu, Francis L. K. *The Challenge of the American Dream: The Chinese in the United States.* Belmont, Calif.: Wadsworth Publishing Co., 1971.
Huang, Joe and Sharon Q. Wong. *Chinese Americans: Realities and Myths Anthology.* San Francisco: The Association of Chinese Teachers, 1977.
Isaacs, H. R. *Scratches on Our Minds: American Images of China and India.* New York: John Day Co., 1958.
Jacobs, Paul, *et al. To Serve the Devil.* New York: Vintage Books, 1971.
Konvitz, Milton R. *The Alien and the Asiatic in American Law.* Ithaca, N. Y.: Cornell University Press, 1946.
Kung, Shien Woo. *Chinese in American Life, Some Aspects of Their History, Status, Problems and Contributions* (1962). Westport, Conn.: Greenwood Press, 1973 (reprint).
Kuo, Chia-ling. *Social and Political Change in New York's Chinatown: The Role of Voluntary Associations.* New York: Praeger Publishers, 1977.
Lai, H. Mark, and Philip P. Choy. *Outlines: History of the Chinese in America.* San Francisco: Chinese American Studies Planning Group, 1972.
Lee, Calvin. *Chinatown, U.S.A..* Garden City, New York: Doubleday, 1965.
Lee, Elizabeth & Abbot, Kenneth A. "Chinese Pilgrims and Presbyterians in the United States, 1851–1977," *Journal of Presbyterian History,* 55 (Summer, 1977).
Lee, Rose Hum. *The Chinese in the United States of America.* Hong Kong: Hong Kong University Press, 1960.
Lively, Anne O., and Cayton, Horace R. *The Chinese in the United States and the Chinese Christian Churches.* New York: no publisher, 1955.
Lo, Karl & Lai, H. M. *Chinese Newspapers Published in North America, 1854–1975.*Washington, D.C.: Center for Chinese Research Materials, 1976.
Lyman, Stanford M. *The Asian in North America.* Santa Barbara, Calif.: ABC-Clio Inc., 1977.

McClellan, Robert. *The Heathen Chinese: A Study of American Attitudes Toward China 1890–1905.* Columbus: Ohio State University Press, 1971.

McKee, Delber L. *Chinese Exclusion vs. the Open Door Policy, 1900–1906; Clashes over China Policy in the Roosevelt Era.* Detroit: Wayne State University Press, 1977.

Miller, Stuart C. *The Unwelcome Immigrant, The American Image of the Chinese 1785–1882.* Berkeley, Calif.: University of California Press, 1969.

Reynold, C. N. "The Chinese Tongs," *American Journal of Sociology,* 40 (March, 1935).

Riggs, Fred W. *Pressures on Congress: A Study of the Repeal of Chinese Exclusion* (1950). Westport, Conn.: Greenwood Press, 1972 (reprint).

Schwendinger, Robert J. "Chinese Sailors: America's Invisible Merchant Marine, 1876–1906," *California History,* 57 (Spring, 1978).

Seward, George. *Chinese Immigration: Its Social and Economic Aspects* (1881). New York: Arno Press, 1970 (reprint).

Sih, Paul K. T., and Leonard B. Allen, ed. *The Chinese in America.* New York: St. John's University, 1976.

Speer, Rev. William. *The Oldest and the Newest Empire, China and the United States.* Hartford, Conn.: S. S. Scranton and Co., 1870.

Steiner, Stan. *Fusang: The Chinese Who Built America.* New York: Harper & Row, 1979.

Sung, Betty L. *Mountain of Gold.* New York: Macmillan, 1975.

Sung, Betty L. *A Survey of Chinese-American Manpower and Employment,* Report to Manpower Administration. Washington, D.C.: U.S. Department of Labor, 1975.

Tsai, Shih-shan H. *China and the Overseas Chinese in the United States, 1868–1911.* Fayetteville: University of Arkansas Press, 1983.

Tung, William L. *The Chinese in America 1870–1973, A Chronology and Fact Book.* Dobbs Ferry, N.Y.: Oceana Publications, 1974.

Vernon, Philip E. *The Abilities and Achievements of Orientals in North America.* New York: The Academic Press, 1982.

Wang, Ling-chi, *et al. Chinese-Americans: School and Community Problems.* Chicago: Integrated Education Associates, 1972.

Wu, Cheng-tsu, ed. *Chink! Evidence of Anti-Chinese Prejudice Pervading Our Country.* New York: New American Library, 1972.

Zo, Kil Young. *Chinese Emigration into the United States.* New York: Arno Press, 1978.

VI. Regional Historical and Sociological Works

Adams, Romanzo. *Interracial Marriage in Hawaii.* New York: Macmillan, 1937.

California Historical Society. *California History Special Chinese American Issue.* San Francisco: California Historical Society, 1978.

Char, Tin Yuke. *The Sandalwood Mountains: Readings and Stories of the Early Chinese in Hawaii.* Honolulu: University Press of Hawaii, 1975.

Chin, Art. *Golden Tassels: A History of the Chinese in Washington 1857–1977.* Seattle, 1977.

Chiu, Ping. *Chinese Labor in California, 1850–1880.* Madison: Department of History, Universtiy of Wisconsin, 1963.

Dillon, Richard H. *The Hatchetmen, Story of the Tong Wars in San Francisco's Chinatown.* Sausalito, Calif.: Comstock Editions, 1977.

Edson, Christopher. *Chinese in Eastern Oregon, 1860–1890.* San Francisco: R & E Research Association, 1970.

Fang, Ting C. *Chinese Residents in Chicago.* San Francisco: R & E Research Association, 1974.

Farrar, Nancy. *The Chinese in El Paso.* El Paso: Southwestern Studies Monograph, 33, 1972.

Kingston, Maxine Hong. *The Woman Warrior: Memoirs of a Girlhood Among Ghosts.* New York: Knopf, 1976.

Kuo, Chia-ling. *Social and Political Change in New York's Chinatown.* New York: Praeger, 1977.

Kwong, Peter. *Chinatown, N.Y. Labor and Politics, 1930–1950.* New York: Monthly Review Press, 1979.

Lai, H. M., Genny Lim, and Judy Yung. *Island, Poetry and History of Chinese Immigrants on Angel Island 1910–1940.* San Francisco: Chinese Cultural Center, 1980.

Loewen, James W. *Mississippi Chinese: Between Black and White.* Cambridge: Harvard University Press, 1971.

Lowe, Pardee. *Father and Glorious Descendant.* Boston: Little, Brown & Company, 1943.

Nee, Victor G., and Brett De Bary. *Longtime Californ': A Documentary Study of an American Chinatown.* Boston: Houghton, 1974.

Quan, Robert Seto, and Julian B. Roebuck. *Lotus Among the Magnolias: The Mississippi Chinese.* Jackson: University Press of Mississippi, 1982.

Rhoads, Edward J. M. "The Chinese in Texas," *Southwestern Historical Quarterly,* 81 (July, 1977).

Sandmeyer, Elmer C. *The Anti-Chinese Movement in California* (1939). Urbana: University of Illinois Press, 1973 (reprint).

Saxton, Alexander P. *The Indispensable Enemy: Labor and the Anti-Chinese Movement in California.* Berkeley: University of California Press, 1971.

Telemarque, Eleanor Wong. *It's Crazy to Stay Chinese in Minnesota.* New York: Thomas Nelson Inc., 1978.

Tom, Kim Fong. *Participation of Chinese in the Community Life of Los Angeles.* San Francisco: R & E Research Association, 1974.

Wong, Jade Snow. *No Chinese Stranger.* New York: Harper & Row, 1975.

220